# Architecting Cloud Computing Solutions

Build cloud strategies that align technology and economics while effectively managing risk

**Kevin L. Jackson**
**Scott Goessling**

BIRMINGHAM - MUMBAI

# Architecting Cloud Computing Solutions

**Commissioning Editor:** Vijin Boricha
**Acquisition Editor:** Shrilekha Inani
**Content Development Editor:** Devika Battike
**Technical Editor:** Mohd Riyan Khan
**Copy Editor:** Safis Editing
**Project Coordinator:** Judie Jose
**Proofreader:** Safis Editing
**Indexer:** Tejal Daruwale Soni
**Graphics:** Tom Scaria
**Production Coordinator:** Deepika Naik

First published: May 2018

Production reference: 1280518

Published by Packt Publishing Ltd.
Livery Place
35 Livery Street
Birmingham
B3 2PB, UK.

ISBN 978-1-78847-242-5

www.packtpub.com

# Contributors

## About the authors

**Kevin L. Jackson** is a globally recognized cloud computing expert, technology thought leader, and CEO/founder of GovCloud Network, LLC. Mr. Jackson's commercial experience includes being vice president of J.P. Morgan Chase and worldwide sales executive at IBM. He has deployed mission applications to the US Intelligence Community cloud computing environment (IC ITE), and he has authored and published several cloud computing courses and books. He is a Certified Information System Security Professional (CISSP) and Certified Cloud Security Professional (CCSP).

> *Thank you to my coauthor, Scott Goessling, whose knowledge and insight has greatly enhanced me both professionally and personally. My love and sincere admiration go out to my children Lauren, Lance, and Karl, who, in their journey through life, fill me with pride every day. And finally, AMLAD to the best part of my own life's journey, my wife, Lisa. You are my everything!*

**Scott Goessling** is the COO/CTO for Burstorm and helped create the world's first automated Cloud Solution Design platform. He has lived and worked in the Philippines, Japan, India, Mexico, France, and the US. Being an expert in many technologies, Scott has also been a part of several successful start-ups, including a network hardware innovator that was acquired for over $8B.

Scott's perspectives combine many real-world experiences. He is interested in nutrition therapy, home renovation, custom car restoration, cooking, photography, sculpture, and, most importantly, parenting.

> *Thank you to my co-author Kevin Jackson whose knowledge, experience, and patience continue to enhance me both professionally and personally. None of this would have been possible without the endless love, understanding, and support from my wife, Laura, and young son Grayson. Thank you for your unconditional love.*

# About the reviewers

**Sivagurunathan** has over 10 years of experience in establishing and managing successful technology companies with strong expertise in cloud computing, Virtualization, networking, and security. Having co-founded his first start-up at the age of 21 and bootstrapped it into a multi-million dollar venture within 3 years. Siva is an alumni of IIM Bangalore and also has a double major in engineering from Bits, Pilani. He currently focuses on hybrid cloud initiatives bridging public clouds and on-premise data-centers.

**Travis Truman** has 20+ years of experience in the technology industry. His previous roles include software engineering, software product architecture, SaaS platform architecture, and VP of engineering in several Philadelphia-area start-ups. Travis is a regular contributor to open source software, and he has contributed code to OpenStack, Ansible, GopherCloud, Terraform, Packer, Consul, and many other projects powering modern cloud computing. He currently works as a cloud architect focused on OpenStack, AWS, and Azure for a Fortune 50 media and technology company based in Philadelphia.

# Packt is searching for authors like you

If you're interested in becoming an author for Packt, please visit authors.packtpub.com and apply today. We have worked with thousands of developers and tech professionals, just like you, to help them share their insight with the global tech community. You can make a general application, apply for a specific hot topic that we are recruiting an author for, or submit your own idea.

`mapt.io`

Mapt is an online digital library that gives you full access to over 5,000 books and videos, as well as industry leading tools to help you plan your personal development and advance your career. For more information, please visit our website.

# Why subscribe?

- Spend less time learning and more time coding with practical eBooks and Videos from over 4,000 industry professionals

- Improve your learning with Skill Plans built especially for you

- Get a free eBook or video every month

- Mapt is fully searchable

- Copy and paste, print, and bookmark content

# PacktPub.com

Did you know that Packt offers eBook versions of every book published, with PDF and ePub files available? You can upgrade to the eBook version at `www.PacktPub.com` and as a print book customer, you are entitled to a discount on the eBook copy. Get in touch with us at `service@packtpub.com` for more details.

At `www.PacktPub.com`, you can also read a collection of free technical articles, sign up for a range of free newsletters, and receive exclusive discounts and offers on Packt books and eBooks.

# Table of Contents

# Preface

Cloud adoption is a core component of digital transformation. Organizations must align modern technology and current economic models to business strategy. Transformation requires a new approach that balances cost and technology choices with company direction and client consumption models. *Architecting Cloud Computing Solutions* presents and explains many critical Cloud solution design considerations and technology decisions required to successfully consume the right cloud service and deployment models based on strategic, economic, and technology requirements.

This book starts with the fundamentals of cloud computing and its architectural concepts. It then navigates through cloud service models (IaaS, PaaS, and SaaS), deployment models (public, private, community, and hybrid), and implementation options (Enterprise, MSP, and CSP). Each section exposes and discusses key considerations and challenges that organizations face during cloud migration. In later chapters, this book dives into how to leverage DevOps, Cloud-Native, and Serverless architectures in your Cloud environment. Discussions include industry best practices for scaling your cloud environment, as well as details for managing essential cloud technology service components such as data storage, security controls, and disaster recovery. By the end of this book, you will be well versed in all the design considerations and operational trades needed to adopt cloud services no matter which cloud service provider you choose.

Chinese lanterns symbolize wishes for a brighter, more prosperous future. The lanterns on the book cover symbolize our desire to help you and your organization attain that brighter and more prosperous future with cloud computing.

# Who this book is for

This book teaches you how to architect effective and organizationally aligned cloud computing solutions by addressing cloud computing fundamentals, cloud architecture considerations, cloud technology service selection, and cloud computing security controls. It is ideal for the following people:

- IT administrators, Cloud architects, or a solution architects looking to lead an organization through cloud adoption
- Small business owners, managers, or consultants looking to develop and execute a goal-oriented cloud computing strategy
- Software developers leading or participating in DevOps or DevSecOps processes

No prior knowledge of Cloud computing is needed, but a basic understanding of current information technology operations and practice is highly desired.

# What this book covers

Prologue, Ground rules, covers baseline assumptions the authors took when writing this book.

# Part 1: What you hear about cloud computing

Chapter 1, *What is Cloud Computing?* explains foundational definitions and explanations.

Chapter 2, *Governance and Change Management*, explains how organizational governance and change management affect cloud computing transitions.

# Part 2: How a cloud architect sees cloud computing

Chapter 3, *Design Considerations*, provides direction on how to think through design, economic models, risk profiles, strategies, and technology decisions.

Chapter 4, *Business Drivers, Metrics, and Use Cases*, provides key considerations when looking at the economic impact of cloud solutions.

Chapter 5, *Architecture Executive Decisions*, explains how organizational executives lead the changes in mindset, process, and approach in order to accelerate organizations, motivate teams, and increase control over cloud computing strategy, economics, and risk.

Chapter 6, *Architecting for Transition*, discusses about interpreting the current environment and maintaining situational awareness during the cloud transition process.

Chapter 7, *Baseline Cloud Architectures*, explains how to use the baseline cloud architectures as foundational building blocks to cornerstone design ideas.

Chapter 8, *Solution Reference Architectures*, discusses about blending different deployment and service models to deliver on organizational goals.

# Part 3: Technology Services – It's not about the technology

Chapter 9, *Cloud Environment Key Tenets and Virtualization*, explains essential elements used to modify existing architectures, application layouts, and solution dependencies to modernize deployments at lower risk.

Chapter 10, *Cloud Clients and Key Cloud Services*, discusses important cloud services and service access methods.

Chapter 11, *Operational Requirements*, explains Cloud operational levers used to create business opportunities and alternatives. It discusses standards for interoperability and portability related to cloud computing applications, ecosystems, and applications.

Chapter 12, *CSP Performance*, discusses how to measure, evaluate, and compare service providers.

Chapter 13, *Cloud Application Development*, discusses key concepts to address when developing for cloud-based applications.

# Part 4: Cloud Security – it's all about the data

Chapter 14, *Data Security*, explains security planning from a data-centric point of view.

Chapter 15, *Application Security*, discusses challenges that need to be considered when developing cloud-related applications.

`Chapter 16`, *Risk Management and Business Continuity*, explains how to manage both the risk and risk mitigation when making future state choices.

# Part 5: Capstone – end-to-end design exercise

`Chapter 17`, *Hands-On Lab 1 – Basic Cloud Design (Single Server)*, provides an example of a small cloud solution design.

`Chapter 18`, *Hands-On Lab 2 – Advanced Cloud Design Insight*, provides an example of a small-medium solution design.

`Chapter 19`, *Hands-On Lab 3 – Optimizing Current State (12 Months Later)*, provides an example of a small large solution design.

`Chapter 20`, *Cloud Architecture – Lessons Learned*, discusses important solution design lessons.

`Epilogue`, Sensomorphic.

# To get the most out of this book

This book is designed to guide organization digital transformation and cloud transition. To get the most out of this guide, the main goal should be to design and build architectures supporting specified business or mission use cases. The target should be the use and aggregation of cloud architectures to deploy and securely use business and/or mission software applications.

# Conventions used

There are a number of text conventions used throughout this book.

`CodeInText`: Indicates code words in text, database table names, folder names, filenames, file extensions, pathnames, dummy URLs, user input, and Twitter handles. Here is an example: "Please type `dyn` in the search box"

**Bold**: Indicates a new term, an important word, or words that you see onscreen. For example, words in menus or dialog boxes appear in the text like this. Here is an example: "At the top of the same page in current view, there is a **Text Search** box."

 Warnings or important notes appear like this.

 Tips and tricks appear like this.

# Get in touch

Feedback from our readers is always welcome.

**General feedback**: Email `feedback@packtpub.com` and mention the book title in the subject of your message. If you have questions about any aspect of this book, please email us at `questions@packtpub.com`.

**Errata**: Although we have taken every care to ensure the accuracy of our content, mistakes do happen. If you have found a mistake in this book, we would be grateful if you would report this to us. Please visit `www.packtpub.com/submit-errata`, selecting your book, clicking on the Errata Submission Form link, and entering the details.

**Piracy**: If you come across any illegal copies of our works in any form on the Internet, we would be grateful if you would provide us with the location address or website name. Please contact us at `copyright@packtpub.com` with a link to the material.

**If you are interested in becoming an author**: If there is a topic that you have expertise in and you are interested in either writing or contributing to a book, please visit `authors.packtpub.com`.

# Reviews

Please leave a review. Once you have read and used this book, why not leave a review on the site that you purchased it from? Potential readers can then see and use your unbiased opinion to make purchase decisions, we at Packt can understand what you think about our products, and our authors can see your feedback on their book. Thank you!

For more information about Packt, please visit `packtpub.com`.

# Prologue

140 million results are returned in 0.48 seconds when you search for cloud computing in a Google search. With that much information available, and that many conversations active around the globe, do we really know what cloud is? Are we confident in knowing what cloud can do? Can we explain why the cloud is changing everything?

If 10 people were asked what cloud computing is and why it is important, we would get at least 12 different answers. Where is the disconnect? We know leaders want it. CFOs support it. Strategists recommend it. Technical teams request it. Users demand it. Isn't cloud easy? Cloud is often associated with acceleration, cost control, added flexibility, increased agility, lower complexity, and rapid innovation. Cloud is never described as easy. It takes an incredible amount of work and planning to be simple. CIOs are stating that cloud skills are a top hiring priority in 2018. What do we need to stay relevant? How do we keep up with an industry that is changing every day?

Cloud computing is changing strategies and enabling innovation at every turn. Cloud is changing IT economics. Cloud is blurring the lines and breaking down traditional silos. Cloud is blending roles and redefining boundaries. Regardless of which industry we are in, or the position we hold, cloud computing is changing everything: how we work, how we play, and how we communicate.

## Ground rules

This book is meant as a guide to help you sort through the noise related to cloud computing. We intend to help explain what cloud really is and how it affects strategy, economics, and technology simultaneously, and discuss how to stay professionally relevant through the tremendous changes occurring daily in our industry.

Our targeted audience is anyone involved in the cloud conversation. There are many people asking questions and many more trying to find and/or provide answers.

 Three of your closest provider friends are not representative of the market. Now combine the extremely high cost of failed implementations and incorrect strategies and you quickly realize that the old way of thinking, the manual tools of Excel, PowerPoint, and email, can no longer help someone trying to embrace cloud or lead any kind of digital transformation within their organization.

In designing this book, we've taken an agnostic view of the market. Digital transformation and cloud adoption have many paths. Just like any other journey, there are multiple ways to reach the destination, with some paths more optimal than others, depending on what is required for a successful outcome. Many books are extremely technical, detailing technology knobs and dials, configuration formulas, and technical tasks. Many books discuss various concepts for business and strategy. Our approach was to create a book that simultaneously aligns strategy, technology, and economics. Fundamentally, we believe these cannot be separated. Technically optimal solutions may not fit within economic goals. Strategy requirements may alter technical choices. Risk always needs to be offset by economics. We believe our industry needs a way to reference and apply these.

There are thousands of service providers in the market offering services out of tens of thousands of locations. Many of them have thousands of products with what seems like endless potential combinations The combinatorial effect of options equates to trillions of possible solutions available in the market today. How do we begin to sort through the data? How do we analyze a representative sample size to make a well informed, market-conscious decision?

In construction, it would be costly to finish half a building just to have a fatal flaw cause you to tear it down. The high cost of failure is astronomical. Not to mention the costly person-hours expended in the preliminary work needed to design, architect, and fund such a project. Cost is why every major modern design process today uses computer-aided design, which is particularly the case if the marketplace has a high cost of design coupled with a high-cost failure. Industries from computer chip design using Cadence to construction using Autodesk have evolved in this way. Can you imagine trying to develop computer chips using paper and pencil?

We see the same thing in the IT industry. IT today is all about hybrid platforms and cloud computing. Failure is very, very expensive. Going back to the construction idea mentioned previously, it is very cumbersome and expensive to have finished with 40 stories of a skyscraper and realize it must be torn down due to a fatal flaw in the foundation.

Today's market is rapidly changing, with new options, pricing, locations, concepts, and solutions appearing almost daily. The opportunities to identify, evaluate, and apply new solutions and strategies are endless. Today, we have limited data and no way to work in real time as we compare, optimize, and choose between options and strategies. The tools we use are usually manual, disconnected, expensive, and filled with stop and go serial-built processes. Working with limited data in a disconnected way makes it virtually impossible to make good decisions as the market has changed before we can act confidently. In a situation with little automation, limited data, and disconnected processes, it is impossible to align strategy, technology, and economics to move forward quickly. These challenges mean we need automation, connected ecosystems, and computer-aided design in our IT toolbox:

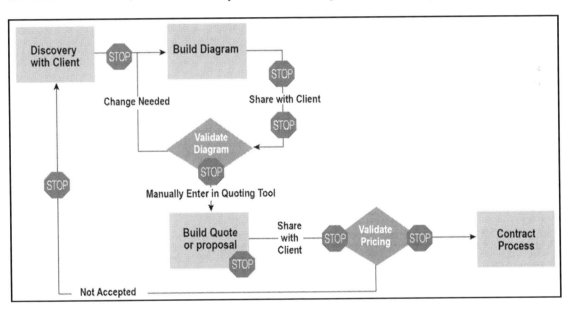

This book will teach a modern approach to IT solution design. In our design process, economic, technical, and strategic attributes must always align. Executives have always needed to balance economics, return, and risk. As executives modernize their thinking, they are having to blend deeper technical detail with the economic and strategic aspects. Solution designers and architects must also modernize their thinking by adding economics, risk, and strategy with technical detail to make high-value recommendations. Product managers updating skill sets and processes require the same level of strategic and economic prowess as they do technical. As solutions and answers to modern IT challenges are assembled, they must simultaneously align strategy, economics, and technology.

The examples in this book will use enterprise and mission goals to visualize, map, match, and compare solution design patterns modeled using modern computer-aided design platforms. Hybrid is not just a term to describe cloud solutions. It is also used to describe the modernization of skill sets required when architecting business, economic, technical, and risk strategies, new business models, and leading-edge technology solutions.

This book is not meant to be read front to back. Just like architecting strategy or architecting technical solutions, the journey can take different paths, with things of interest moving you in one direction or another. The examples in this book help the reader progress through architecting interactions in compounding layers. As choices, not decisions, are made, scenarios, insights, comparative analysis, and outcomes change. The examples in this book will show how multiple choices, and combinations of choices, can derive additional data, present unique insights, and identify optimal scenarios that simultaneously satisfy risk, economic, strategic, and technical requirements.

As discussed, architecting is done at many layers and levels. Our examples in this book will show how to do the following:

- Collect accurate real-time solution design data and analytics
- Leverage automation and high-speed solution design tools
- Update your skill set to include business fundamentals, economics, and risk management
- Rapidly model solutions, quickly interpret insights, and gain advantage through safe failures leading to success

A final important aspect of our approach is that we are looking at cloud computing with an architecting focus, not a solution design focus. It will often be stated throughout the book that successful architectures, not designs, must satisfy strategic, economic, and technical requirements simultaneously. Designs do not. The focus of this book is on cloud computing and the various architectures associated with it. There are many moving pieces and intertwining facets for successful cloud architectures. The design is one important part.

# What is Cloud Computing? 1

We hear that the cloud simplifies, yet it makes things more complicated (at first). It saves us money, yet unusually high bills have surprised many IT leaders and executives. The cloud is flexible, agile, and nimble, yet many get locked into single providers with less than optimal architectures and with substantial migration costs to change. We also hear that the cloud is not as secure as our data center, even though this has been proven false time and again.

In many ways, cloud computing reflects human nature. Everyone believes their idea is best. People sometimes blindly follow their beliefs regardless of the data. No single cloud provider, cloud service, or cloud architecture is perfect. They all have things that we wish were different. They have rules to follow, and they all peddle the line of being the only way to the truth and the promised land.

The cloud is **not** an answer for everything. It is a tool in the toolbox that has a purpose. When used appropriately, it is an incredible addition. When used incorrectly it can be painful, expensive, and career altering. Let's sort out what it is and what it is not.

We cover the formal definition later, but in essence, *cloud computing is a new business model for the consumption and provisioning of information technology software, infrastructures, and related services.* Additionally, this chapter covers:

- Cloud computing history
- Cloud computing definition
- Essential characteristics of cloud computing
- Cloud service models
- Cloud deployment models
- Similar technology models
- Cloud washing

# Cloud computing history

For our purposes, the first age of computing was the 1970s when the focus was on big infrastructure. Green-screen terminals, in vogue back then, eventually evolved into personal computers. Networks went from a centralized, hierarchical design to a decentralized design. Decentralization moved the processing closer to the user meaning applications moved from thin client (processing on the server) to thick client (processing on the user/client side). Green screens were tightly coupled interfaces to the data-laden backend. Decentralization enabled developers to track process steps and state information on the server side while allowing client-side computers to do much more of the processing. The period was the birth of client-server architectures, which are central to today's modern technology-driven business.

With much of the processing moving closer to the actual user, the connectivity of the user became the main limitation. Lack of connectivity led to the second age of computing. The 80s heralded the rise of the internet. Better connectivity between distributed computing systems quickly led to the development and near ubiquity of easy-to-use, visually attractive computing devices. Businesses moved quickly in exploiting this new **Internet Protocol (IP)**-based connectivity as local area networks expanded to globally inter-connected wide area networks. Users, however, became frustrated with poor application performance, network latency, and application timeouts. Developers were again forced to place more compute load closer to the user. Tightly coupled centralized applications did not have the functions, flexibility, or the responsiveness of a well-designed well-built decentralized application. Additionally, the late 80s gave way to a major shakeup in the telecommunications industry. The then monopolized local exchanges were mandated to separate into independent competing companies. The competition forced faster innovation, lower costs, and higher levels of reliability and service.

The following diagram depicts the various cloud computing phases:

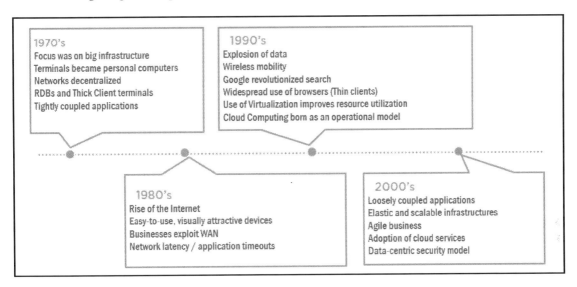

As connectivity and services improved and competition continued to drive reliability up and costs down, the third age of computing began. The amount of data generated exploded. Wireless began to take off, leading to things such as widespread cell phone adoption and mobility solutions. Google revolutionized the internet searches by automating it with MapReduce, no-SQL, and the AppEngine (an early Platform-as-a-Service). During the 90s, the fast growth of wireless networks and the rapid adoption of mobile devices led to the rebirth of the thin client in the form of a **browser**. Better connectivity and browser-based mobile application interfaces enabled much of the computing to remain on the server side with content and responses sent to the client's browser. Servers began utilizing a newer form of virtualization (IBM started a form of virtualization on mainframes in 1964) improving resource utilization and changing the way applications are developed and deployed.

Today, applications are loosely coupled architectures that can take advantage of modern elastic and scalable infrastructures. As mentioned earlier, virtualization has been around for a while taking different forms. The real innovation came in the form of modernized billing systems and economic models. The true innovation is that we can now purchase a fraction of a core or a fraction of a GB of RAM, consume it for a fraction of a minute and turn it off and not pay for it until we need it again. The real power of modern computing is to be able to buy what you need, when you need it, and give it back when finished. The model has led to entirely new business ideas, business strategies, operational models, economic models, and entirely new categories of business.

Technology innovations typically run in 10-year hills where we climb through a level of adoption and face significant challenges that level off adoption until innovation resolves the current challenges, then we start to climb the next hill of adoption. The second hill is usually the largest increase in adoption with major game-changing innovation usually occurring in the third hill that restarts the clock. Situational awareness is critical for business leaders. Which hill are you climbing? Are you early adopting with significant challenges ahead? Is your company late to the game and about to be washed out by innovation? Leaders must always offset risk with economics.

Leaders face many challenges as they try to modernize their business and business models. For example, an executive driven initiative to reduce costs through the adoption of cloud services renders current traditional infrastructure-centric security models worthless. To remain relevant, enterprise security professionals must now adopt a modern data-centric security model. Technical teams traditionally funded as an overhead cost must transform to become trusted revenue-enabling information technology partners to business leaders. To stay relevant, traditional technologists must now update, not only their technical skills but also their non-technical skills. This updated approach includes business risk, economics, finance, and strategy. Innovations such as cloud computing that are driven by economic innovation are lasting and force everyone to adapt. Every known business model is affected by cloud computing: strategy, operations, security, economics, risk, deployment, and more.

Cloud computing, also known as IT-as-a-Service, was quickly adopted due to its ability to deliver value in three significant market sectors.

The first, and most significant by revenue standards, is the software marketplace where it was able to reduce software consumption costs, especially in the area of application and software licensing, and reduced software application support costs. More importantly, this is accomplished while simultaneously improving business backend system capabilities.

The second marketplace was really in the application development arena. Application development platforms, also known as integrated development environments, were delivered with the embedded support of multiple languages and frameworks. The Platform-as-a-Service model exists in multiple technology environments, with greater flexibility. Environment flexibility opened up choice, reduced vendor lock-in fears, and also created an ability to auto-scale applications based on the number of actual users.

The third-most significant IT-as-a-Service marketplace was infrastructure. Infrastructure enabled global scale at an affordable price point. Here is where modern converged networks are used to deliver variable IT capacity pools. It also ushered in the concepts of information technology self-service, and on-demand capacity.

All these models delivered dramatic improvements in cost control, flexibility, speed to market, reliability, and resilience.

The following diagram depicts the various components of IT-as-a-Service:

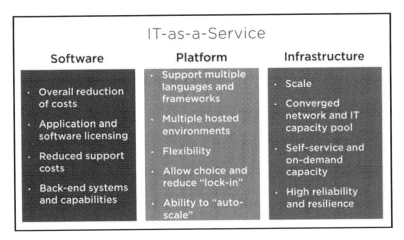

# Cloud computing definition

*"Cloud computing is a model for enabling ubiquitous, convenient, on-demand network access to a shared pool of configurable computing resources (for example, networks, servers, storage, applications, and services) that can be rapidly provisioned and released with minimal management effort or service provider interaction."*

*– US National Institute of Standards and Technology*

This definition is the most widely quoted and used version globally. Many countries and industries have adopted it, and this is the highly recommended starting point for your organization's working definition for the cloud. This definition is so important that we should take a few minutes to review it in detail.

Cloud computing is a model. It is not a specific technology. You cannot go and buy a cloud computer. The term is used to describe an economic and operational model for the provisioning and consumption of IT infrastructure and associated services. The term can also be extended to cover both business and public-sector mission models. What do these models enable? Why cloud?

They enable ubiquitous, convenient, on-demand network access to a shared pool of configurable computing resources. Universal, convenient, on-demand network access means from anywhere and at any time. The network may include the global public internet, but it may also refer to a global private network. The concepts of ubiquitous, convenient, and on-demand take the viewpoint of the cloud service provider's intended users. Shared pool means that the individual user or organization does not pay for all the resources in the pool. The end user pays only for what they use when they use it. This concept is the heart of the cloud computing economic model. If you need to pay for the resource even when you are not using it, you are not leveraging the cloud computing economic model. Configurable means that the service capability can be changed essentially in real time to meet a specific user's requirements.

That final phrase, "*...can be rapidly provisioned and released with minimal management effort or service provider interaction,*" implies a high degree of automation. Cloud service providers operate a highly automated, services-oriented platform that requires relatively few people. Automation is enabled through brutal establishment and enforcement of rigorous IT standards. Automation also enables self service, so if a prospective service provider cannot offer their capabilities without human interaction, you should be worried.

# Essential characteristics of cloud computing

When the United States **National Institute of Standards and Technology (NIST)** published the cloud computing definition, they also defined the essential characteristics of this new model. These have come to be more important than the definition in that the characteristics have helped to define and protect the marketplace against all the marketing hype that has accompanied the cloud.

The first characteristic of cloud computing is that it is an on-demand, typically self service model. On-demand, meaning that it can be purchased when needed, for as long as needed, and given back when finished. Self service refers to the consumer's ability to buy, deploy and shut down services without any assistance from the service provider. This speeds up the process controls cost and moves control to the consumer. (Refer back to earlier paragraphs where we discussed the de-centralization and continual innovation of pushing compute and control closer to the edge of the consumer's control and consumer-controlled devices. The same applies here.)

From a security perspective, this has introduced governance challenges about the acquisition, provisioning, use, and operation of cloud-based services. Interestingly, these new services may violate existing organizational policies. By its nature, cloud computing may not require procurement, provisioning, or approval from finance due to its low initial cost, self-service nature, and immediate deployment options. Cloud infrastructure and services can be provisioned by almost anyone with a credit card, also known as **shadow IT**. For enterprise customers, this low-entry cost, quickly deployed on-demand model may become one of the most important characteristics as it instantly wreaks havoc on governance, security, long-term cost, strategy, internal politics, and collaboration.

The second characteristic, broad network access, is required. Ever heard the phrase the *network is the cloud*? Anything referred to as-a-service requires a network connection. How would it be accessed, managed, operated, or utilized without some network connection, typically to the internet using standard protocols that promote use by disparate client platforms? Because the cloud is an always-on and always-accessible offering, users have immediate access to all available resources, and assets. Think convenient access to what you want, when you need it, from any location. In theory, all that is required is internet access and relevant credentials. The mobile device and smart device revolution have introduced an interesting dynamic into the cloud conversation within many organizations. These devices are often able to access relevant resources that users require; however, compatibility issues, ineffective security controls and non-standardization of platforms and software systems have made the first adoption climb more difficult for some enterprises.

The third characteristic, resource pooling, is the characteristic that, in essence, lies at the heart of all that is good about cloud computing. Combining many smaller compute resources into farms or pools that can serve many consumers simultaneously enables dynamic resource allocation and re-allocation, cost predictability, IT resource control, and higher rates of infrastructure utilization. Utilization and consumption patterns directly affect cost. Resource pooling enables different physical and virtual resources to be allocated and re-allocated according to consumer demand. As mentioned earlier, the true cloud innovation was economic, allowing us to stop billing and give back the resource when finished. More often than not, traditional, non-cloud traditional deployments see low-utilization rates for their resources, typically between 10 and 20%. Cloud deployments from pools used across multiple clients or customer groups can see as high as 80 to 90% utilization (100% is not ideal in most cases). Resources can automatically scale and adjust to dynamic needs, workload or resource requirements. Cloud service providers or **cloud solution providers (CSPs)** typically have scores of resources available, from hundreds to thousands of servers, network devices, and applications, enabling them to quickly and economically accommodate, prioritize and implement the varied size, and complexities each client presents.

The fourth essential characteristic of cloud computing centers on elasticity, the ability to dynamically match the need. Product and service capabilities are developed, acquired, priced, and provisioned elastically, enabling rapid response to continuously changing user demand. To the consumer, capabilities often appear unlimited and easily deployed in any quantity at any time. Because cloud services utilize a consumption-based pay-per-use model, you only pay for what you use. As mentioned earlier, cloud innovation and adoption are being driven mainly by economics that affects strategy. For cyclical loads, applications with intermittent use, seasonal or event-type business cloud eliminates the need to pay for 100% of a physical server (CAPEX) when only 5% is used 2% of the time (OPEX). Think of selling thousands of tickets to an Olympic event. Leading up to the ticket release date, little to no computing resources are needed; however, when the tickets go on sale, they may need to accommodate 100,000 users in the space of 30 minutes-40 minutes. This is where rapid elasticity and cloud computing can be beneficial. Enterprises no longer require traditional IT deployments with substantial capital expenditure up front (CAPEX) to support the temporary project load.

The final key characteristic mentioned here is that the cloud is a constantly measured service. Cloud computing natively offers a unique and important component that traditional IT deployments have struggled to provide—measurement and control of resource consumption and utilization. As mentioned often, billing was the big innovation. Cloud resource consumption needed to be measured and billed for accurately. Once that was possible, the true power of the cloud, which included the ability to shut it off, was realized. The capability enabled automated reporting, monitoring, and alerting which provided much-needed transparency between the provider and the client. Like a metered electricity service or cell phone data usage, consumers have transparent and immediate access to usage data enabling immediate behavior change if needed. Itemized billing provides transparent trendable data providing insight that may lead to needed change. Proactive organizations can now utilize this well measured, transparent, granular, trendable data to charge departments or business units for their actual consumption. IT, product development, and finance can now move toward operating collaboratively as a revenue-driving team that can quantify, qualify, and justify exact usage and costs per department, by business function, per leader, and so on—something that was incredibly difficult to achieve in traditional IT environments.

The following diagram is a graphical representation of the five essential characteristics of cloud computing:

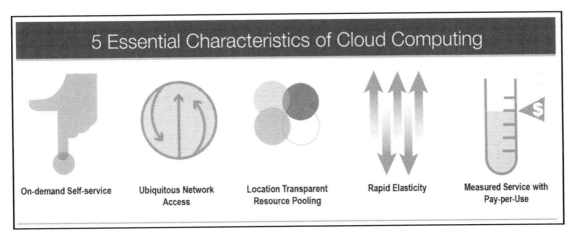

As a side note: people have been utilizing the cloud for years without realizing it. It is not a new thing, but it has just started to port over into more popular arenas. Let's look at internet access as an example.

- **Characteristic 1**: Based on the first characteristic mentioned earlier, how many people dig up the street to put in connectivity when they want to access the internet? None. We pay for it as a service that allows us to use it when we choose.
- **Characteristic 2**: Do we need a network to access the internet? Of course.
- **Characteristic 3**: Do we have dedicated switches, routers, SONET ring, and so on in our living space? No, those resources are pooled by the service provider and shared with all the clients in the area or region.
- **Characteristic 4**: Can we utilize more if we need it? Absolutely. We only use what we need with the ability to scale all the way up to the maximum performance for which we are willing to pay. If more is needed, we call and change what performance level we pay for to match up with the changing need.
- **Characteristic 5**: Are we paying as we go? Is our service metered and measured? Definitely yes. If we choose to stop paying for the service, the service is shut off. We get a bill every month and often have a portal that we can log in to that details what we pay for, what we use, performance details, uptime, downtime, and so on.

# Cloud computing operational models

There are many paths to the cloud. Each path is grouped based on how the services are offered, deployed, and consumed. The cloud is not a technology. A cloud layer does not exist. Each path to the cloud is a response to a requirement or set of needs based on the consumer's current situation, desired future state, available skills, and resources, as well as tolerance for risk. Cloud products and services often establish reusable and reoccurring architectural patterns (building blocks) used for designing, building, and managing applications and infrastructure.

There are primarily three cloud service models: **Internet-as-a-Service (IaaS)**, **Platform-as-a-Service (PaaS)**, and **Software-as-a-Service (SaaS)**. Deployed as needed, all three models require network connections to change resource pools that are measured in great detail, dynamically. However, each consumption model differs in its approach to a technical solution, economics, complexity risk, and level of acceleration. Deployment models also differ in that they could be public/shared, private/dedicated, community, and hybrid. Each model is unique in how it addresses organizational risk tolerance, economic models, and management preferences.

Often the motivator for a move to the cloud is some event that triggers probing questions. Events could be anything from a magazine article, a blog post to a security breach, infrastructure downtime, a complaint about responsiveness, difficulty managing to the desired level of service, or staff/leadership change. Questions can be typically reduced down to three Es: Expectations, Economics, and Execution. As an example, someone expects more delivered work with smaller budgets and less time, or project execution unexpectedly fails due to budget and staff constraints.

As questions get asked, and solutions considered, strategy details, economics, and technology must align. Solutions that are technically perfect may be too expensive. Low-cost solutions may not match up to chosen strategies going forward. In all cases, economics need to balance or offset chosen risk level. For example, very inexpensive self-managed public cloud servers may not match up to the desired level of isolation and security required for transactional database servers.

Next we discuss ways to think through the three primary models available today. How do we recognize situations in which a cloud model should be a consideration? What are the characteristics of each model? What are the benefits? The following diagram is an overview of the three main service models:

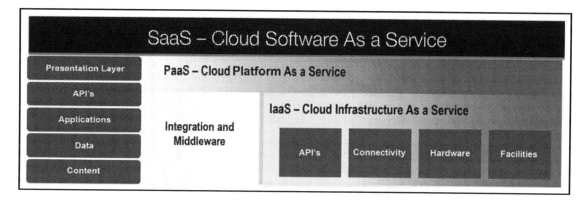

# Cloud service models

The different cloud service models are described here in the following sections.

# IaaS – background

Across the industry, hardware has been largely ignored for a very long time. Servers were not sexy. There was no glory for servers. Servers were just a support for the more important applications. Applications got all the credit for solving business challenges. Applications were the things that users interacted with directly. Servers got stuck in dark closets, forgotten and neglected until a problem occurred.

Because servers received no glory, very little to no maintenance and no budget for patching, upgrading, and so on, many servers are now well beyond their service life and prone to failure. Incredible amounts of money will be spent over the next several years rewriting applications, developing new applications, migrating legacy applications, and updating to new cloud-ready functions needed to replace old applications and neglected hardware currently stuck in old closets and worn out in-house data centers.

IaaS gave many the opportunity to upgrade, refresh infrastructure, and move from excessive capital spending to a monthly pay-as-you-go incremental spend. The shift enables strategy changes, go-to-market changes, differences in software development, and changes in handling IT workloads. Think of what hundreds of servers can do in one hour versus one server for hundreds of hours.

# IaaS – things to consider

IaaS is often deployed on-demand in small increments (cores, RAM, storage, network) with billing occurring in small increments of time. Instead of spending the capital (CAPEX) for a large four or eight-core server (which is the smallest currently available from some manufacturers), a right-sized virtual server can be acquired and deployed as a service, matching infrastructure size to cost and immediate need. This flexibility allows for infrastructure to be quickly matched to business strategies and economic constraints.

IaaS can include many of the infrastructure components included in traditional deployments. Firewalls can be virtual or physical. Compute and storage can be deployed across many different styles and platforms. Each service provider has their unique mix of technology and services. Ultimately the goal when using IaaS is to forget about infrastructure management and details and acquire the mix of services needed, when needed, solving the requirements at that time.

IaaS  was one of the first cloud models available and has seen significant adoption in nearly all sectors. With IaaS, the user does not manage or control the infrastructure directly, only the software and functions loaded onto it (that is operating system, application). There are different types to choose from with varying levels of management and monitoring available for the underlying hardware, virtualization layers, firewalls, SANs, switches, routers, **network interface cards** (**NIC**), and related **service level agreements** (**SLAs**). The controlled risk and lower economic entry points for IaaS are attractive to new cloud adopters as well as savvy veterans. Controllable cost and controllable risk provide extra incentive to those trying to modernize through the adoption of the cloud.

The delivery of on-demand capacity is typically handled via self-service online customer portals. The portal provides complete visibility and control of the IaaS environment. Self-service portals enable and automate functions for adds, moves, changes, managing, and reporting without engaging and waiting for other resources internally or within the provider. IaaS can have many different consumption models matching various OPEX and CAPEX requirements. When using IaaS, there is no need to invest capital up front based on compute and storage resources forecasts. IaaS enables infrastructure to be purchased in increments, as needed, to match utilization.

For organizations, IaaS usage metering provides a higher level of detail used to trend utilization and chargeback specific departments or functions based on actual utilization. Detailed measurements and reporting also allow for instant, and in some cases, automatic, scaling up, and down based on dynamic need requirements. Resource flexibility is particularly useful when there are significant spikes, dips, or cyclical loads for infrastructure.

A few examples of current IaaS providers are Amazon Web Services, Microsoft Azure, and Google. They offer many different styles of compute, storage, and network, as well as many supporting solution services. They each offer several different economic models to match up to SLAs, OPEX and CAPEX requirements, risk and deployment options.

# SaaS – background

As many small and medium-sized organizations looked for additional ways to control cost, modernize strategy, and consume on-demand solutions, software licensing became a very complicated issue. An example of this is Oracle, a company that was a bit late to the cloud licensing game. New server configurations were much more substantial with more sockets, more cores, and more RAM. Even with no change in utilization or software configuration, Oracle client charges increased to over a million dollars due to new server sizing. This affected strategy, economics, and eventually technical decisions on how to move forward in the face of shattered budgets and ROI calculations.

Many organizations lack the skills or resources to create custom software applications. Freeware and opensource software helped some organizations, but they still required skills sets and significant adjustment for adoption. Software providers are starting looking for ways to offer online cloud-based solutions at lower cost and universal access. These new models would center around new licensing models tied to multiple users, a certain level of access, and SLAs rather than the size of the software infrastructure deployment.

With SaaS, the subscriber uses the provider's centralized application deployed using cloud infrastructure. SaaS enables access from any approved client device, browser, or custom interface. The user/subscriber does not have access to the underlying infrastructure, application code, or individual application attributes except for a set of named user-specific application configuration settings.

In the SaaS space, some applications have stabilized/normalized meaning they are widely adopted and have significant competition and innovation driving licensing costs downward, for example, office suites, collaboration software, and communications software. Software-as-a-Service providers offer a complete software application to customers using a license-based model that accesses the application on-demand via a self-service interface.

# SaaS – things to consider

Using SaaS, organizations have potentially limitless possibilities for running applications that may not have been otherwise possible given the limitations of their corporate systems, infrastructure, or resources. If the right middleware and associated components are deployed, SaaS can present massive incentives and benefits. Organizations can quickly realize benefits from scalability, flexibility, and on-demand self-service capabilities. Customer adoption accelerates as access to data and applications can be from virtually anywhere, at any time with internet access. Additional benefits include:

- Cost control, cost reduction
- Licensing or support becomes a built-in component for the provider and the subscriber benefits from economies of scale
- The purchasing of up-front bulk licensing and the associated capital expenditure is removed and replaced by demand-based pay-as-you-go licensing models
- User-based internal support requirements reduce significantly as the software cloud service provider can typically handle more of the support at scale
- Ease of use and limited administration
- Automatic updates and patch management
- Improved security
- Standardization and compatibility
- Global accessibility

Notable providers of SaaS include Google, Microsoft, Oracle, Salesforce, and SAP.

# PaaS – background

PaaS takes both IaaS and SaaS and adds yet another twist on trying to solve the problem. As described earlier, people are trying to control costs, eliminate large major cash outlays, accelerate, modernize strategies, and move to only paying for what is needed, when it is needed. IaaS helped but still required a lot of people, skills, and money to support the applications. Based on our direct research, software required between 8x and 32x the annual cost of the server annually in management, maintenance, monitoring, and support. A $6,000 server written down over a 3-year use cycle would cost between $16,000 and $64,000 each year for software support. The cost was dependent on the specific software and organizational efficiency. These operational changes meant that new infrastructure and software models were required to keep businesses innovating and moving forward.

The next challenge was that the as-a-service model was not available with every software package. Some software was just not adaptable to modern cloud models. A complicating issue was that, for most companies, only about 15%-20% of software was off-the-shelf. Most of it was custom developed, homegrown, and built for specific functions and purposes within each business. Nearly every company still had to develop proprietary applications, middleware, services, connectors, workflows, and more. Each of those projects required different programming languages with different frameworks and libraries. How can things accelerate? How can costs be controlled?

Interestingly, people realized that the combinations of languages, libraries, and frameworks used were often the same or very similar. Consumers needed the ability to quickly build and deploy applications coded with provider-supported programming languages, services, libraries, and tools. The end user did not want to manage or control the underlying cloud infrastructure, but they did need to control the deployed application's configuration settings. CSPs responded by integrating all of the needed components and subsystems into a solution stack that could now be offered as a service or rented as-needed. This new PaaS enabled faster development at a lower cost. The environment was now ready to use, managed, and monitored, enabling developers to be productive immediately using the latest components available. This has led to many other variations where raw materials are integrated into environments that enable the building and assembling of new creations quickly and cost-effectively.

# PaaS – things to consider

Cloud PaaS has revolutionized software development and the means through which it is delivered to customers and users. Market entry barriers have been reduced dramatically by lower cost, accelerating time to market, and promoting innovative cultures within many organizations.

As PaaS providers are considered, the languages and frameworks supported are key. A provider that supports multiple relevant languages and frameworks can help avoid productivity pitfalls later. Developers need to write code in their preferred language that meets specified design requirements. Recent advances include options for open source development stacks and many new infrastructure deployment styles including OpenStack infrastructure, various containerization engines, and serverless (FaaS) options. PaaS providers that support multiple languages and deployment options reduce vendor lock-in and interoperability issues as applications grow and deployment locations change.

Applications are never static. They are continually changing, updating, and growing. Being able to deploy and move the application across different hosting environments is also a key PaaS benefit. Supporting multiple hosting environments helps the developer or administrator easily migrate the application if required. With this option, PaaS can also be used for contingency operations and business continuity to ensure continued availability. It is important to consider the final environment as platforms used by early users to test for functionality. These environments transition to a run environment at some point. The final environment may not be the same as originally intended as many things change throughout the process and testing. Multiple deployment options are an important consideration when picking a platform provider.

Many platform providers started with the idea of adding value by assembling platforms. Make the platform proprietary with their unique workflows, combinations, components and create a sort of lock-in mentality. Providers wanted clients to use only their specific platform and direction. The goal was to make things very sticky with limited ability to transition between provider platforms. Recent changes have added much-needed flexibility matching developer needs and requirements. To stay relevant, platform providers needed to respond or lose the developers and their communities to more flexible environments and open source options.

The **application programming interfaces (APIs)** are required for nearly every form of software in our space today with RESTful being elevated to the de-facto standard in most cases. A service provider always offers specified APIs or integration. Developers could run their application in various environments based on common and standard API structures. This ensured consistency and quality for customers and users. PaaS pushed forward infrastructure concepts like auto-scaling where software could now take the responsibility of scale up and scale down and manipulating the infrastructure through APIs, as needed. This would help accommodate cyclical, less predictable demand patterns, seasonal business, and event-driven activities. Mother's Day would bring down Hallmark's online card servers every year until they were able to implement auto-scaling. Before auto-scaling, Hallmark would have to build and engineer infrastructure for a guesstimated utilization level. With auto-scaling, the platform allocates resources and assigns them these applications, as required. This capability is a key driver for any seasonal organizations that experience spikes and drops in usage.

When thinking through platform providers, look for flexibility and future migration options. Look for the right combinations of services and support with expertise in areas relevant to project needs and direction. Look for providers that not only provide the platform but also offer the other versions of the cloud as well. Where your project starts is not where it stays. Plan to move and change. It may not change often, but change happens. Plan for it up front.

Notable PaaS providers include Microsoft, Lightning, and Google.

# Other cloud service models

You have probably heard of many other X-as-a-Service offerings such as Storage-as-a-Service, Desktop-as-a-Service, Network-as-a-Service, Backend-as-a-Service, Function-as-a-Service. These other models are merely subsets or aggregations of SaaS, IaaS, or PaaS. Categorizing them into the three standard models simplifies any cloud conversation you may have.

# Cloud deployment models

We have discussed the three standard cloud service models. The service model defines the what. What is unique about each model? What are they trying to solve? What are their strengths and weaknesses? Each of the discussed service models adheres to the five characteristics mentioned, possibly adhering in different ways. Within each of the service models, there may also be multiple ways to enable and deploy the service. The service model is the what, the deployment model is the how.

Many cloud services are straightforward to comprehend. For example, network as mentioned earlier. Most do not realize that the network was one of the very first types of IaaS, therefore, one of the original types of cloud. True, there are many types of services, and with that, an even greater number of ways to refer to them. In this section, we introduce the deployment models and some of the jargon. The discussion also addresses how the different deployment types are referenced, marketing names, labels, and currently used buzz words.

This section also demystifies some of the marketing hype which makes it easier to *quiet the noise* when participating in the often jargon-filled conversations. How is this bare metal different to a dedicated cloud? What is a public cloud? What is a private cloud and how is private different to dedicated? Is it different? Is private on-premises still considered as the cloud? Is a private cloud from a service provider also the cloud? If it is called a cloud, it must be a cloud?

# Public

Public is the typical IaaS-compute deployment model most people think of when referring to the cloud. A public cloud service provider offers IT resources as-a-service and, as part of the service, is responsible for building, monitoring, and maintaining physical data centers and IT resources that are for dynamic public consumption. This IT service environment is shared among many customers which normally reduces costs for each customer. By leveraging economies of scale, the CSP enables higher average utilization of resources through the extensive use of virtualization, workload binding, offsetting clients workload patterns, and performance tiers.

The general public uses a public cloud infrastructure. The infrastructure may be owned, managed, and operated by a business, academic, or government organization, or some combination. The infrastructure is always on service provider premises as they have taken ownership of operations and maintenance. Amazon is a good example. The business started off by selling books. It then started to sell excess server and storage capacity to the general public. The infrastructure remained on-premise at Amazon locations.

A public cloud can fall into two sub-types within IaaS, self managed or fully managed. Both of these sub-types are discussed in greater detail later in this chapter. A public cloud is highly scalable, immediately deployed, portal driven, and can be parked or turned off when not in use.

Public cloud benefits include:

- Ease of use and inexpensive setup, low cost of entry to the cloud
- Streamlined and easy-to-provision resources via a self-serve portal
- Scaled to meet customer needs
- No wasted resources because customers pay only for what they consume
- Basic security services included

Public cloud considerations are:

- How are noisy neighbors handled?
- Does security line up with my requirements?
- Is there any network access or storage limitations?
- Cost of access or data transfer in/out?
- Portability? Grow into other instance types and service types?
- What other services connect to it?
- What is the price/performance metric?

Providers often mentioned in this space include Amazon, Microsoft, and Google, among others.

# Private and dedicated

There are a lot of marketing, jargon and buzz words that come along with the cloud. Companies are fighting hard to create separation from the pack. Sounding unique and different was one way to try and differentiate. What is the difference between a dedicated and a private cloud? What is a virtual private cloud? Is a virtual private cloud different to a private cloud? Do these different versions adhere to the five characteristics of the cloud? Many factors drive interest in single-tenant infrastructure. Dedicated and private both, by definition, are single-tenant environments with the infrastructure only accessible by a single company or client. The difference ultimately comes down to economic model and access.

## Private cloud

A private cloud is typically an on-client premise solution with the infrastructure leased or purchased by the company/entity using it. These environments can also be deployed within a service provider data center utilizing collocation services. This would still be considered an on-premises solution as the collocation space is just another leased location for the infrastructure owner. A private cloud is typically managed by the organization it serves; however, outsourcing the general management of this to trusted third parties may also be an option. A private cloud is typically available only to the entity or organization, its employees, contractors, and selected third parties. The private cloud is also sometimes referred to as the internal or organizational cloud.

The factors driving the use of infrastructure may include legal limitations, trust, and security regulations. Private cloud benefits include more control over data, the underlying systems, and applications, ownership, retention of governance controls; and assurance over data location. Private clouds are typically more popular among large, complex organizations that have legacy systems and heavily customized environments. Additionally, where significant technology investment has been made, it may be more financially viable to utilize and incorporate these investments within a private cloud environment than to discard or retire such devices.

Is a private cloud really a cloud? It has cloud in the name. Having cloud in the name was not one of the five characteristics of the cloud. It is interesting to debate, you decide. Compare a private cloud to the five characteristics and come up with an answer.

# Dedicated cloud

A dedicated cloud is very similar to a private cloud. It is also a single-tenant solution. Ownership and access differ. In a dedicated cloud, ownership of the infrastructure shifts to the service provider. The infrastructure is housed within the provider's data center. A dedicated environment is for use by the single tenant. Network, compute, and storage are dedicated to the single tenant.

The economic model for dedicated solutions is usually a combination of **non-recurring cost (NRC)** which is a one time fee up front, and **monthly recurring cost (MRC)**, which is a monthly payment paid over a term (number of months or years). Dedicated solutions enable a shift from all capital upfront models (CAPEX) to smaller payments over a longer period (OpEx). Management and operations can continue to be in-house, outsourced, or a combination of both.

Is a dedicated cloud really a cloud service? It also has cloud in the name. This is also an interesting one to debate, you decide. Compare a private cloud to the five characteristics and come up with an answer for your conversations. When sorting out the answer, look at the economics. The cloud is an economic innovation. Ultimately, can you turn it off and give it back? Does billing stop? Do you stop paying for it when you shutdown?

# Virtual private cloud

As with many things in our industry, the lines often get blurred (marketing may have something to do with it). Dedicated is an isolated environment deployed within the provider's data center. A **virtual private cloud (VPC)** is a variation of a dedicated cloud. A virtual private cloud combines concepts from a public and a dedicated cloud. VPC takes the concept of shared infrastructure and the economies of scale for servers and storage then combines it with an isolated network.

The very high cost of a dedicated cloud and the network challenges of noisy neighbors in a public cloud led service providers to the virtual private approach. VPC is the blending of strengths while trying to control some of the weaknesses. The name drives the blurred line in this service. A private cloud is typically deployed on client-owned infrastructure as an on-client-premise solution. A VPC is deployed on the service provider-owned infrastructure. This service would be more appropriately named a virtual dedicated cloud. Some providers have changed the name to eliminate some of the confusion within their product and solution sets.

## Community

In a community cloud, an IT infrastructure is provisioned for use by a specified community of end users. The community participants are from organizations that have shared concerns and governance requirements. Typically, these requirements link to mission, security, policy, or regulatory compliance. It can be owned, managed, or operated by a community member, a third party, or a combination. Community clouds may exist on or off premises.

A community cloud provides most of the same benefits as a public cloud deployment while providing heightened levels of privacy, security, and regulatory compliance.

## Hybrid

A hybrid cloud is any solution that combines a cloud model with any other cloud or non-cloud deployment model. Most organizations tend to gravitate to the hybrid models as no single model or deployment type matches up to the multiple applications and services needed to support a business. Many applications cannot migrate readily to new services. Application dependencies may introduce additional risk for migrated applications. There is rarely a situation where everything is forklift moved all at one time from current state to future state. Hybrid is the typical path to the cloud for currently deployed applications and infrastructure.

In a hybrid IT environment, private clouds, public clouds, community clouds, traditional data centers, and services from service providers can be integrated and interconnected. Applications and services can then be deployed to and consumed from the most appropriate combination of services and environments.

Key benefits of the hybrid model are retention of ownership and oversight for critical tasks, reuse of earlier technology investments, tighter control over critical business components and systems and more cost-effective options for non-critical business functions. Cloud bursting and disaster recovery options can also be enhanced by using hybrid cloud deployments.

The basic understanding of the cloud deployment models are shown here:

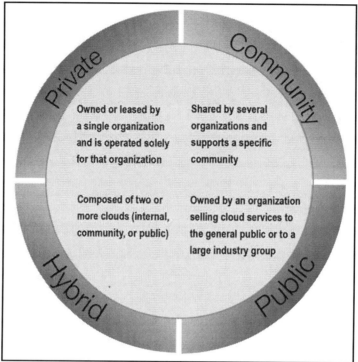

## Other delivery models

The cloud, and technology in general, has a notion of fashion to it. Some things are in vogue while others fade from favor quickly. As cloud conversations happen, it is vital to see ahead of the curve and keep in mind overall direction. For decades, a consistent direction has been to place more power in the hands of the end user/consumer. Our cell phones today have more compute power and run more applications than many desktop computers sold a few years ago. Think forward a bit to IoT. Significant compute power and data are at our fingertips. Connected cars are currently built with nearly 40 processors, almost 100 sensors sending out 25 GB of data per hour. Connected cars are described as rolling data centers.

As technology continues to innovate and progress at incredible speeds, it is essential to raise your awareness of immerging trends. It is also important to quickly distinguish tech fashion from tech innovation. Real innovation always has an economic driver that is sustainable. Starbucks coffee did not invent coffee. Starbucks was when the first-time coffee and culture became inseparable. The iPhone was not the first mobile device; however, it was the first time a mobile device connected many of the most important facets of our home, work, and play lives. The cloud was not the first deployment of virtualization. The cloud is the first innovation that has directly connected the concepts of technology, strategy, and economics forever changing the way we build, deploy and consume technology and services.

The shortlist here includes some very innovative ideas that build on and extend the core concepts of cloud computing. These are a few things to watch as they climb the two hills of innovation. More on that later in this book:

- **Grid computing**: Distributed and parallel computing capability where a virtual computer is composed of a cluster of networked and loosely coupled individual computers which act in concert to perform very large tasks.
- **Fog computing**: A distributed computing model that provides IT services closer to the fog client. Sources are near-end user edge devices. Fog computing can handle data at the network level, on smart devices, and the end-user client side instead of sending data to a remote location for processing.
- **Dew computing**: Dew computing is positioned at the ground level for the cloud and fog computing. When compared to fog computing, which is designed to support IoT applications that are sensitive to network latency and require real-time and dynamic network reconfigurability, this variant pushes the computing applications, data, and low-level services to the end users and away from centralized virtual nodes.
- **Edge computing**: Edge computing extends cloud computing by pushing the processing, applications, and data as far away from centralized resources as possible. Moving work to the edge also means that devices may not always be connected to the internet (that is, mobile, laptop, tablet). This means that processing would also need a high level of redundancy with content highly distributed.
- **IoT**: IoT is connecting the physical world with the logical one. Sensing and processing technology are being placed where needed when needed. Cloud computing is rapidly morphing to help catch, process, and utilize the vast amount of data already being generated by IoT initiatives and projects.

- **AI, neural networks, and machine learning**: These concepts have been pulled together because they are hard to separate and sometimes they are used interchangeably even though there are distinct differences. AI has been around for decades, it is not new. However, cloud computing has removed many of the barriers that were slowing innovation; 300 computers for one hour can process a staggering amount of data, connect it, correlate it, learn from it and apply it. Cloud computing innovation has truly helped this field leap forward recently.

# Cloud washing

Cloud washing is a term used to refer to the often deceptive attempt to rebrand an existing product or service by associating the buzzword cloud with it. Within a financial construct, there is a parallel that describes the practice of inflating financial results for a company's cloud business by redefining existing services and products as cloud services. A typical example of this is referring to access to any application or service over the internet through a browser as cloud computing, just because you are receiving the service over the internet.

Another example is the traditional **application service provider** (ASP) model where a third party offers individuals, and companies access over the internet to applications and services that would normally have been located in their own personal or enterprise computers. This is often marketed as a SaaS, but there are many significant differences between the two models. ASP is a software delivery method with a revenue model that is disconnected from the software itself. At its core, these are single-instance, single-tenant legacy software deployments. The revenue model is like renting a server with an application installed on it. This approach failed in the marketplace because it lacks scalability for the vendor, too much customization is required, and there is a single customer for the instantiation. There is also no organic aggregation of data, and no network effect data available for collection and aggregation.

SaaS, on the other hand, is an all-inclusive business architecture that is a value delivery method. Its built-in multi-tenancy design allows for shared resources and shared infrastructure. SaaS is scalable and offers true economies of scale to the service provider. This approach reduces overall costs, operational complexities, and customization. Multi-tenancy can also be leveraged to improve customer service and retention, reduce sales cycles, accelerate revenue, gain competitive advantage, and even directly monetize additional services.

Managed service arrangements are also sometimes referred to as cloud hosting. The difference here is that the day-to-day functions are outsourced to a particular vendor to realize an increase in efficiency around processes associated with data center operations. When doing this, the client also pays for all the capital investment (either up front or embedded in the recurring fee) and commits to regular payments over a minimum term. These payments are not driven by use but are a calculation related to total operational and customization costs over the minimum term, financial interest rates and a minimum profit for the service provider. In all cloud service models, the cloud service provider bears all capital cost and offers the same standard service to all marketplace customer. Payment is related directly to actual customer use, and there is no minimum term commitment.

# Cloud computing taxonomy

The cloud computing taxonomy was initially developed by the United States **National Institute of Standards and Technology (NIST)** as a tool for standardizing conversations around cloud architectures. Since then, this basic model has been enhanced by the community and broadly adopted to discuss basic concepts. The major taxonomy components are described here:

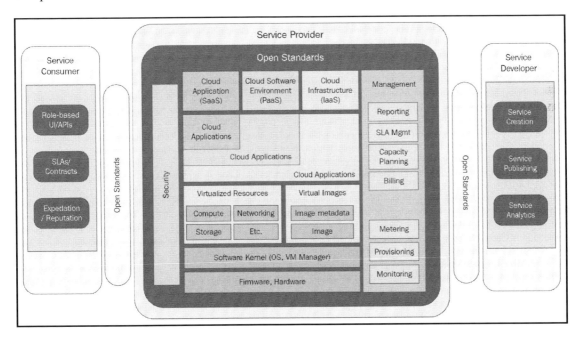

The **service consumer** is the entity (enterprise or end user) that actually uses the cloud service. Users will normally have multiple programming interfaces. These interfaces present themselves like any normal application and the user does not need to understand any cloud computing platform details. User interfaces can also provide administrative functions like virtual machine or storage management.

The **cloud service provider** (**CSP**) creates, manages, and delivers information technology services to the service consumer. Provider tasks vary based on the service model:

- For SaaS, the provider installs, manages, and maintains all software. Service consumers only have access to the application.
- For PaaS, the provider manages and provides a standardized application development environment. This is typically in the form of a development language framework.
- For IaaS, the provider maintains and operates the facilities, hardware, virtual machines, storage, and network associated with the delivery of any information technology service. The service consumer, however, is responsible for service design, operations, and delivery.

Critical to the service provider's operations is the management layer. This layer meters and monitors the use of all services. It also provisions and deprovisions services based on user demand and service provider capacity. Management also includes billing, capacity planning, SLA management, and reporting. Security is applied across all aspects of the service provider's operations.

The service developer creates, publishes, and monitors cloud services. Typically, these consist of line-of-business applications delivered directly to end users. During service creation, analytics is used for remote debugging and service testing. When the service is published, analytics is also used to monitor service performance.

Standards and taxonomies will affect cloud use case scenarios in four different ways:

- Within each type of cloud service
- Across the different types of cloud services
- Between the enterprise and the cloud
- Within the private cloud of an enterprise

Within each type of cloud service (IaaS, PaaS, or SaaS), open standards help organizations avoid vendor lock-in by giving users the freedom to move to other cloud service providers without major application or operational modifications. Standards within an enterprise are normally driven by interoperability, auditability, security, and management requirements.

# Summary

As you move forward in cloud conversations, please keep in mind the five characteristics of the cloud. These characteristics will help you stay focused on aligning technology, economics, and strategy. The cloud's big innovation was economic, not technical. Strategy changing economics are driving rapid transformation and digitization. There are many different services, different economic and deployment models along with many different strategies to use them. The cloud is another tool in the toolbox. It is not the answer for everything, but it is quickly becoming the foundation for everything.

The next chapter starts the conversation on governance and change management. You may think that a cloud solutions architect's success depends on the technology chosen. That thinking couldn't be further from the truth. While cloud computing is foundational to digital transformation, successful cloud computing solutions must be built on top of an effective change management and IT governance foundation.

# 2
# Governance and Change Management

Solution adoption requires cultural change. Cultural change requires relevant, insightful data; well-planned governance, and relentless change management. Change is difficult in many ways and for many reasons. Without governance and change management, driving adoption for new solutions can be exhausting, unpopular, expensive, and slow. Governance and change management are inseparable but not interchangeable. One is not synonymous with the other. Governance and change management are tightly coupled and dependent on one another. Changes in one can certainly affect the other. What are they and how are they different?

Governance address the things that need to be accounted for as change is implemented. Governance is the operating agreement for how changes will take place for the things involved. Governance definitions and operating rules may define organizational structures, decision rights, workflows, processes, stakeholders, authorization points, and toll gates. The goal of governance planning is to talk through how things operate today versus how things will operate during and after the change. Well-planned governance ideally creates a target workflow that aligns and optimizes the use of business entity resources with the goals and objectives of the business.

Change management focuses on the people and how people will be assisted through changes being implemented. Changes to our norms can be real challenges. It is difficult to veer away from comfortable modes of normal operation, accepted and adopted workflows, team structures, roles and responsibilities, and known rules of engagement. Change management helps people transition through changes by providing things such as messaging and communication plans, engaging support, interactive training, and coaching, co-ownership in successes and wins.

In this chapter, we will cover the following topics:

- IT governance
- Change management
- IT service management
- Architecting cloud computing solution catalogs

# IT governance

Governance addresses things needed to implement change. Typically, this process will start with a series of questions that determine outcomes, responsibilities, and process. The desired outcome is always first. Without knowing the desired outcomes, it is impossible to determine who is involved and what is needed to get there.

Three questions to help start the IT governance process are shown in the following diagram:

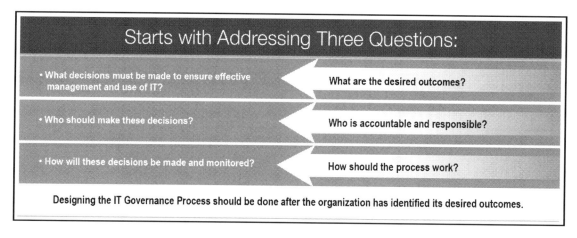

Figure 1: Effective governance starts with addressing three questions

Organizational leadership and management must articulate desired outcomes, who is accountable and responsible for these outcomes, escalation criteria and triggers to progress, the process for progression, and what metrics and counter metrics to be used. The delivery of desired outcomes must be continually monitored and evaluated for direction toward desired outcomes, adoption levels, impact to metrics, and affects to counter metrics. Is the change providing the necessary transparency? Is it following expected timelines? Are stakeholders and decision makers adjusting accordingly? Scorecards are extremely helpful to compare, visualize, and guide as governance is monitored through change.

### Counter metrics

A second value to watch that may signal unexpected results or behaviors away from the actual change. For example, new storage is implemented with much faster throughput. The server is responding much quicker and taking more load. The metric being measured is disk i/o and data transferred statistics for the server. The countermeasures may include dramatic changes in load balancing metrics because one server is getting all the traffic now due to first responder algorithms being used. Higher utilization on network ports, high CPU or RAM utilization may also be the metrics to watch to see if the change is causing adverse behaviors in other places not directly affected by the change.

The next diagram shows an example of an IT governance scorecard with notational outcomes and metrics:

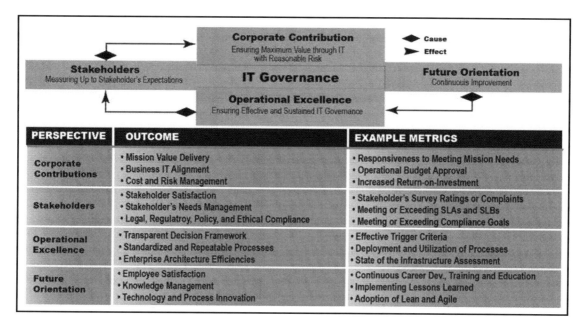

Figure 2: Notational IT governance scorecard

IT governance does not have a *one size fits all* approach. Change comes in all shapes and sizes with as many or more unique challenges to navigate. IT governance is unique because the same change with the same desired outcome requires different governance when the change is deployed into different operation and deployment models.

Complete scope and strategy are things to consider when building IT governance plans and processes. It is important to have a clear understanding of what business processes and which applications may be affected. This analysis must also consider cost, benefit, risk, and shortcomings that may lead to unexpected outcomes as operation models and deployment models are chosen. Different models will require different governance plans and processes. As mentioned previously, if there are changes to governance, there will also be changes in change management.

# Implementation strategy

To illustrate, there are three main categorical ways to consume IT products and services. The first is in-house. In-house refers to a typical enterprise implementation, where the organization pays for ownership of all applicable resources. The enterprise also employs the required operations staff to operate the deployed solutions. In this model, the enterprise has complete and total control of IT governance.

The second, **managed service provider** (MSP), is an arrangement where the enterprise contracts with an outside service provider to provide and/or manage IT resources. In this model, the enterprise retains some level of IT governance control by negotiating and enforcing a binding contract known as a service level agreement. The enterprise also funds all the MSP incurred costs plus a mutually agreed to profit. This option can be cheaper than the traditional data center due to economies of scale. If the MSP is more efficient and/or more automated, the same desired outcome may be less expensive but will require some change to governance as some responsibilities will be shifted from in-house enterprise resources to the service provider.

The third option uses a **cloud service provider** (CSP). The CSP funds all hardware and software. The CSP also pays the salaries and benefits for the required operations staff. The required IT function is consumed by the enterprise completely as-a-service. In this model, the CSP has complete and total control of IT governance.

The following diagram here illustrates a few differences between the outsourcing models, MSP, and CSP. When choosing IT strategies, associated governance plans must also adapt to service models, deployment models, and implementation options:

| Managed Service Provider | Cloud Service Provider |
| --- | --- |
| Consumer dictates the technology and operating procedures | CSP dictates the technology and operating procedures |
| Network operations center (NOC) service | No network operations center (NOC) service |
| Customer help desk service | No help desk service |
| Remote monitoring and asset management for the customer | Customer responsible for monitoring and managing assets |
| Proactive maintenance of assets under management | Customer responsible for maintenance of assets |
| Predictable billing model | Pay by use billing model |

# Change management

Cultural/organizational/policy friction occurs through changes to established norms, not because of the technology being used. When adopting cloud computing, companies must focus on the benefits from business model changes. Many changes are needed as businesses search for ways to support new growth, modernized product strategies, and constant economic pressures. The transition to cloud computing can be complex for many different reasons. Some of the most common include:

- New knowledge required
- Dynamic nature of infrastructure
- New cloud service management tools
- Rapid innovation and fast-moving market
- New management models
- Distributed ownership
- Continuous optimization

During cloud transitions, organizations are not only changing from a technology perspective, but they are also changing their mindset and culture, simultaneously. The following is a list of typical domain changes associated with moving from traditional models to the cloud. With each of these, there is also a simultaneous change to organizational culture, required skill sets, and individual mindsets:

| Domain | Transition From | Transition To |
|---|---|---|
| Security Framework | Infrastructure-centric | Data-centric |
| Application Development | Tightly Coupled | Loosely Coupled |
| Data | Mostly Structured | Mostly unstructured |
| Business Processes | Mostly Serial | Mostly Parallel |
| Security Controls | Enterprise responsibility | Shared responsibility |
| Economic model | Mostly CAPEX | Mostly OPEX |
| Infrastructure | Mostly physical | Mostly virtual |
| IT Operations | Mostly manual | Mostly automated |
| Technology Operational Scope | Local/Regional | International/Global |

Ideally, before cloud services begin to be utilized, focused change management strategies should be implemented. Change management plans should quickly focus on raising awareness, understanding the change, accepting the changes, and the commitment of the organization to the expected outcomes and the people associated with them. The focused change management and communications plans must relentlessly focus on providing data and messaging that support organizational change, modernizes mindset, and skill sets, highlights benefits, and raises awareness. The organization should review metrics and counter metrics to gauge culture change rates and determine if all communication channels are being leveraged with correct messaging and correct timing.

Cloud computing is transformational. The hardest part of any transformational strategy is changing the hearts and minds of the people in the organization. It is critical for leaders to be keenly aware of what to look for and to have metrics and counter metrics in place to show changes in organizational culture, transformation rates and progress toward desired outcomes. A key question to ask is if each team member knows what the vision is; that is, do they see the whole elephant or do they only see the part they are connected to? Do they understand how their part is connected to the whole? Refer to the following photograph:

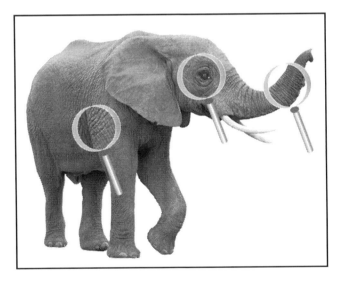

Figure 3: Does the staff see the elephant and how their part is connected?

Indicative questions may include:

- Do they believe that this transformation is achievable?
- Are customers and service providers on the same page?
- Do they think they have sufficient resources to meet the schedule?
- Are the staff the right kind, in the right place, doing the right work?
- Do the various groups that are working together understand and accept the interfaces and hand-offs?
- Are accepted and consistent vocabularies and definitions being used across the enterprise?

Think of the IT industry as a tribe. The industry has its language, terminology, and standard phrases. The cloud has a bit of its dialect within the IT tribe. There are common practices, rituals, and super-secret handshakes among tribe members. As with any other tribe or culture, standard practices and dialect enable quick identification of outsiders, newbies, and those that may be a threat to the tribe. Is change likely to be adopted when the path forward lacks awareness for current practices or the messaging is communicated used a completely different vernacular? Not possible.

As cloud and things-as-a-service increase in adoption, change management, and communication plans are paving the way. A deep dive into effective communication planning and IT governance strategy could fill several volumes. Some guidelines for effective plans and strategies are:

- Communicate using the tribe vernacular
- Use industry standard terms and definitions
- Provide authoritative sources if possible
- Provide data and insight with each communication
- Reinforce benefits of change at every opportunity
- Ensure leaders are familiar with tribe language, customs, and rituals

Companies should also explicitly link demand-side governance with supply-side governance to improve efficiency and effectiveness as detailed in the following diagram. Metrics should be evaluated to create, modify, or delete as part of an enterprise continuous improvement process:

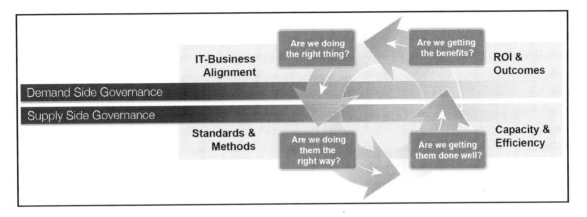

Figure 4: Linkage between IT governance and efficient implementation

# IT service management

Cloud computing solutions are implemented using service management frameworks. In designing any solution, the cloud solution architect must account for how well the organization is prepared to manage, operate, and continually improve that service. The most widely adopted industry standard process for efficiently and effectively providing **IT service management (ITSM)** is based on the **Information Technology Infrastructure Library (ITIL)**. ITIL structures ITSM into four domains:

- **IT infrastructure**: The technology components directly related to an IT service, for example, a **Red Hat Enterprise Linux (RHEL)** OS instance running on a server.
- **Supporting services**: The underlying infrastructure required to operate the customer-facing IT services, for example, the DNS server required to reach the RHEL instance by use of the hostname. Supporting services could be referred to as IT-internal services.
- **IT service**: The services requested by customers. Each IT service is implemented using the corresponding IT infrastructure. The IT service, therefore, complements a set of IT infrastructure components by adding service definitions such as SLA information and cost. In our example, the RHEL instance could be offered as a gold and silver service. Gold might include 24 x 7 support while silver offers 8 x 5 support at a lower cost.

- **ITSM framework**: Standards and processes that orchestrate all the activities required to deploy an IT service. This is not a collection of infrastructure components but rather the framework used for the deployment, operation, and decommissioning of IT services. The ITSM framework ties the IT infrastructure, supporting services and IT services together and provides the needed operational functionality. IT services are presented to potential customers, they, in turn, need to be able to order them:

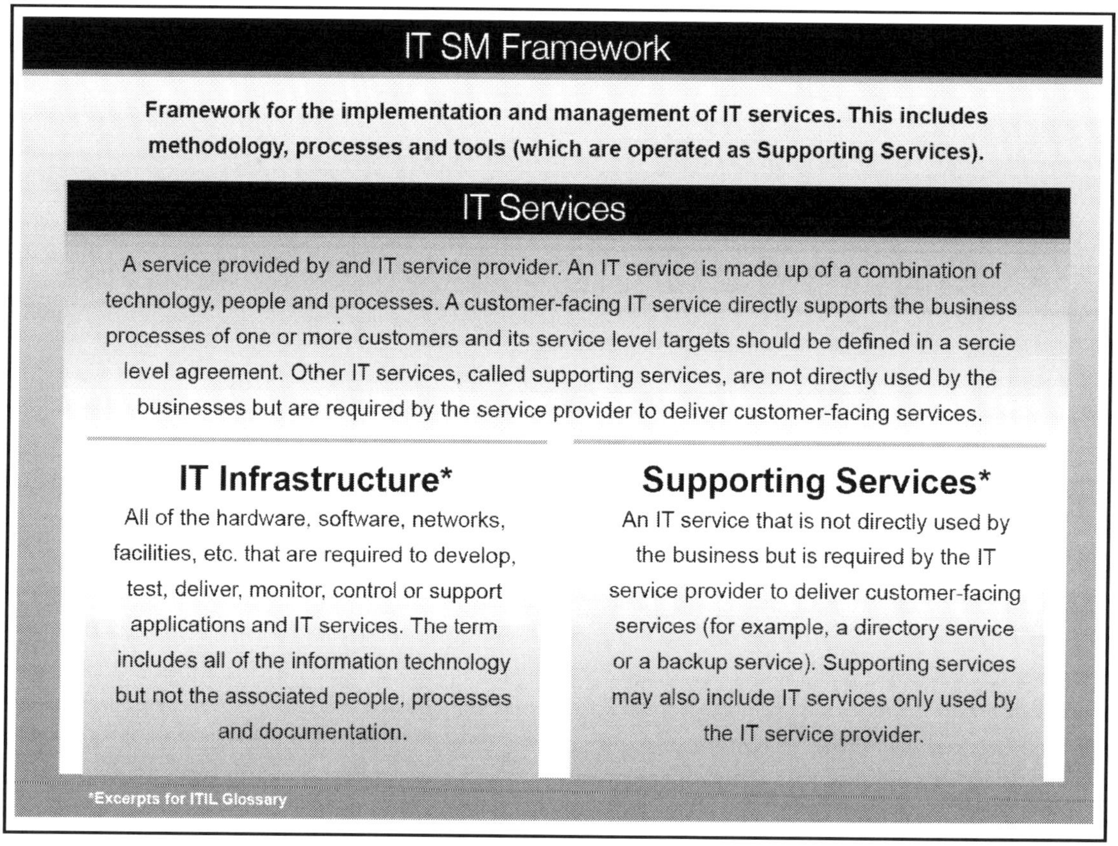

---

## IT SM Framework

**Framework for the implementation and management of IT services. This includes methodology, processes and tools (which are operated as Supporting Services).**

### IT Services

A service provided by and IT service provider. An IT service is made up of a combination of technology, people and processes. A customer-facing IT service directly supports the business processes of one or more customers and its service level targets should be defined in a sercie level agreement. Other IT services, called supporting services, are not directly used by the businesses but are required by the service provider to deliver customer-facing services.

### IT Infrastructure*

All of the hardware, software, networks, facilities, etc. that are required to develop, test, deliver, monitor, control or support applications and IT services. The term includes all of the information technology but not the associated people, processes and documentation.

### Supporting Services*

An IT service that is not directly used by the business but is required by the IT service provider to deliver customer-facing services (for example, a directory service or a backup service). Supporting services may also include IT services only used by the IT service provider.

*Excerpts for ITIL Glossary

---

Figure 5: IT service management framework

The ITSM framework should not be confused with the deployment of an IT infrastructure required by a service. The focus is on orchestrating all the activities required to deploy an IT service as opposed to a collection of infrastructure components. If the customer requests the RHEL gold service, it is not only about deploying the OS image using Red Hat Satellite, but also about modeling the service in the **Configuration Management Database (CMDB)**, configuring the event and impact management, making sure that the corresponding OLA are rolled-up into the promised SLA, and reporting it in a service view on a customer-facing portal. The ITSM framework ties everything together into a coherent service offering.

In addition to implementing ITSM, the following best practices should also be practiced:

- **Enforcement of brutal standardization across the enterprise**: A small number of non-optional constraints is often the most effective means of achieving agile governance. Jeff Bezos at Amazon famously mandated in 2002 that "*All [Amazon] teams will henceforth expose their data and functionality through service interfaces*" that could eventually be exposed to a public-facing market. The form and style of the interfaces were left to the teams to determine, but critically, anyone who didn't follow the edict was subject to termination. Vigorous enforcement of a lightweight set of requirements is a recurring theme in successful modern IT management. If this is not possible to globally enforce due to organizational considerations, it becomes even more important to demonstrate success via well-scoped pilot projects that can showcase the new model.
- **IT standardization**: Standardization is critical to gaining operational efficiency, reducing overall cost, and reducing the time required to deliver new capabilities. Across all commercial industries, average standardization savings are on the order of a 2/3 reduction of servers. Increasing the utilization percentage realizes these. Most of the economic value in this type of transition is accomplished through standardization in the software development platform and support personnel efficiencies enabled by standardized operational processes, as shown:

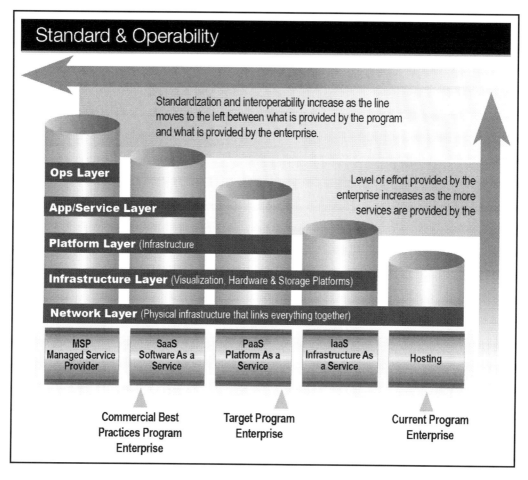

Figure 6: Achieving a shared services environment

- **IT change management standardization (processes and tools)**: As part of the adoption of ITIL, it is critical that the organization has positive knowledge of its IT assets. This is typically the first transformational step towards ITIL. Once a baseline of assets is collected, configuration control and processes must be put in place and religiously followed. This is needed to efficiently handle incident management (restore services, analyze incident types and trends, and improve communications), problem management (root cause analysis, document known errors), and change management (reduce unexpected outages, track approvals for compliance, new service support). Variations in these processes are problematic and are easily seen by the customer. The goal is to provide transparent, efficient, and consistent processes and services.

- **Transition from customer-mandated to a customer-focused model**: In a customer-mandated model, the solution design is primarily driven by a targeted end user's requirements and dictates. This approach can lead to wide technical variations across operationally similar solutions. In a customer-focused environment, the architects design solutions that can be used to meet a broad marketplace of users. These offerings are focused on the target audience for the provided services. For example, Amazon Web Services provides only limited patched versions of windows and Linux/Unix. This allows them to provide these service solutions at a very inexpensive rate on-demand to customers.

- **Leverage all applicable shared services**: The interoperability and efficiencies gained through cloud-based offerings are depicted in the following diagram. As more and more components become standardized the level of effort to provide them decreases as well as the overall system complexity. As the enterprise and the cloud offering matures, the enterprise performs more and more of the work performed and eventually, the business process-specific applications can be deployed as specialized IT service extensions.

- **Use common standardized delivery patterns**: Ideally, all cloud computing solutions should be designed as real-time aggregations of existing cloud services. The following diagram depicts the concept of providing a common set of standardized delivery patterns. In this diagram, the far left depicts some enterprise-wide patterns or sets of software that could be used to support specific lines of business. The diagram also includes the notion of a common development environment. This common development environment can be a PaaS or a standardized company environment that uses specified software components for targeting specific deployment patterns. By matching a certified and accredited development environment to a specific certified and accredited operational environment, an organization can rapidly develop and deploy industry-accredited solutions quickly.

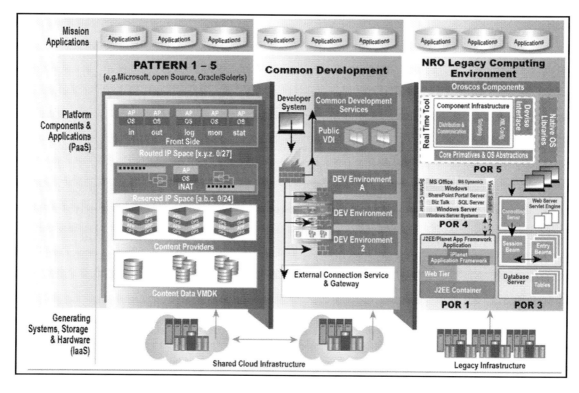

Figure 8: Common standardized delivery patterns

# Architecting cloud computing solution catalogs

To align with ITIL recommendations, enterprise IT services should be a customer-facing representation of the available technology services. An organization's IT services catalog should, in turn, provide all the information a customer should need to review, select, and acquire cloud solutions. Although both top-down approaches (from the business view) and bottom-up approaches (based on a technology and an available technology services view) have been used, industry best practices indicate that the bottom-up approach is far more efficient, because it is based on something tangible—the technology or technology services available to an organization.

A mapping of technology services to a cloud solution requires standards regarding both architecture and delivery. Without this standardization, a mapping across the IT external and internal boundary is not possible, (for example, if IT doesn't maintain a standardized build and delivery method for RHEL, the customer would receive a different build every time a RHEL gold service is ordered). A failure by the organization to set and enforce standards across the entire technology space, both regarding architecture and delivery would be contrary to the exact purpose of IT service management.

The challenge of the cloud computing solution task is primarily in the structuring and organization of available services to allow for a standardized, efficient, and reproducible mapping. This is referred to as service design in ITIL. During service design phases, all aspects of the solution must address new and evolving business needs. Business aspects often considered for cloud solutions include:

- Business process and the definition of the functional service needs, for example, telesales, invoicing, orders, credit checking
- The service (or solution) being delivered to the end user or business by the service provider, for example, email, billing
- Service level agreements that specify the level, scope, and quality of service to be provided
- Infrastructure—all of the IT equipment necessary to deliver the service to end users which includes servers, networks, switches, client devices, and so on
- The environmental requirements needed to secure, and operate the infrastructure
- Data is necessary to provide the service and deliver the information required to execute the business processes
- The application needed to manipulate or modify the data and provide the functional requirement of the business processes
- The **operational level agreements** (**OLAs**) and contracts, as well as any foundational agreements needed to deliver the SLA-dictated quality of service
- Support services necessary to execute all required operations
- All processes or procedures needed in the execution and operation of the delivered service
- Internal support teams that provide level 2 and level 3 support to end users and any of the service components
- External third party suppliers which are necessary to provide level 2 and level 3 support to end users or service components

The cloud is not the answer for everything. Components must first be considered in isolation. If the cloud presents advantages for the component in isolation, the component should then be considered among its other relationships, interactions, and dependencies to other components and services. If advantages remain the same or increase, the cloud becomes a viable option. This approach will result in an effective, well-researched, and easily communicated solution that aligns technical, strategic, and economic business needs within acceptable risk profiles.

Following ITIL recommendations, each solution component should be documented using configuration management artifacts across nine categories:

- **Description**: Describes the individual solution components by the use of standardized diagrams and a short textual description.
- **Life cycle:** Defines the organization's specific lifecycle for solution components. That life cycle is different (lagging) from the vendor life cycle because vendor products may need to be customized to meet internal standards.
- **Provisioning**: Describes the technical provisioning of solution components, the provisioning process required by solution components is covered in the artifact processes and runbooks.
- **Configuration management**: Document a solution component's requirements with regards to the implementation in a configuration management framework. This includes both CMDB templates as well as configuration management reports.
- **Security**: The technical and process aspects of a solution component's security requirements that must be met during the deployment and operating phase.
- **Monitoring**: Functionality required for monitoring the operational status of the solution components.
- **Processes and runbooks**: One-time activities related to a solution component, such as provisioning. The runbook focuses on normal activities along with any anticipated abnormal activities associated with the specific solution component, such as house cleaning, backup/restore, auditing, failover. Both the process descriptions and the runbook should cover the complete lifecycle of a solution component, including provisioning, operations, and decommission.
- **Financials**: Technology-based cost for **Capital Expenditure (CAPEX)** and **Operational Expenditure (OPEX)**. This does not include any IT service-oriented cost items such as system administrator support, as they can vary depending on the associated IT service offering.

- **Blueprints:** Detailed descriptions of the technical implementation of the solution component. For the engineering teams, the blueprints define how a component is to be developed for customers, they include detailed technical information about the component.

The solution itself should be documented in the following 12 categories:

- **Description**: Describes the individual solutions by the use of standardized diagrams and a short textual description.
- **Non-functional requirements (NFR)**: Solution requirements defined in a standardized and unambiguous fashion. There are two categories of NFRs:
  - Capabilities, which describe the features and functions provided by the infrastructure components
  - Qualities of service requirements that expand the infrastructure capabilities to cover additional end-user expectations
  - **Recovery Point Objective (RPO)** and **Recovery Time Objective (RTO)** are referenced for failover within a data center as well as failover between data centers
- **Required solution components**: Solution components required by a solution.
- **Life cycle**: The solution life cycle is mainly based on the life cycle of the individual solution components required by the solution.
- **Provisioning**: Provisioning of a solution consists of the provisioning of individual solution components. However, some solutions might require the prior provisioning of other solutions.
- **Configuration management**: Document a solution's requirements with regards to the implementation in a configuration management framework. This includes both CMDB templates as well as configuration management reports.
- **Security**: The security of a solution should be built into the individual solution components and not added on a solution level. Most solutions don't require any additional security considerations.
- **Monitoring**: The monitoring of the overall solution is essentially a collection of the individual solution components monitoring functionality. If applicable, the solution level monitoring should define how events from the different solution components are correlated and de-duped. These definitions must correspond the scenarios outlined in the resiliency assessment artifacts.

- **Resiliency assessment**: The description of all possible technical failure scenarios (operational errors are out-of-scope). This includes a description of the failure, how the failure is detected by the monitoring components and what remediation is possible. The impact of the failure is then captured regarding QoS type NFR, mostly downtime and data loss. The worst QoS NFR of all scenarios defines the QoS NFR for the solution as a whole.
- **Process and runbooks**: A collection of the corresponding artifacts on solution component level. Because of the mapping of solutions to IT services, there are IT services-specific process steps which are placed as a wrapper around the component processes.
- **Financials**: Technology-based cost for CAPEX and OPEX for each component used by the solution.
- **Blueprints**: This artifact lists the blueprints associated with the solution. There is no solution-specific blueprint for a solution that consists of solution components and doesn't provide technical functionality outside of the solution components.

It is essential that the ITSM framework supports the mapping of IT services to solutions and maintains the relationship between solution components, solutions, and delivery patterns. This can be done in the following manner:

- Customer orders an IT service
- IT service is mapped to a solution
- Solution components and composite solution components required for a solution are identified (solutions can't be deployed as a unit. Solution components are what is deployed)
- Solution components are deployed as individual components
- Solutions are re-constructed from solution components and mapped to IT services

# Summary

A cloud computing solution can only be successful if it is built on top of an effective IT governance and change management foundation. This chapter expanded that critical point by addressing cloud implementation strategy options and IT service management details. It also delved into solution catalogs through which service providers present and explain the available technology services.

# 3
# Design Considerations

Cloud computing is not a technology; it's an economic innovation. There are many ways to think through design, economic models, risk profiles, strategies, and technology decisions. The section will talk through some ways to navigate the thought process, how to eliminate some of the noise surrounding the cloud, and how to stay focused on what the challenges are and how solutions get mapped to those business challenges.

We will cover the following topics in this chapter:

- Foundation for design – the thought process
- Foundation for design – the cloud is economic, not technical
- Foundation for design – the plans
- Understanding business strategy and goals

## Foundation for design – the thought process

The cloud was supposed to be simple. It was supposed to be fast. It was supposed to solve many, if not all, of the problems. As people started digging into cloud designs, they began to discover that things were not always as simple, things were not always less expensive, and things were not always performing as expected. In many cases, they experienced significant challenges with social adoption. The design did not match expectations for various reasons. Throughout this book, we talk about how perceived requirements are merely starting objectives that accelerate towards requirements with the gathering of additional insight and data. Ultimately, successful designs must simultaneously harmonize economics, strategy, technology, and risk. This balance leaves risk and economics offset at equilibrium.

Cloud computing is one of the rare things in our industry where nearly everyone is impacted or affected by the change. Adoption of the change is the big challenge. People must embrace the transition while they adapt to process and work method changes. Without mental and emotional buy-in, projects can stall, exceed budgets, and, potentially, fail. The only path to acceptance and cultural change is through data.

As an example, consider a developer who is required to utilize a different cloud provider for all projects going forward. That developer must change processes and working methods and, potentially, go through a significant learning curve for new systems, applications, and tools. This example is not about the transition to the cloud, but about transitioning between clouds. How well does this go over if the developer enjoyed working with the previous supplier? What if that developer was very efficient in using the toolsets and could quickly navigate current processes? What if the developer was with presented data showing that the new provider could provide machines at 30% lower cost? The developer then can acquire and utilize three times the number of servers for the same budget. Consequently, what if productivity then increased tenfold when more compute resources are combined with integrated toolsets and automated processes? Data helps drive adoption in all cases.

As we begin to think through design considerations, a consistent thought process is required. Consistent, methodical, process-oriented thinking will help accomplish several things, such as:

- Eliminating the noise
- Enabling quick navigation through the complexity
- Maintaining focus on constraints and objectives
- Allowing fast and accurate interpretation of relevant insight
- Accurately identifying optimal solutions satisfying constraints
- Quickly identifying opportunities to optimize strategy

# Foundation for design – the cloud is economic, not technical

Contrary to what most believe, the cloud is not a technological innovation; it is an economic one. Although the cloud is based on virtualization technology, virtualization is not a new technology. Virtualization has been around for more than 50 years, starting with IBM mainframes in the early 60s, namely the CP-40. For decades, we have been trying to match better hardware and system utilization to the task or workload we are working to complete. Virtualization started with scientists and mathematicians from both IBM labs and MIT trying to perform complex calculations. They were trying to get more work done and, at the time, one task was limited to one system. IBM came up with the idea of virtualizing memory, which creates separate instances and completing more tasks could take place in the same amount of time. The birth of virtualization happened around 1963, with the first commercially available virtualized system going to market around 1967.

This book often discusses the fact that strategy, technology, and economics must align for successful design. Cloud computing and virtualization are not technical innovations. They are not strategic innovations, as the strategy of utilizing computing to its fullest extent, at its lowest possible cost, has been around as long as or longer than virtualization. The cloud is truly an economic innovation. The cloud was not a technical problem; it was a billing problem. The problem was that people could not find a way to accurately bill for a fraction of a processor or a fraction of RAM for a fraction of the time; a second, a minute, or so forth. The real innovation came when an instance of compute could be consumed for a period of time at a specified cost, with the ability to shut it off and give it back and only be billed for resources and time used (everyone considers Amazon Web Services as the early IaaS pay-as-you-go model). It is the ability to consume expensive compute on a pay-as-you-go model (OPEX versus CAPEX). It eliminated the need for massive capital up front and extended the growing movement of as-a-service models.

Much time and effort are spent aligning strategy, economics, and technology early in the book, because the cloud requires a new skill set, a new thought process, and a new approach to design. Successful architectures must simultaneously solve for strategic, economic, and technical requirements. A technically perfect design that is too expensive equates to poor design. A technically perfect design that is economically feasible may solve for the wrong strategy, also equating to poor design. All three must simultaneously resolve before the design can be viewed as successful. Because of this, cloud architects require a new thought process: a process of reflection that systematically navigates in layers utilizing discriminating attributes and characteristics rather than service names and marketed functions. Cloud architects need an updated skill set that includes economics and risk strategy, along with their technical prowess. Successful cloud architects must think more like selling CFOs than technical geniuses. Successful cloud architects need to be aware of the associated risks to the business if proposed changes are implemented. What is the impact on the business economically, short-term and long-term? What cultural impact will the changes have in the business, business unit, or division? Will personnel be affected? Does the company structure need to change? As you can see, technical information is no longer enough for the cloud architect. Cloud architects must be as comfortable in strategy conversations as they are in a technical one. Business finance and economics training are equally as important as, if not more important than, technical training.

Because the cloud is an economic innovation, and not a technical one, we quickly see that technical information will be pushed later towards the end of the thought process. In many cases, technical information becomes the tiebreaker, rather than the requirement. If you start with a good set of non-negotiable, and work through basic ideas and their economic impact, you can quickly see what fits strategically and what doesn't. If there are too many solutions, you can change requirements, potentially optimize strategy, revisit economic requirements, and so on. No one is saying that technical information is not required or valuable. The idea is to use technical detail to fine-tune, optimize, and perfect; think of a modern robot-driven, laser-guided surgical scalpel, as opposed to a medieval broadsword.

The cloud architect thought process is as shown in the following diagram:

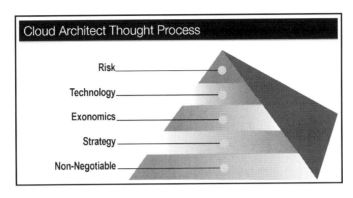

Every building project requires a solid foundation. Cloud design is no different. It is costly and difficult to change directions part-way through. Think of a high-rise building. It is tough to be twenty floors into construction and find there was a fatal flaw in the foundation, requiring the whole project to be torn down and started over. In cloud design, several elements create the base for a successful design. Many modern day designers begin with basics, such as storage, compute, or perhaps the network. They gradually get deeper and deeper technically, never knowing if they are headed in the wrong direction or not, unless they get told no by someone else who owns strategy or the project budget. This framework changes that dynamic. Technical elements come later in the process. This updated cloud architect thought process begins with the base of things that are truly non-negotiable. Non-negotiable constraints include things such as legal requirements, geography, sector and industry-specific requirements, project goals, strategic elements, and so on. These limitations form the basis on which everything else is built. If any of these elements can change, they are not true requirements and they certainly cannot be labeled non-negotiable. Once an exact set of non-negotiable are set, we can then look at additional details that will help define overall success factors, including basics such as business drivers, strategy, value prop, economic models, and corporate/industry preferences. Every design will follow the same thought process, beginning with non-negotiable constraints working upward through each layer as data and insight satisfy the objectives and constraints of the previous tier.

Every situation, scenario, design, and component will follow the same thought process and the same line of questioning:

- What are the non-negotiable constraints and characteristics?
- What are the economic attributes and their impact?
- How does this affect strategy?
- What is the discriminating technical attributes and characteristics?
- Is there an abnormal or excessive risk associated and does it affect economics?

# Foundation for design – the plans

There are no pre-built plans. Architects and designers are the ones tasked with developing the plans. Buildings cannot be built without a set of plans. The perimeter boundaries are surveyed. The site plan is created. The dimensions of the building are laid out. All of this is establishing scope and size for the architect or designer, who must stay within those confines. Anything outside of those boundaries will be unacceptable and labeled as poor design.

Cloud architecture and design operate in much the same way. We must establish a set of boundaries to work within. We must identify what is acceptable and what is not. All of our questionings must lead us toward a clear understanding of what leads to success and what leads to failure. It is just like building a house; if I put in a five-car garage, but I don't have room for a kitchen, that would be a poor design. I did not account for all requirements and, most likely, missed one that was non-negotiable. The same is true for cloud computing. If I'm not considering the correct requirements, my design will fail. So, the question becomes: How do I identify the right requirements?

We must discover the correct requirements through progressive questioning. We must start with questions that help us identify wants and needs. We must identify what is non-negotiable. What is the foundation? What is the base? What are the things that, no matter what changes, those answers are always the same? They will not change based on better pricing or something else suddenly becoming more interesting because of the latest magazine article. The base foundation elements are truly non-negotiable. They are based on what you know at this time and on the current data you have. They outline what needs to happen as a result of your design creating our base layer and non-negotiable foundation. We have now drawn the boundaries of our property before we start laying out the building. We know where our limits are.

Non-negotiable must always include a combination of economic, strategic, and technical elements. All successful designs must have these elements. Therefore, they must also be included in the design foundation. For the foundation to be correct, these non-negotiables must harmonize. A balance must be met within these limits and boundaries for the design to proceed.

Many factors need to be considered when navigating towards a successful design. Successful design requires boundaries. It requires an understanding of where the no lines are. By trying to find where unacceptable meets acceptable, we are then able to focus on what does work rather than chasing something that was never going to work from the start. It is a bit like some are essential and non-negotiable. These things are set, they cannot be changed. For example, geography. Geography is typically non-negotiable. Services get deployed where they are needed. If services are needed in California, they are not likely to be moved to Singapore because the price is a bit more favorable. Non-negotiable can change with every solution and every design scenario. The point is to uncover what is the foundation for the design. Find the things that absolutely cannot change and go from there. The following are some of the more common non-negotiable attributes within design:

- **Enterprise size**: While the size of an enterprise can positively influence certain factors of design, the enterprise size itself does not dictate design. For example, there is no minimum company size required to utilize the cloud. Enterprise size may affect design factors, such as scale, economics, risk, distribution, service mix, and so on. Each of these factors must be looked at from a strategic, economic, and technical point of view to make. A Microsoft study showed that the vast majority of organizations of all sizes use both **Software-as-a-Service (SaaS)** and hosted infrastructure services. Both SaaS and hosted infrastructure services are used most by organizations with less than 100 employees. Smaller companies are also more likely to use **Platform-as-a-Service (PaaS)**.

- **Relevant industry sectors**: Different industries have different requirements, different levels of compliance, and different appetites for risk. Government and education industries lead in the use of SaaS with a Microsoft study showing more than 60% of organizations reporting active use. While information technology is the ubiquitous horizontal layer underlying all industry sector verticals, security requirements strongly influence implementation specifics. This was highlighted by a cloud computing adoption study that documented the difference between regulated and unregulated industries.

Among regulated industries, insurance companies prefer private clouds because they are considered more secure than public clouds. Even though many studies have shown this to be a false assessment, this misconception is shared across many industry sectors. Even so, industry association community clouds have increased in popularity. While the banking industry is also concerned about security, the industry's forced transition from OS/2 to Windows 7 in 2014 drove a rapid adoption of newer and more sophisticated technology. Additional upheavals caused by subsequent transitions to Windows 10 have made cloud computing an attractive option for administrative and back-office processes like email, file sharing, and sharing of notes. While opportunities to use cloud computing in a variety of ways do exist across the government sector, most users misunderstand them. Today's largest opportunity is in using the public cloud, but many in government also fear security problems. Government-wide efforts such as the **Federal Risk Authorization and Management Program (FedRAMP)**, however, have gone a long way toward educating this sector.

Across unregulated industries, the story differs greatly. Cloud implementations in the retail market have been mostly IaaS or PaaS solutions. Security, availability, and vendor maturity are all aspects that retailers consider when deciding which functions to deploy as a cloud service. Media companies have gone all in on utilizing cloud computing. Today, the media audience can access any content through a variety of channels. These new opportunities are why cloud service providers and application developers are exploring a cloud-based ways to enable multi-screen entertainment. Industries are using cloud integrate, automate, and enable innovations in logistics, sales support functions, HR, product development, and lifecycle management, as well as some manufacturing operations.

- **Geography—Where am I? Where do I need to be?** Cloud computing is composed of physical data centers with five primary considerations influencing where data centers are built:
  - Physical space required to build the data center buildings
  - Availability of high-capacity network connections
  - Inexpensive electricity
  - Applicable jurisdictional law, policies, and regulations
  - The cloud computing export markets are shown in the following figure:

## Cloud Computing Export Markets

**Top Cloud Computing Export Markets (through 2016)**

| | |
|---|---|
| 1. Canada | 11. China |
| 2. Japan | 12. France |
| 3. United Kingdom | 13. Netherlands |
| 4. Brazil | 14. Italy |
| 5. South Korea | 15. Sweden |
| 6. Germany | 16. Singapore |
| 7. Switzerland | 17. Spain |
| 8. India | 18. South Africa |
| 9. Mexico | 19. Chile |
| 10. Australia | 20. Malaysia |

The first three are governed by physical constraints based on environmental variables:

- Physical geography
- Weather and natural disaster risks
- Renewable energy resource availability (such as water, geothermal, or wind) for cooling and power
- Safety concerns fueled by crime, terrorism, and corporate espionage

After that, proximity to high-capacity internet connections is key, because a data center's value is measured by the number of users it can support. Proximity to the internet backbone, or the main trunks of the network that carry most of its traffic, is another important driver. Data centers consume huge amounts of energy to cool servers. Areas with cheap energy are highly attractive. Considerations associated with jurisdictional laws, policies, and regulations are addressed later.

While US companies lead the cloud computing marketplace globally today, that doesn't guarantee leadership in the future. Some foreign companies, such Germany's SAP or Japan's Fujitsu, have become strong global competitors, while others, like Alibaba in China, have become formidable global competitors.

Public cloud services are rapidly becoming more important strategic factors in business. Public cloud will constitute more than half of worldwide software, server, and storage spending growth, by 2018, according to IDC. An example of this is General Electric, a global company that currently has over 90% percent of its applications in a public cloud. Greater public cloud adoption has also spurred wider SaaS usage, accounting for approximately 55% of all public cloud spending by 2018.

- **Legislation and other external regulations that apply**: The laws, policies, and regulations of a particular jurisdiction can have a significant impact on the cloud provider and the cloud user. The many law and policy problems that may affect its use by a company include:
    - Security with the assurance that unauthorized access to sensitive data and source code will be guaranteed by the cloud provider
    - Confidentiality and privacy of data held by the CSP with an expectation that the cloud provider, third parties, and governments will not be able to monitor their activities
    - Clear delineation of liability with regards to operational problems
    - Protect of intellectual property
    - Regulation, control, and ownership of data that is created or modified using cloud-based services
    - Fungibility and portability which is described as the ability to easily move or transfer data and resources from one cloud service to another
    - Ability to audit users to verify compliance with regulatory requirements
    - A clear understanding of legal jurisdiction

The manner in which an organization will approach cloud computing policy vary and will be driven by organizational priorities. One of the largest challenges will be associated with user security and privacy. Since many data centers are located in the United States, some of these concerns will be caused by the USA PATRIOT Act, the Homeland Security Act, and other intelligence-gathering instruments employed by the federal government to for release of information. One of the most disturbing aspects of these policies is the restrictions placed on a CSP that prevent notification to a user if the government issues a subpoena for a user's information. Other policy issues that can impact cloud use include **Health Insurance Portability and Accountability Act (HIPAA)**, Sarbanes-Oxley Act, Gramm-Leach-Bliley Act, Stored Communications Act, federal disclosure laws, federal rules of civil procedures, and e-discovery.

Adopted by the European Commission to strengthen data protection for all European Union citizens, the **General Data Protection Regulation (GDPR)** was approved in April 2016. With an effective date of May 25, 2018, GDPR compliance is challenging for companies of all sizes. With cloud computing, the problem may be even worse. Studies have shown that only 1 percent of cloud providers have data practices that comply with GDPR regulations. In fact, only 1.2% of cloud providers give users encryption keys that the customer manages and just 2.9% have secure password enforcement that is robust enough to pass GDPR muster. Only 7.2% have proper SAML integration support.

# Understand business strategy and goals

The second layer of the design triangle is having a thorough understanding of organizational strategy and goals. The cloud solution design must support and advance the organization's strategy and goals or it will be deemed a failure. To ensure alignment, the solution architect must discuss goals and strategy with the business owner and agree on the key metrics and target values. Some of the most popular cloud computing goals are as follows:

- **Agility**: Cloud computing delivers improved agility because it has on-demand self-service and rapid elasticity. These attributes enable enterprises to quickly innovate, introduce new products and services, enter new markets, and adapt to changing circumstances. Business agility also requires the ability to create new business processes and change existing ones. Cloud computing can eliminate procurement delays often associated with development and testing by enabling development resources to be available on-demand. Resource scaling enables service levels to be maintained and reduces cost. Cloud-based strategies can also help an enterprise acquire capabilities without the need for training.

- **Productivity**: The cloud can provide a more productive environment for collaborative working. The use of cloud-based tools for email, instant messaging, voice communication, information sharing and development, event scheduling, and conferencing are well known. The cloud can also provide shared logic in a business ecosystem.

- **Quality**: The cloud can deliver better quality-IT because usage information gives the enterprise an understanding of how IT is operating. Better understanding enables effective planning, equitable resource sharing, and increased resource efficiency. The ability to use web portals to automatically provision and configure resources gives the cloud service consumers substantially better management capabilities versus non-cloud system. Economies of scale also make the cost and effort required to of duplicate systems for disaster recovery relatively small. Server consolidation, resource optimization, increased asset utilization, and thin client use enhances cloud computing efficiency and reduces the carbon footprint.

- **Reduced cost**: Cloud computing reduces IT costs by delivering effective resource optimization, by being able to move processor, memory, storage, and network capacity among users almost instantly. Significant cost reductions can be obtained by replacing expensive client devices with cheaper client devices that provide just a user interface to the application server. Community clouds provide an easier path for a community of enterprises to share the cost of common resources. If the organizational goal is maximizing financial capital use through the improved use of the debt and equity funds, the OPEX opportunity provided by cloud computing will directly support that strategy.
- Identification of new business opportunities through morphing a company into becoming a cloud service provider. A company that excels in the quality of its IT may easily become a public IaaS or PaaS provider. Implementing services in the cloud would make them accessible to a large, global market.
- Operational risk/reward balance can be improved by moving low-risk activities to an on-demand service environment. Other on-demand business opportunities may be unveiled exist by mitigated risk management through partnerships and risk sharing. High risk can be reduced by sharing selected business process operations that are strongly correlated to operational or legal failures. This may include corporate risks linked to identifiable software applications, infrastructure components, or specified services. Corporate benefits should be traded-off against these corporate risks with consideration of whether business activities with low corporate returns can be commoditized for competitive advantages. This strategic direction could identify opportunities to improve market share, revenue, profit, or cost management through on-demand delivery of cloud services.
- Modifications to the business products line could be both transformative and disruptive. Opportunities to exploit existing markets with current products and services could be profitable as a utility or commodity offering. A company may be able to offer existing services in a self-service model that has been augmented and enhanced with on-demand features. Unique products services sourced and delivered via an on-demand portal could also be disruptive to existing product lines. If this is the case, the cost-benefit exchange here must be analyzed. Rapid scaling and expansion of offered services could deliver additional value.

- Reducing investment in non-differentiating processes through the use of SaaS could significantly improve an organization's bottom line. Areas where this has been particularly helpful include:
    - Business management area, which includes skills management, benefits administration, compensation planning, and **human capital management (HCM)**
    - **Financial management (FM)** in the areas of accounting, financial and compliance reporting, real estate management, **Sarbanes-Oxley (SOX)**, finance taxes, BASEL II, order to cash, business performance management, and risk management
    - **Customer relationship management (CRM)** that supports sales, **business intelligence (BI)**, **customer experience management (CEM)**, business analytics, call center management, campaign management, **sales force automation (SFA)**, and sales analytics
    - **Supply chain management (SCM)**, especially procurement, **supplier relationship management (SRM)**, inventory management, logistics, and import compliance processes
    - **Manufacturing management of product lifecycle (PLM)**, resource and capacity, and workforce
    - **Information technology (IT)** services associated with IT architecture design, data center operation, and software development

- Corporate headquarters activities such as research and development (R&D), communications, strategy, and portfolio management, legal, and marketing:
  - Internal business process scope and complexity can be adjusted by considering what niche business processes could be moved to a CSP. This could range from moving a specific IT operation to an on-demand provider or commoditizing a service for competitive low-cost advantages. Both large organization-wide operations and smaller, localized activities should be considered. Management should also make specific decisions on which specific business processes need to stay under the control of the business for competitive advantage or whether complex processes can be improved by reducing the number or complexity of the steps involved.
  - Cloud computing has a history of improving collaboration/information sharing through the use of on-demand personal productivity tools. This area can also be used to addresses debates around whether personal information and assets created by individuals should be classified as the private intellectual property of the corporation. Collaboration across a community of users can raise similar issues, by raising intellectual property issues regarding creating assets on a shared platform or ecosystem business service environment. When addressing private information, corporate rules that identify and define data ownership and the partitioning of corporate information from that which is private should be part of the strategy process. This will often drive decisions regarding the suitability of secure storage and access control service.

- In the case of public information, corporate and personal data rules should prohibit the storage of, and access to, personal and corporate information from public locations. Local and national legislation affects this as well. Information held publicly must be monitored and managed at a level that meets legal e-discovery standards. Personal and corporate information must be classified, partitioned, and effectively isolated for storage and use in public locations. The various components of the business process are shown in the following diagram:

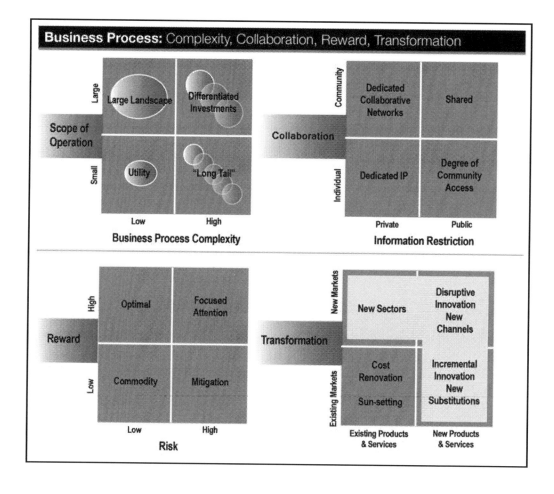

An architect's success in overcoming the two big hills to adoption of cloud computing services will be influenced mostly by a solution's alignment with relevant business drivers and strategies. The solution must also pay homage to the intended customer value proposition.

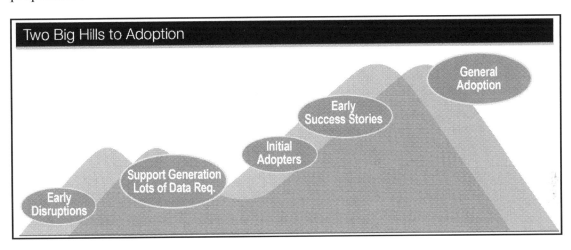

The most broadly recognized cloud computing business drivers are:

- Cost flexibility, which shifts fixed cost to variable cost and allows the implementation of the pay-as-and-when-needed model
- Business scalability that provides flexible, cost-effective computing capacity
- Market adaptability, which enables faster time to market and supports business or mission experimentation
- Masked complexity that helps expand product and service sophistication while simultaneously allowing for greater end-user simplicity
- Context-driven variability that is used to better define the user experience which, in turn, increases product relevancy
- Ecosystem connectivity, which fosters new commerce value nets, which can drive and create new business models

Business strategies most often supported by these business drivers are:

- Product and service optimization that enhance the customer value proposition improve current industry value chains and uses the cloud to incrementally enhance their customer value propositions while improving their organization's efficiency.

- Marketplace innovation that aims at extending the customer value proposition through the transformation of industry value chain and improving customer value. This strategy choice often results in brand-new revenue streams and ecosystem role modifications.
- Market disruption is focused on inventing new customer value propositions and creating new industry value chains by generating new customer needs and segments.

Value chain enhancement is accomplished by building new industry value chains or disintermediate existing ones. Cloud adoption can also aid an organization that is struggling to maintain its place within an existing value chain. This is accomplished through increased efficiency and improved capability to partner and collaborate. Transformative organizational goals can be attained through the development of new operational capabilities, changing the organization's existing industry role or by deciding to enter a completely different marketplace or industry.

If organizational goals revolve around improving the customer value proposition, companies can garner incremental revenue through improvements in current products and services and enhancement of customers' experiences. Cloud computing services can help a company explore or create new distribution channels or payment methods. This could attract existing or adjacent customer segments. This vector could also lead to the creation of a new marketplace need which would attract new customer segments and generate unique revenue opportunities.

The various economic options cloud enables often drives innovative business models. This is accomplished by having a model that ensures a dollar of revenue for every dollar of expense. Cloud computing economic payment options include:

- On demand, in which you only incur cost for the service your organization actually consumes
- Reserve, where a company is obligated to pay for a predetermined quantity of service provider resources at a discounted price
- Spot market, which is an open marketplace auction model that varies resource cost by varying demand for that resource

# Summary

Cloud computing requires consistent, methodical, and process-oriented thinking. It is not about any specific technology, but rather operational, economic, and business models built on highly standardized and automated IT infrastructures. Success depends on establishing and working within formalized boundaries. These boundaries must be documented and enforced by organizational IT governance. The cloud solution design must support and advance the organization's strategy and goals or it will be deemed a failure. To ensure alignment, the solution architect must thoroughly understand the business or mission goals and strategy. More importantly, the architect and business/mission owner must agree on the key metrics and target values that will define success.

# 4

# Business Drivers, Metrics, and Use Cases

There are many ways to evaluate projects from a financial perspective. Cloud solutions, like most IT projects, are easily compared with ROI metrics. However, ROI does not typically tell the whole story. The cloud can pull many financial levers as well as optimize and increase efficiencies in several related, but not necessarily direct, inputs to ROI calculations. This section looks into some of the considerations when looking at the economic impact of cloud solutions.

## Return on Investment

**Return on Investment (ROI)** is the most often used measurement when making project investment decisions. It measures the rate of return versus the cost of the investment. Because ROI is a percentage, it is very easy to make quick comparisons when evaluating multiple options. There are only four ways to either increase revenues or lower costs, improving ROI numbers. The four financial levers are the following:

- Decrease investment
- Increase revenue
- Decrease costs associated with the activity
- Reduce the time required to attain revenue

Cloud computing can operate any of these levers but the simultaneous achievement of all four is impossible. The relationship between these factors is the most important aspect of cloud ROI, not the absolute values. For example, a project moving to a public cloud may resemble the following: initial investment decreases, operating costs may increase, revenue may remain flat, but margins may increase due to lower investment, and return may accelerate due to lower overall investment at higher return margins. Increasing revenue in this situation would accelerate the rate of return and shorten the time needed to attain revenue goal.

These financial dynamics change with every project, service model, and deployment model. Private deployments have completely different dynamics. In-house versus external, in-house versus in-house, each will have different return rates. ROI can be improved, or made worse, with strategy choices because of the relationships of revenue and speed of return. Revenue may increase by improving features and quality, commanding higher market values. Automation may help a business scale, driving greater revenues at controlled costs.

Cloud requires balance in its approach. Data-driven methodologies will help to define goals and expected outcomes, and identify ways to manage risk. A data-driven approach can guide the organization to optimal strategies and identify better choices. There are many data points and fundamental drivers that can impact cloud ROI numbers. Many data points are captured from related productivity, speed, scale, and quality measurements. Typical ROI calculations are straightforward: there is a cost for a given return. ROI for cloud is a bit different in that there are other factors, including efficiency improvements, opportunity costs, and investment patterns. When evaluating cloud versus traditional IT strategies, additional layers of data must also be considered, such as the following:

- Increased turnover and profits due to increased efficiencies
- Revenue loss due to the inability of existing systems to respond to dynamic demands
- Costs of managing a standalone and non-standardized environment
- Reduction or avoidance of capital cost related to the purchase, development, and deployment of new systems or services
- Success-based growth and investment, as needed
- Smaller increment investment for cloud versus larger capital investment for traditional models

The factors that drive ROI are the following:

- Productivity, which is enabled by utility-based services that provide on-demand provisioning that meets meet actual customer usage. Increased productivity can avoid infrastructure capital expenditures, avoid infrastructure investment opportunity cost, and improve customer satisfaction through better responsiveness.
- Resource utilization, which eliminates the practice of dedicating servers to specific functions or departments by using active management to size and handle peak loads that are underutilized at off-peak times.
- Usage-based pricing translates higher provider utilization into lower infrastructure costs for consumers. SaaS does this by reducing the traditional licensing cost associated with ownership, number of users, support, and maintenance costs:

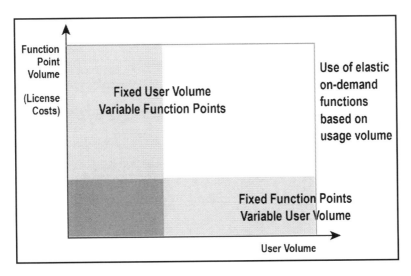

Software license cost as they relate to number of users

- Specialization and scale that gives the CSP an ability to drives lower IT costs through skill specialization and economies of scale by amortizing costs over a larger user base:

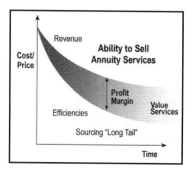

Revenue generated on the basis of the cost and the time

- Increased speed in provisioning IT resources, which enables enterprises to acquire the resources they need faster. This model also increases visibility into resource configurations, which accelerates the choice when many options are available. This factor can dramatically cut the time to deployment of new products and services. Elastic provisioning creates a new way for enterprises to scale their IT to enable the business to expand. Rapid execution saves time and enables new business operating models:

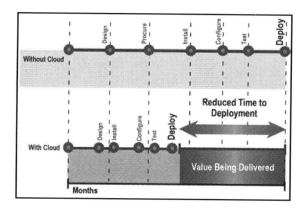

Traditional IT deployment versus an IT deployment using cloud computing

- Faster execution of lifetime cost models through increased speed of execution. This factor positively impacts lifetime cost models by reducing the cost of a product or service as the depreciation cost of purchased assets decreases and efficiencies are realized. This higher rate of cost reduction means that profitability increases more quickly, giving shorter payback times and increased ROI:

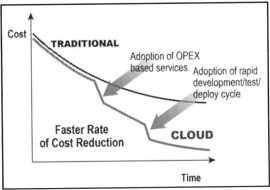

Traditional rate of cost reduction versus that with cloud computing

- The IT asset management process accelerates reducing the risk of decoupling IT choices and its impact on long-term operations and maintenance IT service costs. This factor also enables the ability to select hardware, software, and services from defined design configurations to run in production environments. This reduces the design-time/runtime divide while simultaneously optimizing service performance:

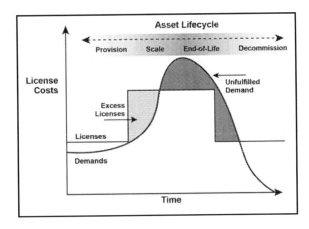

Traditional software license Return on Investment graph

Cloud computing is an economic innovation, not a technical one. Infrastructure is aging and is going to require significant funding to modernize. How can we optimize the ratio of spend to return across the entire asset portfolio? The same traditional deployments are going to lead to a traditional return. A change in model and economics is required to modernize. Cloud enables an enterprise to change economic models, achieving a faster, cost-effective asset management lifecycle for the entire IT portfolio. Designs can utilize current capabilities and components, optimizing runtime performance. Cloud services also lower entry cost with faster deployment time, quicker time to market, increased competitiveness, and more business and leads generated across a much larger operational scale. Additional high-value services are quickly and efficiently delivered to clients and customers through the use of cloud-based collaboration services for communication, information exchange, and virtual meetings.

Cloud economics is creating many new business opportunities that were not possible previously. Opportunity is often associated with the **Long Tail** shown in the preceding figure. The illustration shows as efficiencies improve, opportunities for a revenue increase and margins rise over time. Innovation driven by economics increases efficiency, lowers cost, and as a by-product creates additional opportunities for revenue. The revenue opportunities may be related to underserved markets that are now accessible. New segments and sectors may now be financially feasible that previously were considered economically undesirable. Opportunities that may have previously been undesirable from a risk point of view may now be interesting revenue opportunities as the lower costs and higher margins may offset perceived risk.

Interestingly, we see the same behavior in the IT infrastructure market. The cost of computing resources is dramatically dropping while the cost of managing traditional deployments is rapidly rising. This creates new opportunities within cloud-based ecosystems as well. We are seeing many new cloud service providers entering the market. Merger and acquisition activity has increased. Innovations driven by economics are always disruptive. These types of shifts create many opportunities for specialists and related enterprises to make big plays as new service providers or acquirers.

Because cloud innovation is economic and not technical, new revenue opportunities can be people-based and IT-based. Opportunities may be a new type of service or an existing service with a new economic model. Revenue opportunities may enhance the quality of existing services as reinvestment is now possible due to improved margins, increased scale, and larger scope for current operations. Cloud computing enables better utilization of resources and assets, increasing efficiency, and accelerating operations and delivery at lower cost. Cloud computing is disruptively influencing both buyers and sellers.

As available services, combinations of services, and pricing models continually change, the quality of the service must be considered. A recent performance comparison of a single server from a single service yielded some surprising data. The provider offered the same cloud service out of multiple locations. Two locations were chosen. The same instance type and same server configurations were chosen. The only difference was the location. Each server was benchmarked using the same CPU and memory test. Testing reported a 700% difference in performance within the same provider, with the only difference being location. When the benchmarking was run across multiple providers, using the same size of server with the same configuration, we noticed very different performance, with the price varying by more than 3,200% from low to high, for the same configurations. What is the difference? Why would the deviation be so high? Aren't all clouds equal? Cloud is cloud, correct? Not exactly.

Basic ROI calculations are pretty straightforward: cost versus expected return. As we examine the other surrounding benefits of utilizing the cloud, we are reminded of a few things:

- Cloud is an economic innovation
- Every benefit of the cloud has an economic impact
- Next-generation designers, architects, and IT leaders need a blended foundation that includes principles of business and strategy, general economics, and technology, as well as a good understanding of business risk and economic mitigation

Why would the same server vary 700% in performance and 3,200% in price for the same configuration? Other layers and benefits must be accounted for in our cloud ROI calculations. There are many metrics to consider; not all need to be used, for example, **service level agreements (SLAs)**. SLAs are a simplified way to try and express a quality of service numerically. The higher the number, 99.999 versus 99.90, the higher the quality of service is perceived to be. What does the quality of service actually mean? This topic will be explored more throughout the book. Is the service redundant? How resilient is it? Is it delivered via cheap unknown white box machines out of a neighbor's garage or is it within an impenetrable fortress using a brand name, high performance, and the latest and greatest hardware? How is it supported? How up to date are patching and security? Is it hardened OS? Is there 24x7 support? What is the quality and level of the support engineering teams? Many things can contribute to pricing differences, including margin.

Cloud computing differentiation is not just through the provisioning of utility computing services, but also higher-level services that enhance and build customer value. These attributes are why there is rapid movement from technology-centric services to business-value-centric services. This change extends to nearly every service and every industry, with utility infrastructure services at one end and complete function and application business-centric services being provided by nearly every provider in the market.

# ROI metrics

When designing and building a business case for a cloud computing solution, the following metrics can assist with aligning a prospective solution with the business or mission need:

- **Time**: Cloud solutions optimize time required to deliver or execute business processes by decreasing the time required to provision resources or time required to consider multi-sourcing options. It can also decrease the time required to achieve specified goals associated with information technology services. This value also leads to a faster realization of reduced IT total ownership costs.

- **Cost**: Cloud computing can optimize ownership use by reducing the application portfolio total cost of ownership. This is realized through license cost reduction, open source adoption, and SOA reuse adoption. Cloud also optimizes the cost associated with delivering a specified IT service capacity by aligning IT costs with IT usage. The CAPEX versus OPEX utilization balance can be more effectively managed with pay-as-you-go savings.

- **Quality**: Cloud can improve service and product quality through customization and enhanced user relevance. It can also reduce ecological damage through reduced carbon footprint and advance organizational green sustainability goals.

- **Optimizing margin**: Metrics associated with the cost to deliver/execute business and supply chain cost is reduced, which increases product/service margin. Increased flexibility and choice across providers and feeder services can also help to optimize margin.

# Key performance indicators

The **key performance indicators** (**KPIs**) are used to measure goal attainment. Advance agreement on the relevance of the following cloud computing KPIs can assist in solution/business alignment:

- Time:
    - **Availability versus recovery SLA**: Indicator of availability performance compared to current levels
    - **Timeliness**: Degree of service responsiveness, which can be used to indicate rapidity of service choice determination
    - **Throughput**: Transaction latency or the volume per unit of time throughput which measures workload efficiency
    - **Periodicity**: Frequency of demand and supply activity or the amplitude of the demand and supply activity
    - **Temporal**: The event frequency to real-time action and outcome result

- Cost:
    - **Workload-predictable cost**: Indicator of CAPEX cost of on-premises ownership versus cloud
    - **Workload-variable cost**: Indicator of OPEX cost for on-premises ownership versus cloud
    - **CAPEX versus OPEX cost**: Indicator of on-premises physical asset TCO versus cloud TCO
    - **Server consolidation ratio**: Ratio of servers in legacy infrastructure to the number used in the cloud infrastructure
    - **Workload versus utilization percentage**: Indicator of cost-effective cloud workload utilization

- Workload type allocations:
    - **Workload size versus memory/processor distribution**: Measures percentage of IT asset workloads using cloud
    - **Instance to asset ratio**: Measures percentage and cost of IT consolidation
    - **Degree of complexity reduction (%)**: Measures the number of guest operating system instances versus the number of physical resource assets
    - **Tenancy to instance ratio**: Measures tenants per resource, which measures CPU and memory utilization

- **Ecosystem (supply chain) optionality**: Tracks the use of commodity assets used to deliver company services after the function is migrated to a CSP
- Quality:
  - Experiential—the quality of the perceived user experience of the service
  - Basic quality of service metrics (availability, reliability, recoverability, responsiveness, throughput, manageability, security)
  - User satisfaction
  - Customer retention
  - Revenue efficiencies
- Margin increase per unit revenue:
  - Rate of increase of annuity income
  - SLA response error rate
  - Frequency of defective responses
  - Intelligent automation—the level of automated response (agent)
- Margin:
  - Revenue efficiencies—ability to generate margin increase per revenue.
  - Rate of annuity improvement
  - Market disruption rate—rate of revenue growth versus rate of new product customer acquisition

# Business goal key performance indicators

Business goal KPIs that should be considered include the following:

- The speed of cost reduction
- Cost of adoption/de-adoption
- Optimizing ownership use
- Rapid provisioning
- Increasing margins
- Dynamic usage
- Elastic provisioning and service management
- Risk and compliance improvement

# Economic goal metric

In a similar vein, measurable economic goal metrics include the following:

- Capital expenditure avoidance
- Consumption billed as a utility
- Lower barriers to market entry
- Shared infrastructure costs
- Lower management overheads
- Immediate access to the application
- Immediate termination option
- Enforceable SLAs
- High benefit-cost ratio

There are also metrics for performance and price-to-performance that can provide very clear comparisons between providers, services, and strategies. Using these next-level metrics can move the ROI conversation forward quickly when aligning solutions to an organization's goals and expected outcomes. This type of transparent data also helps build consensus, eliminate politics, and facilitate cultural adoption within the enterprise.

# General use cases

You can refer to a baseline set of use cases a cloud solution architect can use to identify the best solution target for the enterprise at `https://www.scribd.com/document/17929394/` `Cloud-Computing-Use-Cases-Whitepaper`(Saved copy).

These are illustrative examples of the most typical cloud use cases and are not meant to be an exhaustive list. Active use case components are shown in color.

Additional details on the operational requirements summarized here are provided in `Chapter 11`, *Operational Requirements*.

# Summary

ROI is always a key topic when organizations invest. Investing in cloud computing solutions is no different. The architect must be clear on how the proposed solution will deliver value and that value must be described in business or mission terms. The metrics outlined in this chapter have been effectively used across many industries. Key business drivers must be identified early and a direct linkage to solution functions and capabilities made clear. General use cases are useful for outlining *day in the life* scenarios, which, in turn, can be effectively leveraged when communicating solution value to business or mission owners.

# 5
# Architecture Executive Decisions

The cloud is changing everything. Change occurs every day in the cloud services market. Changes to solutions, services, pricing models, consumption models, and locations all lead to different strategies, technology choices, economic impacts, and risk profiles.

Today, it is a normal process for the consumer to express what solution and solution components they require in the form of an RFI, RFP, RFQ, or some other type of requirements document, emailing a spreadsheet, for example. The consumer expresses what their experts need based on a mix of data sources, including business requirements, current state information, and the latest innovative articles read by a partially involved IT leader. Requirements are sent to one or more providers with the providers expected to respond to what is requested. Pricing is normally added and the response returned with minimal, if any, insight given. There may be a few phone calls and some back-and-forth, enabling the service provider to respond as accurately as possible.

Current processes feel very transactional: I want a blue shirt, or I want a French cuff, button-down, blue dress shirt; please show me the blue shirts you have and how much they are. This process pattern is very manual and very slow. The process is filled with stop-and-go workflows and communication patterns. This kind of process is also serial, meaning that each step must be completed before the next can start. Tools used to communicate and share data are also manual, disconnected, and slow.

Today's process looks something like the following diagram. This view is from the service provider side as they formulate a response. Everyone involved in the process (consumer, provider, integrator, consultant, and channel partner) follows virtually the same engagement pattern:

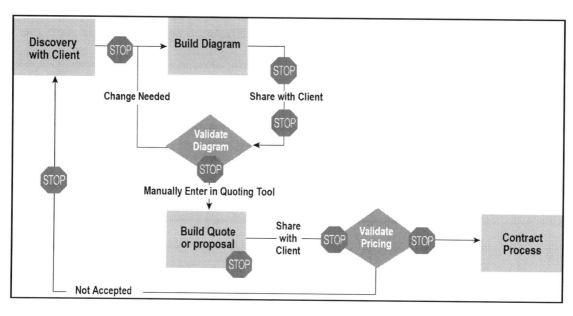

The cloud is completely turning this engagement method upside down and sideways. This method no longer works. The market is changing too fast. Products and services are released, updated, changed, or retired almost daily. How can the consumer side possibly build accurate solutions in a vacuum and pass it to a service provider for a response? It is impossible. The service providers can barely keep up with the pace of knowing their own product catalogs. There is no way the consumer can keep up with the thousands of available products and services from a service provider. Multiply that by the hundreds and thousands of potential service providers available in the market. Talking to two or three suppliers is no longer a representative sample set. Multiply those numbers by the hundreds of locations available globally. There are trillions of potential combinations available. How can a consuming enterprise possibly gather the data, normalize it, compare it, optimize design, and pick a strategic partner using the slow, manual, disconnected tools, and processes available today?

What needs to change? As stated, the process needs to be completely inverted. The tools need to be automated. Collaboration needs to be in real time. Insight needs to become a requirement, not an unexpected differentiator. Instead of pricing requirements, we need to design with economics in mind. Instead of building technical designs, we need to collaborate for solutions that align technology, strategy, economics, and risk. Instead of telling service providers what is required, business challenges and risks should be communicated. The thinking must change and begin to map solutions to business challenges and match technology to tasks.

With changes in mindset, process, and approach, executives can accelerate organizations, motivate teams, and increase control over strategy, economics, and risk. Engaging in insightful, collaborative ways can transform the previous slow, serial, stop-and-go methods into the following high-velocity, streamlined, parallel operating method:

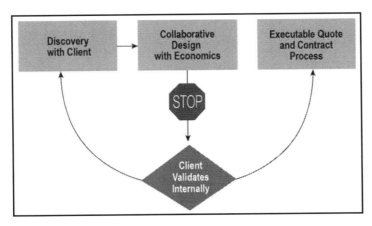

# Invert for insight – process

Today, we are bound by a process that no longer matches our industry, nor does it align with industry direction. As stated, consumers express what they believe they require, confining service providers to respond with services they have that match the request. The RFI process allows for some insight to be given, yet is still void of any real collaboration. It is still a version of a question and answer session. If the questions go unasked, or the wrong questions are asked, opportunities for greater insight are missed.

# Real-time collaboration

With the level of change, and the rapid pace of change, in the current market, anything less than real-time collaboration will miss the mark. It is no longer possible to keep up with the moving pieces in our industry. The constant changes to product strategies, economic and business models, consumption models, deployment models, and pricing can't be accurately gathered, normalized, and compared for one or two vendors, certainly not the hundreds available today.

# Express challenges, not requirements

Cloud is changing everything. Cloud allows us to buy a fraction of a resource needed for a fraction of time, consume it, and return it when finished. The length of time could be in seconds, hours, days, months, or years. The beauty is that we cannot align what we need to when we need it and directly match it to a specific challenge or situation. Thinking can now shift away from acquiring solutions then mapping as many problems as we can to it, to now expressing well-defined challenges and only acquiring what is needed, when it is needed, to satisfy the challenge and be able to give it back when we are done with it, eliminating much of the cost.

Expressing challenges also improves relationships and partnerships with those wanting to help solve them. Service providers listen and respond to global market needs every day. The challenge for a service provider is trying to interpret requirements and translating them into challenges. Service providers rarely participate in conversations directly expressing client challenges. The normal conversation covers requirements, not business-focused needs. Consumers avoiding deep discussions related to their challenges may occur for many reasons: internal politics, ego, inexperience, poor planning, oversight, policies, confining processes, and so on. Service providers have learned that insightful, proactive, collaborative engagements are the most successful, with the highest levels of loyalty and commitment. Express challenges to receive insight.

# Automate and enable

Executives continually balance investment, return, and risk. Today, many of the tools and processes we use are manual, disconnected, and slow. In a rapidly moving market, executives need more data and insight quicker. Automation, integration, and enablement are critical for success in today's cloud universe. Any platforms, systems, tools, and processes invested in should align strategy, technology, economics, and risk in an automated integrated way. Collections of data do nothing without mapping, matching, and comparing to expose real-time insight used to make aligned decisions.

# Stop talking technology – Strategy

Many people start talking about technology choices very early in conversations. There may have been significant recent investigation aimed at a technology component or direction. There may be team structures aimed at supporting technology commitments previously made. Financially, there may be a perception that change is going to be difficult and expensive. There may also be those that are afraid of change as it may politically change their value, roles may change, team structures could change along with current responsibilities, or skill sets may need significant changes for those late in their career path.

Strategy determines direction; technology implements it. Technology can influence strategy, but cannot dictate it. Before the cloud, projects were designed and engineered for the anticipated high-water mark of utilization, even if it was for 1 minute. The anticipated workload determined infrastructure size and scale. Cloud has now enabled us to design and architect for the low side baseline workloads and dynamically burst as needed into demand-based configurations using automation and scripting, improving economics, and matching technology to strategy.

# Economics, not pricing – Economics

It is important to switch the thinking from what the cost is for assembled technical answers and move to using economic data as an integral part of the solution design process. Today, we go through the design process four or five times, first for assembling a reasonably correct technical answer then pulling it apart in layers, trying to back down to something that is within economic reach yet in a technically desired direction.

If we switch that model and move to looking at designing with economics from the very beginning, we can eliminate nearly all recirculating effort as designs are built then redesigned in the current process. It is also important to keep in mind that much of the technical detail affects implementation details more than it does strategy or economics. If it does not materially affect strategy or dramatically change economics, move on to implementation discussions after confirming a solution strategy and economic direction. If showstoppers rise during implementation conversations, you are still money and time ahead, able to switch directions as needed since you have not done the four or five rounds in traditional processes:

The perfect technical solutions are sometimes unaffordable or miss the strategy. Low-cost solutions may not balance with technical requirements or introduce too much risk. All factors must balance for successful solution design.

# Solutions, not servers – Technology

Technology no longer needs to drive economic and strategic conversations. Due to the economic innovation of cloud, technology is now better able to align with strategy, economic, and risk requirements. Enterprises can now simultaneously align choices on strategy and direction with technology and economics. As an example, businesses with cyclical needs, meaning that everything is not needed all the time, can leverage services and just-in-time infrastructure deployments as needed to satisfy cycles as needed. Very little investment is required up front, with scalable growth available programmatically.

Successful solutions will utilize services as needed. These services may be internally provided or externally consumed. Strategy and economics will determine the best path forward. In almost all cases, consuming solutions as a service is optimal across nearly all decision metrics and scorecards.

# Lower costs can be bad for business – Risk

Executives often need to balance economics and risk. The more risk assumed, the lower is the cost. Risk and cost seem to have an inverse relationship. Cloud is an opportunity to change paradigms. The shift comes from a change in perspective. Because cloud is an economic innovation, much of its pricing model builds on economies of scale. An entire team of administrators, security experts, technicians, and engineers can be acquired as part of a service for a server priced at pennies per hour. Because of the specialization, deep knowledge, 24x7 operation, automation, and employed best practices, one could argue that this situation is a much lower risk than the overworked, underpaid frustrated internal IT guru who has virtually no training in cybersecurity and is sick of answering calls after hours.

Also mentioned earlier was the situation where the same configured server represented a 3,200% difference in price from a low-cost provider to a high-cost one. It is a guarantee that every provider along that continuum from low to high offers a different level of service quality, automation, support, security, patching, management, and monitoring for that price. Because cloud appears to be lower cost, it does not mean that cloud is optimal for your unique situation and business challenges. Cloud is a tool in the tool bag. Screwdrivers should not get used when driving nails. Cloud is the right tool when used for the right job.

# Adoption is optional – Culture

If you play in the middle of the road, you are eventually going to get run over. Change is hard; adopting change sometimes seems impossible. Cloud is something that goes much better with a firm commitment to it. It is not something to do halfway. You can't *maybe, kinda, sorta* your way into using cloud services. Cloud is a strategic change with very powerful economic levers alongside it. Cloud can transform enterprises in many ways. Cloud is something that you can start at your own pace. There is no reason to lift and shift everything at once. Hybrid strategies are among the safest, easiest to control, and cost-effective ways to beginning the cloud journey. Cloud journeys are not sprints; they do not need to be marathons either. Based on the real-time data, analytics, scenario planning, models, normalized data, and side-by-side comparisons, it should be clear whether cloud services make sense for the given situation. Start with the smallest scope that makes sense and go from there.

Cloud changes can have a rippling effect. They can also have a polarizing effect. It is critical to gather, process, and effectively communicate the right data in the right messaging at the right time. Data helps change the mindset, increase adoption, and, ultimately, remove any cultural challenges.

People get comfortable with routine, processes, structures, roles, and responsibilities. Everything is familiar. A big part of changing mindset is helping others understand the benefits and believe the change is needed. Disruption is difficult when skill sets are lacking. Change is also difficult when the reasoning for the change is unknown or misunderstood. It is very uncomfortable to change processes that people have used for some time. It is hard to reorganize teams or shift responsibilities to others. It is critical to communicate the right data within the right message at the right time. Change management is a huge part of cloud success. A relentless focus on communicating change, retraining, refocusing, and prioritizing is core to any successful culture and mindset change. Every cloud initiative fails without cultural adoption.

Updating skill sets is another big key to success. The market is moving fast. Technology is rapidly changing. Most team members may get one class per year, maybe two if they are lucky. Most have to do it on their own to stay relevant. With technical skills lagging behind, it makes it very difficult when cloud services begin to take hold. Cloud is economics, strategy, and risk. Most technical team members have very little training or, quite honestly, patience to deal with politics, strategy, risk conversations, financial analysis, and metrics. Most technical types would gladly jump off the nearest high bridge. The next generation of architects are going to need a mix of business, financial, technical, and political skills. The next generation of high-value designers and architects will need to think more like CFOs than technical administrators.

# Technology for the executives

Architecting cloud solutions will also require executives to become familiar with a few models as cloud solutions are evaluated and implemented. It is important to have a comfortable level of familiarity with these different concepts as strategies and economics are discussed alongside technology choices and risk profiles. Service models (IaaS, PaaS, and SaaS) dictate the direction for any cloud services consumed and implemented for the scope or that project.

# Cloud service models for executives

Service model choices are driven by the consuming organization's employee skill set. For example, system administrators manage infrastructure. If IaaS is the chosen service model, the enterprise will need to maintain and grow this group's knowledge and capabilities. Because the base infrastructure gets consumed as a service, administrators can refocus on new career growth opportunities beneficial to the enterprise in the longer term. An example might include learning infrastructure scripting skills with languages such as Chef and Puppet:

| Software | Platform | Infrastructure |
|---|---|---|
| • Overall reduction of all costs<br>• Application and software licensing<br>• Reduced support costs<br>• Back-end systems and capabilities | • Support multiple languages and frameworks<br>• Multiple hosted environments<br>• Flexibility<br>• Allow choice and reduce "lock-in"<br>• Ability to "autoscale" | • Scale<br>• Converged network and IT capacity pool<br>• Self-service and on-demand capacity<br>• High reliability and resilience |

Heavy software development shops may choose to consume PaaS services. The platform carries all of the components, frameworks, drivers, pieces, and parts, enabling developers to be productive immediately. There are many different types of platforms for building many different things. Software development is not the only choice or industry with PaaS available, but it is the most prevalent. As an example, in-house developers need to be comfortable with the platform chosen. If Java is their forte, a Microsoft Azure PaaS service may be slow in the adoption of new Java capabilities. Teams may need additional and ongoing training depending on the platform chosen. Additional investment may outweigh the benefits if the platform is too much of a mismatch to current skill sets or lacking capabilities for strategies chosen.

There are opportunities where no infrastructure is needed separately. The software is prebuilt with all the features and functions needed already included for a fee. Licensing is consumed per some unit, usually per enterprise or per user. The SaaS model is rapid to deploy with rapid adoption rates. SaaS does not have an answer for everything, but very helpful when solutions are available.

# Deployment models for executives

Once the organization chooses a cloud service mode, relevant metrics are selected, and targeted values finalized, the architect must then determine the appropriate recommendations for deployment and implementation styles. Each service model may have multiple deployment and implementation models. For example, IaaS is a service model. Within that model, infrastructure is deployed in many ways, including private, public, dedicated, or shared. The deployment of public cloud infrastructure services can traverse many different configuration options as well as different consumption and economic models.

Organizational risk tolerance drives cloud deployment model selection. Risk domains cut across operational, economic, technological, and security domains. Operational risk is a consideration for every deployment model. Private deployments are considered lower risk as they are owned and managed by the consumer. Right or wrong, humans tend to trust themselves more than others. That thinking has been proven invalid many times, yet this reflexive attitude remains.

When choosing deployment options, updating and patching the infrastructure is a key part of cybersecurity. Updates are rolled out proactively when service providers are managing the base infrastructure. In-house management may choose not to install patches or security updates for many reasons. Deployment model choices may need to change depending on the desired outcomes.

When internally managing software and systems, upgrades can take more time, but it does give the owner/manager control to decide how and when the upgrades and updates are implemented, along with as much time as needed for preparation and testing. Another operational risk may include the inability to access a cloud service due to lack of internet access. As cloud deployments grow, typically quicker than traditional deployments, they tend to sprawl, with control becoming more challenging as the number of services consumed grows. If not monitored and managed correctly, this leads to end-of-month cloud sticker shock.

In IaaS solutions, the cloud service provider makes all the decisions regarding technology choices for deployed services, including the type of server, the brand of storage, and the CPU manufacturer. These choices are abstracted away from the end user, with limited visibility into technical compatibility. The separation from the technology choices may lead to portability and interoperability risks in some situations. There can be some concern about data security. Most of these concerns are quickly handled through good design and security-minded questioning. Putting information into services that are accessible over the public internet means that criminals have a potential target. Security is a never-ending battle, with threats externally, internally, and sometimes from the least-expected places. Remember TJX and the HVAC entry point.

# Implementation models and IT governance for executives

Implementation models are largely determined by IT governance. Governance for all cloud services, other than under a private deployment model, is outside of the consuming organization's purview. For this reason, cloud services may introduce some level of legal, security, regulatory, and jurisdictional risks. Realizing there may be some risk associated, cloud services can increase levels of adoption and enforcement of information technology standards. Additional investment commitments in infrastructure, training, and time may be required, depending on the compliance standards being met. A failure to obtain initial compliance and sustaining the level of commitment required will cause failure of even the best cloud computing solution.

Once executive decisions have been finalized, and investment commitments confirmed, a cloud computing adoption strategy can then move forward. The most broadly followed cloud adoption strategies are the following:

- Building competitive advantage, which typically targets organizational strategic reinvention of customer relationships, rapidly innovating products and services rapidly or building new or improved business models.

- Better decisions strategic vector that extensively leverages analytics to pull insights from big data. This also requires the seamless sharing of data across applications and the exploitation of data-driven and evidence-based decisions.
- Deep collaboration aims to make it easier to locate and use expert knowledge across a business ecosystem. This strategy requires improved integration between development and operations and collaboration across the organization and extended ecosystem.

Business model change strategies that can be used to support these adoption strategies are the following:

- Addressing more mission/business requirements via a customer self-service model
- Transitioning from single/limited IT providers into a multiple IT provider ecosystem
- Changing the design/build/maintain and identify/adapt/adopt technology mix from 80/20 to 20/80
- Transitioning from labor-driven HW/SW integration to value-driven IT service management
- Transitioning from dedicated single tenancy to shared service multitenancy
- Transitioning from a cost center that provides support to a business center that delivers tangible value

# Summary

Enterprise executives will make final decisions on just about every aspect of a cloud deployment. Required investment levels and organizational impact makes this inevitable. As a key team member, the solution architect must always understand and manage the viewpoints of any involved executive. These tasks require two-way communication and the effective transfer of difficult concepts and new business, operational, and economic models. In almost all instances, the solution architect tends to be cast to serve the role of lead executive instructor. The challenge of this role was made clear in early 2018 when Facebook CEO Mark Zuckerberg testified before the United States Senate on social media data protection concerns. Although these senior leaders were seriously contemplating the implementation of new social media laws and regulations, their questions on basic cloud computing business models and technologies betrayed a sometimes comical ignorance of modern technology. This chapter should go a long way in assisting you in the performance of your educational duties.

# Architecting for Transition

6

*"Victorious warriors win first and then go to war, while defeated warriors go to war first and then seek to win."*

*— The Art of War, Sun Tzu*

Many people mistake *The Art of War* for a book teaching strategies on how to fight wars and critical battles. To the contrary, *The Art of War* is about how to avoid the fight. Long, drawn-out battles are expensive, slow, and very hard to control. In the first part of the opening quote, *Victorious warriors win first*, Sun Tzu focuses the student on preparation, situational awareness, a controllable environment, attention to relevant details, and determining the outcome before starting. The lessons in the book are about knowing the environment and having situational awareness. Do you have the latest, most accurate information? Do you have reliable sources? Are you thinking clearly? Are you controlling your emotions and biases? Are external influences and detractors in check? Do you see the data for what it is or for what you think it should say?

Cloud transitions, while not wars, can certainly feel like battles. They can feel a bit like religious crusades where believers are willing to do anything for the cause. Cloud transitions do not have a particular pattern, shape, or size. Cloud transitions require the most up-to-date and accurate data possible. Successful cloud transitions are successful before they ever start. They require the same clear focus, preparation, environmental control, and situational awareness. In Sun Tzu, if cloud transitions do not have a clear focus, detailed preparation, and careful planning, the transition will fail before it starts.

In this chapter, we will cover the following topics:

- User characteristics
- Application workload
- Use of **application programming interfaces (APIs)**

# User characteristics

Clouds are like children. They have unique personalities, quirks, strengths, and weaknesses. No two are the same. Just like children, and like some siblings, they behave differently and seem to follow different rules, and sometimes, they misbehave at the worst time.

Cloud solutions are specific to each provider. Successful transitions require due diligence and a thorough understanding of the cloud provider. Cloud transitions require the consumer to know the provider more than the provider needing a deep understanding of the consumer. The traditional IT acquisition process begins with the consumer providing all of the details and requirements for inspection by the provider. The provider then responds with a proposed design that meets said requirements. Cloud solution acquisition cycles now reverse that thinking. Up front, service providers must effectively communicate their capabilities, characteristics, attributes, and supporting services for consideration by consumers. This complete reversal in process and approach is core to the cultural challenge associated with cloud transitions. Strategic, economic, and technical choices are now completely held by the consumer side. Previously, service providers were responsible for nearly all solution due diligence, making recommendations, controlling solution economics, and in nearly all cases conservatively over-engineering solutions as excess capacity was better than too little when needed.

The examination of several characteristics and attributes is now the responsibility of the consumer. These investigative deep-dives often require internal cooperation, and often unwanted politics, across multiple organizations and divisions. The service providers are also adapting in real time as they are now required to share deeper-level detail on how solutions are designed, built, supported, and maintained. Some details potentially requiring additional investigation may include the following:

- Application characteristics
- Application dependencies
- API requirements
- Technology service consumption requirements
- Consuming organization's ability to support IT automation
- Consuming organization's use of scalable design techniques
- Consuming organization's data security and control requirements
- Consuming organization's transformational readiness

Cloud architecture starts by understanding the end user. Cloud service providers use targeted utilization and usage patterns to guide their infrastructure designs. Consumers gain value from a provider's service only if that consumer's operational patterns match the provider's target.

Economy of scale is how CSPs create profit margin. To accomplish this, resource pools are used to share resources across multiple tenants. Both physical and virtual resources are dynamically provisioned and de-provisioned based on user demand. Resource pooling also provides location diversity. For SaaS, the user has no control or knowledge of hardware location. In some cases, the consumer can specify general location aspects such as country or region.

Cloud computing economics typically uses virtualization to automate information technology resource provisioning. This often leads to an assumption that virtualization defines cloud computing. In truth, cloud computing economic depends on customer population metrics, namely the **Number of Unique Customer Sets** (*n*), **Customer Set Duty Cycles** (λ,*f*), **Relative Duty Cycle Displacement** (*t*) and **Customer Set Load** (*L*):

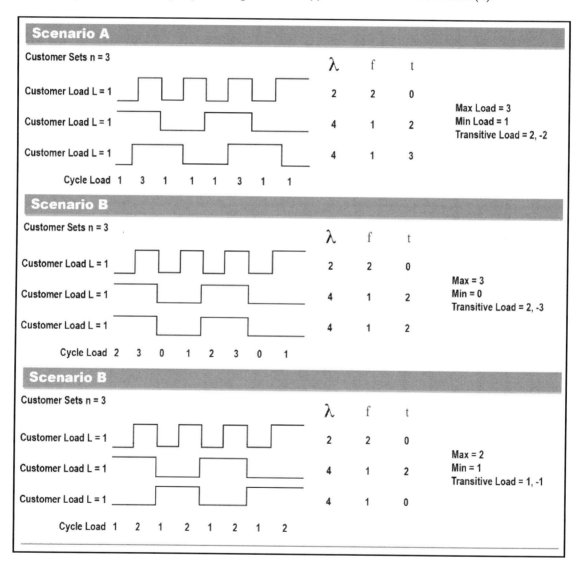

These metrics set the minimum physical IT resource requirements needed to serve a specified maximum level of demand. The preceding figure illustrates this concept. While the three scenarios show different customer sets, each demanding a 1-unit maximum load, and the consumer demand duty cycles are similar, the duty cycle displacement values in each scenario are different. This small difference translates into significant operational differences:

- Maximum demand in **Scenario A** and **Scenario B** is 30% more than that in **Scenario C**.
- **Scenario B** has a zero minimum demand.
- **Scenario C** transitive load requirements are 50% less than the other two.
- If each user set individually owned their resources, three units would be required. **Scenario A** and **Scenario B** would require the same total number of units. **Scenario C**, on the other hand, would only need a maximum of 2 units to support the same demand, resulting in a 30% resource savings.

In leveraging the cloud economic model, CSPs must continuously monitor key user metrics in near real time to enable any required changes in the underlying physical infrastructure. This leads to the desired *illusion of infinite resources* that is characteristic of the cloud computing service experience:

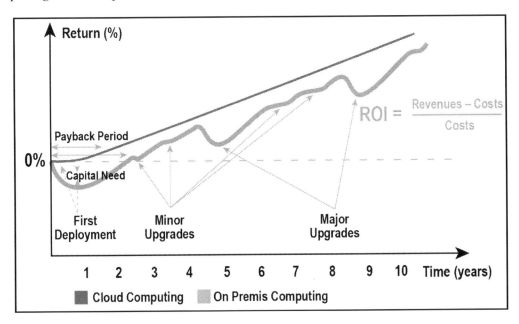

Understanding and knowledge of target user base characteristics will enable a better solution design. The most appropriate service providers are those that provide the best cost and benefit during critical operational periods and duration. If implemented correctly, the cloud computing economic model can materially improve return on investment over on-premises deployments. The preceding figure illustrates this model in a private cloud construct. A 2009 Booz Allen Hamilton study concluded that a cloud computing strategy could save from 50%-67% on the life cycle cost of a 1,000-server deployment.

The study also showed increased benefit-cost ratios when the cloud transition included more servers or a faster migration schedule, as shown in the following figure. A separate Deloitte study shows that cloud deployments deliver more return on investment with shorter payback periods when compared to the traditional data center option:

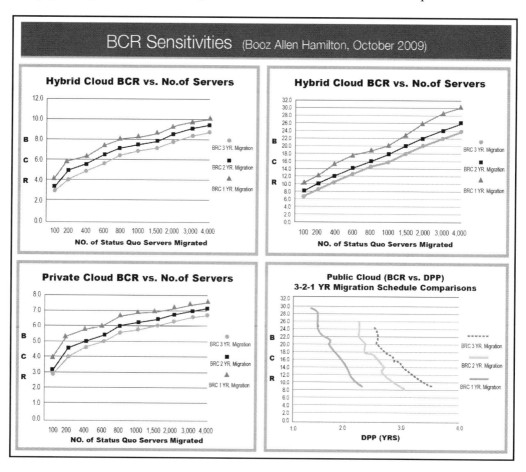

A cloud solution architect should make every attempt to document and verify the following user population characteristics:

- The expected number of concurrent users for every application or service
- User growth rates over an annual period
- The variability of user demand and for any apparent temporal cycle (that is, time of day, day of the week, week of the month, month of the year)
- User consumption differences based on the user's geographic location
- Breadth across the population and frequency in the use of mobile devices and mobile applications
- Types, models, and operating systems of mobile devices used
- Device ownership options
- Variability of user characteristics based on functional entity association, including any economic variable measured or tracked by separate organizational entities or consolidated across the entire user base
- Important business continuity or disaster recovery concerns are driven by end user location, end user devices, operational process considerations, or the usage cycle

# Application design

Many organizations want to leverage cloud computing as a means of reducing the operational costs associated with maintaining legacy applications. In these cases, the cloud solution architect is faced with an application migration task where application maturity may become a decisive factor in whether a cloud environment is beneficial or detrimental. Application characteristics could also profoundly influence the decision regarding CSP choice. Many legacy applications, for example, are tightly coupled to data, specific processes, and other related applications. This makes them very difficult to transition to a commodity-based technology service model. Embedded dependencies and unusually undocumented assumptions don't easily fit into a strictly standardized and not easily tailored environment.

Cloud-friendly applications are loosely coupled, with RESTful interfaces and modular design. This design approach makes them more amenable to modern cloud-based infrastructures. This difference must also be addressed when applications are newly developed for a cloud deployment. Developers have traditionally had the luxury of exploring new design approaches that often leverage the unique capabilities of a specific and targeted technology or vendor. These new approaches are often foundational to a company's market differentiation or customer value proposition. The resultant infrastructure customization or configurations are then presented to the supporting infrastructure system administrators as minimum requirements or must-haves. If the organization is organically responsible for deployment, these minimum requirements are translated into specific technology procurement and technical configurations. If the deployment is to be outsourced to a managed service provider or system integrator, the procurement official translates these requirements into a **request for proposal** (RFP) or **request for quote** (RFQ). Competitive vendors then follow the specified requirements to design and present a priced solution. After technical evaluations and cost-benefit analysis are completed, a contract is awarded and funded for the delivery of a selected solution.

This traditional approach is fatally flawed if the targeted vendor is a cloud service provider. First, cloud computing environments are designed and managed as a commodity service by the cloud service provider. This will typically negate most technology or configuration dictates from the end customer. It also prevents exploitation of most vendor- or technology-specific capabilities designated as minimum requirements or must-haves by the developer. Secondly, the solution design is fixed by the CSP based on previously finalized technology decisions and CSP-funded acquisitions. The technology service price is also dictated by the CSP based on its target marketplace dynamics, not the price sensitivity of any particular customer. In short, RFP or RFQ requirements have virtually zero effect on available CSP technology services or technology service price.

Cloud service acquisition fundamentally represents a 180° shift from traditional IT acquisition practices. This can not only wreck existing procurement process oversight and control, but it will also lead to unexpected deployment challenges, cost, application design changes, and failed migration projects. This pattern has repeatedly been observed across the IT industry. Its root cause is the cloud solution architect's failure to address procurement process differences between traditional IT service acquisition and cloud IT service acquisition.

# Application migration

Application screening is the first step in identifying whether a specific application is ready to move into the cloud. This is normally accomplished using an interview process, with the system/application owner designed to identify cloud migration readiness and the value a migration could provide. As a data discovery exercise, this process will help identify applications for migration, while ensuring that the existing IT and security architecture is well understood, and this also helps to mitigate many complications that may occur when executing a migration strategy. Interviewers should leverage a consistent set of evaluation tested questions that will help triage an organization's application portfolio. Responses should be analysed with a focus on deciding the following:

- The most appropriate target deployment environment, which varies from physical hardware in a user-owned and -operated data center to a virtualized platform, a private cloud, or a public cloud
- Each application's SPAR benefit (scalability, performance, accessibility, reliability)
- Each application's SOAR readiness (security, organization, architecture resilience).

This triage effort should also highlight the most influential business or mission drivers, key readiness strengths, key benefit weaknesses, and key readiness weaknesses.

After identifying the applications that should be moved into the cloud, a data classification (PII, classified information, and so on) of the information processed by these systems should be completed. This should be done with input from the relevant SMEs and the **Governance, Risk Management, and Compliance (GRC)** team. This is an important step to understand because CSPs operate on a shared-responsibility model. The CSP will provide security of the cloud and the customer is responsible securing the information that put in the cloud. Data classification will help determine what information will remain on-premises and what information will be moved into the cloud, and it also helps to ensure that compliance requirements can be achieved.

Application portfolio data should then be compiled across all relevant or interrelated domains. The selection of a service model (SaaS, PaaS, or IaaS) and a deployment model (public, community, or hybrid) should be driven by organizational goals and compliance needs. It is important the think about where data will be stored, is encryption required, how information will be encrypted at rest, how information will be encrypted in motion, and who will manage the encryption. Answers to these types of questions will inform your selection. Screening output should also provides data to inform long-term application strategy decisions. Long-term options typically include retirement, refactoring, rebuilding, or lift and shift.

# Application workloads

Application workload, dictated by user characteristics, represents a major factor in cloud computing solution design. Application scalability and cost efficiency are enhanced by the solution architect's ability to leverage the automated provisioning and de-provisioning of cloud technology services. Dynamic instantiation and decommissioning of virtual machines based on workload variations is often ignored or delayed when a lift and shift application migration strategy is pursued. Failing to design or redesign solutions with application workload variability in mind can nullify any positive return on a cloud deployment investment.

# Static workloads

**Static workloads** show flat resource utilization over time within particular boundaries. Applications with static workloads are less likely to see benefit from an elastic cloud that uses a pay-per-use model because resource requirements are constant. Periodic workloads are very common in real deployments. Examples include monthly paychecks, monthly telephone bills, yearly car checkups, weekly status reports, or the daily use of public transport during the rush hour. Tasks occur in distinct patterns, and the customer realizes cost-savings from the ability to de-provision resources during non-peak times.

# Once-in-a-lifetime workloads

**Once-in-a-lifetime workloads** are a special case of periodic workload in which the peaks of periodic utilization occurs only once in a very long time frame. This peak is often known in advance as it correlates to an individual event or task. Cloud elasticity is used to obtain necessary IT resources. The provisioning and decommissioning of IT resources in this use case can often be done manually since it can be done at a known point in time.

# Unpredictable and random workloads

**Unpredictable and random workloads** are a generalization of periodic workloads as they require elasticity but are not predictable. Unplanned provisioning and de-provisioning of IT resources is required. The necessary provisioning and decommissioning of IT resources are, therefore, automated to align the resource numbers to the changing workload. Many applications experience a long-term change in workload that can be characterized as a continuously changing workload. This is normally seen as an ongoing continuous growth or decline of use. The elasticity of clouds enables applications experiencing continuously changing workloads to provision or decommission resources with the same rate as the workload changes.

The following table provides a cross-reference between the solution use cases outlined in Chapter 4, *Business Drivers, Metrics, and Use Cases*, application workloads described here, and the standard operational requirements also addressed earlier. Once application user requirements are established, the table can be used to develop a documented initial draft of your cloud solution operational requirements:

| | | End User to Cloud | Enterprise to Cloud to End User | Enterprise to Cloud | Enterprise to Cloud to Enterprise | Private Cloud | Changing Cloud Vendors | Hybrid Cloud |
|---|---|---|---|---|---|---|---|---|
| **User Workload Requirements** | Static | | | | | | | |
| | Periodic | | | | | | | |
| | Once-in-a-lifetime | | | | | | | |
| | Unpredictable | | | | | | | |
| | Continuously Changing | | | | | | | |
| | | End User to Cloud | Enterprise to Cloud to End User | Enterprise to Cloud | Enterprise to Cloud to Enterprise | Private Cloud | Changing Cloud Vendors | Hybrid Cloud |
| **Operational Requirements** | Identify | X | X | | | | | X |
| | Open Client | X | X | X | X | X | X | X |
| | Federated Identity | | X | X | X | | | X |
| | Location Awareness | | X | X | X | X | X | X |
| | Metering and Monitoring | | X | X | X | X | | X |
| | Management and Governance | | X | X | X | X | | X |
| | Security | X | X | X | X | X | X | X |
| | Deployment | | | X | | X | | X |
| | Transactions and Concurrency | | | | X | | | |
| | Interoperability | | | | X | | | X |
| | Industry-Specific Standards | | | X | X | | | X |
| | VM Image Format | | X | X | X | X | X | X |
| | Cloud Storage API | | X | X | X | | X | X |
| | Cloud Database API | | X | X | X | | X | X |
| | Cloud Middleware API | | X | X | X | | X | X |
| | Data and Application Federation | | X | X | X | | | X |
| | Operational SLAs | X | X | X | X | X | X | X |
| | Lifecycle Management | | X | X | X | | | X |

# Application categories

The more value an application or business process can exploit from the basic cloud model value proposition, the more valuable a cloud transition becomes. This fact emphasizes the need to categorize enterprise applications by important organizational goals and target deployment options. Several factors can be used to categorize applications. This categorization often drives the selection of an appropriate deployment model for an application being moved to the cloud. These factors include security privacy regulation needs, unique technology requirements, agility, and elasticity needs. The process of categorizing applications is unique for each enterprise, but the cloud solution architect should educate, lead, and advise throughout the process:

## Cloud Deployment Model Selection | High Level Decision Criteria

|  | Local Housing | Managed Service | Cloud - IaaS Public | Cloud - PaaS Public | Cloud - SaaS Public | Cloud - IaaS Private | Cloud - PaaS Private | Cloud - SaaS Private |
|---|---|---|---|---|---|---|---|---|
| **Security** | High | Reasonable | Less Secure | Less Secure | Less Secure | High | High | High |
| **Core Business Function** | All ownership & ops on premis | Retain App Ownership | Retain App Ownership | Retain App Ownership | Totally Outsourced | All ownership & ops on premis | All ownership & ops on premis | All ownership & ops on premis |
| **Unique Business Requirements** | Highly Customizable | Customize App - some infra. | Customize Application | Customize Application | Little Customization | Customize Application | Customize Application | Little Customization |
| **Uniquie Technical Requirements** | Limited to Standard Stack | Ability to Provide Non-standard HW | Limited to Standard Stack | Some Ability to Provide Non-Standard Stack | Don't Care | Some Ability to Provide Non-Standard Stack | Some Ability to Provide Non-Standard Stack | Don't Care |
| **Agility/React to Dynamic Volumes** | Little | Longer Term Agreement | On Demand | On Demand | On Demand | On Demand | On Demand | On Demand |
| **Capital Investment** | Own HW, SW, Apps | Own SW and Applications | Little to None | Little to None | Little to None | Own HW, SW, Appl. | Own HW, SW, Appl. | Own HW, SW, Appl. |
| **Control of Environment** | Total Control | Control Software & Appl. | Control Appl. | Control Appl. | Little Control | Total Control | Total Control | Total Control |
| **Time to Market** | Slow | Medium | Medium | Medium | Fast | Medium | Medium | Fast |

Use of a categorization framework can form the basis for establishing a structured approach for assessing a given application's overall relative cloud migration value against the ease or difficulty in making that migration. It will also identify how valuable essential cloud characteristics are to the application's operational value:

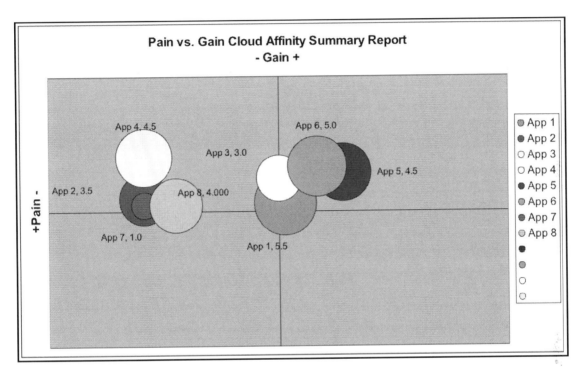

In this example diagram, circle size represents overall cloud affinity. Cloud migration pain is affected by several factors, such as application dependencies, application cloud friendliness, associated security and compliance requirements, and other factors. The gain is derived from scalability, agility, elasticity, and overall organizational cloud transition motivation. Some of the most popular SaaS application categories are shown in the following table:

| SaaS application | Description |
| --- | --- |
| Customer relationship management | Automate marketing and track sales |
| Enterprise resource management | Improve workflow and productivity visibility |
| Accounting | Accurately organize and track finances |

| Project management | Track project scope, requirements, progress, changes, communications, and delivery deadlines |
| --- | --- |
| Email marketing | Automate and optimize marketing and relationship building |
| Billing and invoicing | Reduce billing process time |
| Collaboration | Improve communications and employee productivity |
| Web hosting and electronic commerce (e -commerce) | Automate internet-based business processes |
| Human resource management | More efficient scheduling, payroll automation, and recruiting |
| Public sector, compliance, and EDI | Monitor and enforce regulations to improve compliance and communications |
| Industry vertical applications | Industry-specific application deployment |
| Financial transaction processing | Exchange of financial assets |

# Application dependencies

Application dependencies increase the difficulty associated with putting an application on the cloud. They can dictate application migration order or even determine migration feasibility. Critical application dependencies could include the following:

- Shared communication channel
- Shared architecture
- Identity and access management
- Shared data

The solution architect must explore and gain a consensus on the most appropriate resolution options, which may include the following:

- Creating and deploying a shared service layer
- Replicating the service in the cloud environment
- Replacing legacy services with an available cloud services.

# Use of APIs

Application APIs are the glue that connects applications. They manage the virtual discussions between users and the cloud services being consumed. APIs enable business agility, flexibility, and interoperability. These software modules are more than just connective tissue on the web, they are business model drivers and represent organizational core assets that can be reused, shared, and monetized. Using APIs, companies extend the reach of existing services or provide new revenue streams. In some instances, they are actually end products that, in turn, provide access legacy and third-party systems and data.

Infrastructure APIs are used to provision, de-provision, and scale cloud computing resources. As crucial solution components, the cloud solution architecting process should also consider the following:

- Creation and publication of a service endpoint as an API
- Deployment of APIs on-premises or in the cloud
- Use of versioning to control APIs throughout the solution life cycle
- Management and monitoring of solution-related web services

The predominant API design styles are **Simple Object Access Protocol (SOAP)** and **Representational State Transfer (REST)**.

# SOAP

SOAP uses **eXtensible Markup Language (XML)**, which is very complex when used for requests and responses. Requests are often created manually, leading to fragile applications due to the intolerance of SOAP to errors. **Web Services Description Language (WSDL)** is used with SOAP to define web service usage. With WSDL, the **Integrated Development Environment (IDE)** can fully automate the process. Because of this connection, the difficulty in using SOAP depends on the programming language. An important SOAP feature is its error handling. If a request has an error, the response embeds information that can be used to correct the problem. Error reporting also has standard codes that can be used to automate error handling.

# REST

REST is a lightweight SOAP alternative. It uses a simple URL and can process four different tasks (GET, POST, PUT, and DELETE). REST flexibility lies in its ability to return data using **JavaScript Object Notation (JSON)**, **Comma Separated Value (CSV)**, and **Really Simple Syndication (RSS)**. This means output can be delivered in just about any desired parsing format.

## Advantages of SOAP and REST

The advantages of SOAP and REST are given in the following table:

| SOAP advantages | REST advantages |
|---|---|
| Platform, language, and transport independence | No expensive tools are required to interact with the web service |
| Better support for distributed enterprise environments | Smaller learning curve |
| Better standardization | Efficient (SOAP uses XML for all messages, REST can use smaller message formats) |
| Significant pre-built extensibility sing WS* standards | Fast (no extensive processing required) |
| Built-in error handling | Closer to other web technologies in design philosophy |
| More automation with certain languages | |

# Technical architecture requirements

Cloud computing services are consumed using an on-demand model. Service providers, therefore, meter and monitor the consumption of every resource by every user. Every resource, in turn, uses specific metrics and measurement units to bill users. Most organizations do not measure IT usage in this way. Neither do they typically place resource measurement sensors across their IT platform. IT is usually seen as a shared cost center with only the total cost and total capacity requirements tracked. This makes it extremely difficult to estimate service usage rates and expected cost when an application is transitioned to a CSP. Infrastructure analysis is used to get estimates of resource usage by particular applications, business processes, and organizational segments. This is normally one of the most difficult aspects of developing the business case and resultant cost-benefit analysis. Responses provide insight into the economic comparison between IaaS service options, managed infrastructure service options, and enterprise-owned data center options.

# Legal/regulatory/security requirements

As the global nature of technology continues to evolve, the complexity of adhering to both global and local laws and regulations becomes greater. The most significant trend in the US government market is the move from security compliance to security risk management. Relevant guidance addressing this move is contained in the following:

- The **Federal Risk and Authorization Management Program (FedRAMP)**, which provides a standard approach for security assessments, authorizations, and continuous monitoring of cloud computing products and services.
- The **Department of Defense (DoD)** cloud computing security requirements, which extend the FedRAMP security requirements to meet the unique requirements of the DoD.
- ICD 503, which replaces DCID 6/3 and 6/5 and establishes intelligence community policies for security risk management of information technology systems. This includes security certification and accreditation.

Ensuring compliance with these is challenging within a cloud computing environment increases significantly. Legal, regulatory, and security requirements are used to screen cloud service provider options, select appropriate CSP regions, and verify necessary security controls.

# Business continuity and disaster recovery – BCDR

Cloud infrastructure has some characteristics that can be distinct advantages in realizing BCDR, depending on the scenario:

- Rapid elasticity and on-demand self-service provides flexible infrastructure that can be quickly deployed to execute an actual disaster recovery without unexpected ceilings.
- Broad network connectivity reduces operational risk.
- Cloud infrastructure providers have a highly automated and resilient infrastructure backing all offered services.
- Pay-per-use can mean tremendous cost savings and no capital expenditures to support a BCDR strategy.

Scenarios that should be considered when considering cloud services are the following:

- **On-premises, cloud as BCDR**: An existing, on-premises infrastructure, which may or may not have a BCDR plan already, where a cloud provider is considered as the provider of alternative facilities should a disaster strike at the on-premises infrastructure.
- **Cloud consumer, primary provider BCDR**: The infrastructure under consideration is already located at a cloud provider. The risk being considered is that of a failure of part of the infrastructure of that cloud provider, for example, one of their regions or availability zones. The business continuity strategy then focuses on restoration of service or failover to another part of that same cloud provider infrastructure.
- **Cloud consumer, alternative provider BCDR**: A scenario similar the previous one except instead of the restoration of service from the same provider, the service has to be restored from a different provider. This also addresses the risk of complete cloud provider failure.

**Disaster recovery (DR)** almost by definition requires replication. The key difference between these scenarios is where the replication happens. **Business continuity (BC)** questions are used to identify any critical BC or DR issues that may require more detailed analysis.

# Economics

Cloud service providers typically offer three options to pay for their service:

- On-demand: You pay for what you use as you use it.
- Reserved: You commit to using a specific amount of a service over a specified period.
- Spot: You use a market auction model to match price with demand.

Each has advantages and disadvantages, but all require an understanding of operational requirements and customer sensitivity to price fluctuations. Economic screening questions are used to gauge customer sensitivity to cloud service cost and importance of the various economic payment models.

# Organizational assessment

Digital transformation and cloud computing migrations typically involve transitioning from a non-standardized, minimally documented environment into a highly standardized, rigidly documented one. This is a highly challenging transition that requires effective organizational governance. It may also present significant change management challenges. To be successful, any corporate cloud computing transition strategy needs to be paired with a focused training and education program. This assessment is designed to identify whether such a program is in place or, if not, identify the appropriate organizational POC.

Organizational governance defines organizational structures, decision rights, workflow, and authorization points to create a target workflow that optimally uses a business entity's resources in alignment with the goals and objectives of the firm. Effective governance can only succeed if the organization has defined the desired outcomes and the proper metrics. Organizational leadership and management must be able to articulate what the desired outcomes are, who is accountable and responsible for these outcomes, what the escalation criteria or triggers to move a decision to the next level are, and what metrics will be used to monitor that the system is delivering the desired outcomes. The entire governance process needs to be continuously evaluated to determine that it provided the necessary transparency and timeliness to the decision makers and adjusted accordingly.

During transitions, the organization must simultaneously abandon business as usual and embrace the following across multiple dimensions:

- **Security framework**: Infrastructure-centric to data-centric
- **Application development**: Tightly coupled to loosely coupled
- **Data**: Mostly structured to mostly unstructured
- **Business processes**: Mostly serial to mostly parallel
- **Security controls**: Enterprise responsibility to shared responsibility
- **Economic model**: Mostly CAPEX to mostly OPEX
- **Infrastructure**: Mostly physical to mostly virtual
- **IT operations**: Mostly manual to mostly automated
- **Technology operational scope**: Local/regional to international/global:

| Domain | Transition From | Transition To |
|---|---|---|
| Security Framework | Infrastructure-centric | Data-centric |
| Application Development | Tightly Coupled | Loosely Coupled |
| Data | Mostly Structured | Mostly unstructured |
| Business Processes | Mostly Serial | Mostly Parallel |
| Security Controls | Enterprise responsibility | Shared responsibility |
| Economic model | Mostly CAPEX | Mostly OPEX |
| Infrastructure | Mostly physical | Mostly virtual |
| IT Operations | Mostly manual | Mostly automated |
| Technology Operational Scope | Local/Regional | International/Global |

Before embarking on any cloud transition program, the enterprise should implement a focused organizational change management strategy. There needs to be broad awareness, understanding, acceptance, and commitment across the organization of what is expected and when is it to be delivered by implanting focused organizational change management processes and procedures. The organization should regularly ask, *is the corporate culture changing at the necessary rate and are all communication channels are being leveraged so that the right stuff is being communicated?*

# Summary

Cloud computing is transformational in many ways. Cloud transformation can have a ripple effect throughout the entire organization. The hardest part of any transformational strategy is changing the hearts and minds of the people in the organization. Proper planning, diligent preparation, situational awareness, and environmental control will create a solid foundation for transformation success. Pairing solution strategy, economics, technology choices, and risk profiles with matching cloud service providers will maximize cloud transition value. Change management and communication plans are critical during any major change. Leadership continuously measures and compares accurate, relevant metrics and data, gauging progress, adoption, potential risks, and the pace of cultural change. If progress slows, adoption may follow. If adoption slows, project timelines may slide. Stay environmentally and situationally aware. Continuously monitor, measure, and compare the current situation to transition goals. Preparation is key. Avoid being a defeated warrior going into battle seeking a win.

# 7
# Baseline Cloud Architectures

Cloud transitions can be difficult to begin. As discussed in Chapter 6, *Architecting for Transition*, transitions can be difficult to design and plan, as much of the diligence now falls on the consumer side. This change is a double-edged sword; it cuts both ways. It enables the consumer to have significantly more control over designs, technical choices, economics, and risk. It also places the significantly more of the design and architecture burden on the consumer, who may not have the level of solution design experience that many service providers do.

Baseline cloud architectures are foundational building blocks to cornerstone design ideas. These common design arrangements can be used to jump-start solution efforts. Baseline architectures are useful when leveraging standard cloud computing patterns. Patterns represent cloud service requirements, while baseline architectures provide useful models for handling common architectural components and their associated requirements.

Each of the following sections will build on the section previous. The baseline compute component takes into account a web layer, application layer, and database layer, each having some level of storage. Storage attributes will change based on design requirements. Nearly all modern designs will have web, app, and database layers in their designs.

This type of layering is called **tiering**. Most designs will have three or four tiers. Tiers are typically the number of individual isolated layers between the environment entry point and the destination data. As an example, a three-tier architecture has a web layer, app layer, and database layer. A single-server architecture will have all three layers residing on the same virtual or physical server.

In this chapter, we will cover the following topics:

- Baseline architecture types
- OSI model and layer description
- Complex architecture types
- Architecting for hybrid clouds

# Baseline architecture types

The various types of baseline architectures are as follows.

## Single server

Single server templates represent the use of one server, virtual or physical, that contains a web server, an application, and a database. An example is the **LAMP Stack (Linux, Apache, MySQL, PHP)**. Single server architectures are not very common, as they have inherent security risks as one compromise can compromise all. These architectures are commonly deployed for development work, allowing developers to quickly build functionality without having to deal with connectivity and communication issues between different servers, potentially in different locations.

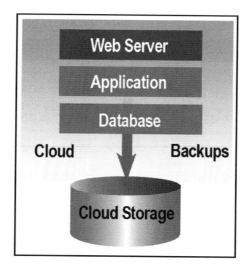

# Single-site

Single-site architectures take the single server architecture and split all of the layers into their own compute instances, creating the three-tier architecture mentioned. With all compute resources located in the same location, a single-site architecture is created. There are two versions of single-site architectures: non- redundant and redundant.

## Non-redundant three-tier architectures

Non-redundant three-tier architectures are used to save on costs and resources but must accept a higher risk. A single failure in any component, a single point of failure, can stop traffic flowing correctly into or out of the environment. This approach is commonly used for development or testing environments only. The following figure shows each layer, or tier, as a separate server, virtual or physical. Using this type of design for production environments is not recommended:

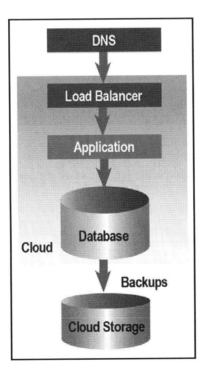

# Redundant three-tier architectures

Redundant three-tier architectures add another set of the same components for redundancy. Additional design components do increase complexity, but are required if designing for failover and recovery protection. Designing redundant infrastructures requires a well thought out plan for the components within each layer (horizontal scaling), as well as a plan for how the traffic will flow from one layer to another (vertical scaling).

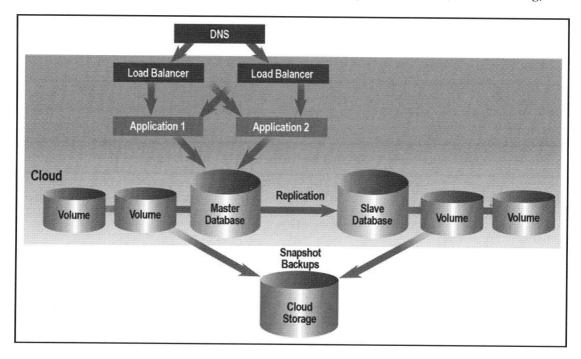

## Single points of failure

In redundant architectures, duplicate components eliminate the single point of failure present when only one device or component is present in the layer. With one component in a layer, there is only one way in and one way out. A second device adds multiple ingress and egress points to the design, eliminating the single point of failure associated with single-component layer designs.

# Redundancy versus resiliency

Redundancy and resiliency are often confused. They are related, but not interchangeable. Redundancy is something that is done to prevent failure, implying that it happens before an issue happens. Resiliency, from the word resolve, relates to how to find solutions after a problem has occurred. Redundancy is before the issue. Resiliency is after. For example, redundant databases with replication can be utilized. Multiple components and copies of data create a redundant design. If the primary side of the database pair fails, the secondary side will promote to primary and begin to pick up the load while the failed side self-repairs. The failover and self-healing functions are resiliency. Both are related, but not interchangeable.

# Horizontal scaling

Working outside in, the XYZ website has a single web server. A recent outage has suddenly identified available budget money for redundant components at each layer of the current design. By the way, every company is one major outage away from adding budget money for redundancy plans. One web server is currently used in the design. To add redundancy, we must horizontally scale the web server layer by adding additional web servers, eliminating the single point of failure. How will traffic be passed to both servers? How does the packet on the wire know which web server to go to and which path to take in and out, and how is all of this physically connected?

Load balancing is a major design component when adding redundancy to designs. A single load balancer will help delegate traffic across multiple servers, but a single load balancer creates another single point of failure. For redundancy, two or more load balancers are added to designs. Load balancers control traffic patterns. There are many interesting configurations to consider when deciding how to control and distribute traffic. Distribution may relate to traffic type, content, traffic patterns, or the ability of the servers to respond to requests. Load balancers help to handle traffic logically; how is the traffic handled at the physical layer?

# OSI model and layer description

The OSI stack is a great tool when working with complex designs. Every layer in the OSI stack must be considered within the design and have a purposeful answer. Designs always start at the physical layer, working up the stack from the bottom to the top. See the following diagram. Many load balancers today work at all layers of the OSI stack. Back to the question: how are multiple load balancers physically connected to multiple servers creating multiple ingress and egress paths? Multiple switches may also be required. Today many load balancers combine the port density of switches, the routing capability of routers, and the logical functions of load balancers, all in a single device simplifying designs and saving a bit of budget money.

| OSI Model & Layer Description | | |
|---|---|---|
| Layer 7 | Application | Communication |
| Layer 6 | Presentation | Applications |
| Layer 5 | Session | SIP, RTP, RTCP |
| Layer 4 | Transport | TCP, UDP, SCTP |
| Layer 3 | Network | Ipv4, IPv6 |
| Layer 2 | Data Link | Ethernet, etc. |
| Layer 1 | Physical Link | Coax, RF Link, etc |

The web layer and application layers can often be collapsed into the same server. From a security perspective, this can be an issue. If the server is compromised, both services are potentially compromised. Many designs collapse these two layers, as they are tightly integrated, and performance can significantly increase using system bus speeds instead of slower network connections and additional devices.

From single server designs to single site to single site redundant, each design builds on the one previous. The following figure adds the additional components, servers, and load balancers to illustrate a baseline architecture for single site designs with redundancy. The following redundant design collapses both web and app onto the same virtual or physical server. Load balancers are added to the design to delegate the load across multiple servers. Database servers are shown as primary-backup with replication between them. This redundant architecture can protect against issues with applications due to system unavailability and downtime. Resiliency considerations may include RAID configurations for database drives, how databases are backed up and restored, how applications and devices handle state and session information, and how databases rebuild after data or drive loss.

# Logical and physical designs

Designs can be logical or physical. It is very important to remain clear on what is represented. Logical diagrams illustrate how things logically flow through the design. Eliminating some of the physical connections may help the viewer focus on logical flows through the design. Conversely, physical layouts may not include many of the logical details and configurations to focus the viewer on physical characteristics and attributes of the design. The illustrations in this section are logical unless specifically called out as physical.

# Autoscaling architecture

A key benefit of cloud computing is the ability to consume what is needed when it is needed. Autoscaling describes the ability to scale horizontally (that is, shrink or grow the number of running server instances) as application user demand changes over time. Autoscaling is often utilized within web/app tiers within the baseline architectures mentioned. In the following figure, an additional server is dynamically added based on demand and threshold settings.

Load balancers must be preconfigured or configured dynamically to handle the new servers that are added.

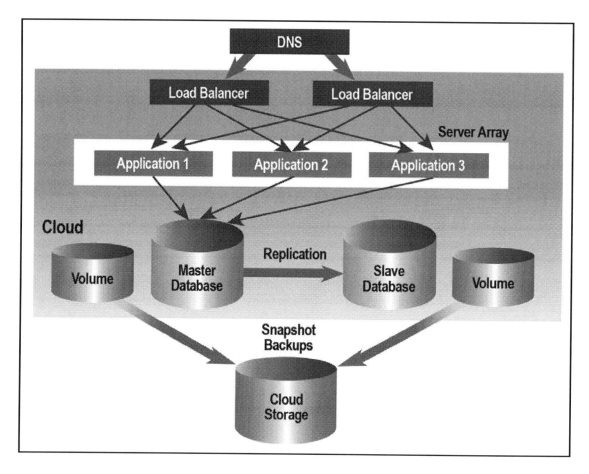

# Complex architecture types

The various types of complex architectures are as follows.

## Multi-data center architecture

Redundant single site designs can often handle many of the more prevalent issues that cause downtime within infrastructure layers. What happens if the entire site is not reachable? What happens if something gets misconfigured in DNS that sends traffic the wrong direction? The single site is now unreachable. Traditionally, the answer to this challenge has been very expensive. The redundant single site design nearly doubled the cost of infrastructure. For geographic redundancy, a second site is needed. This second site effectively doubles the budget of the first site, which already doubled when redundancy was added to the first design.

Cloud solutions are dramatically changing the way we design redundancy, resiliency, and disaster recovery. The cloud changes the fundamentals of base designs. For example, we are now able to design for low-side, base-level traffic flows, instead of designing for anticipated high-watermark levels. The cloud enables dramatic changes in footprint size and the amount of redundant infrastructure needed in single site and multiple site designs. The cloud is also changing the consumption patterns for infrastructure. Some applications traditionally deployed in-house have transformed to SaaS offerings, eliminating the need for the associated in-house infrastructure. The reduction in single site footprints can also reduce the size of second site footprints, helping redundant strategies fit into budgets easier than traditional deployments.

When planning redundancy across multiple data centers, new design challenges need consideration. How is traffic sent to one location or the other? Is one site active and one backup? Are both active? How does fail-back to the primary get handled after the failure occurs? What changes in resiliency plans are needed? How is data synchronization handled before and after failover?

# Global server load balancing

There are many mechanisms to handle the flow of traffic between multiple sites. Nearly all of them rely on the manipulation of DNS information. DNS information can sometimes take hours to update across the globe. If production sites must failover to redundant sites, waiting hours for traffic to pass again is not an option. Global server load balancing enabled the configuration of pre-planned actions to take place in the event of failure. GSLB required expensive publicly accessible devices at each site. Security experts were also required as part of a successful solution to keep devices safe from continuous hacking attempts.

Expensive, traditional, device-based GSLB deployments can be deployed as cloud GSLB services, where GSLB is consumed as a managed service for a monthly fee. Providers are also offering additional options including regional deployments and separated availability zones to help handle geographic diversity and failover. It is up to the consumer to decide the level of redundancy and speed of failover required. Zone level redundancy is different than regional deployments.

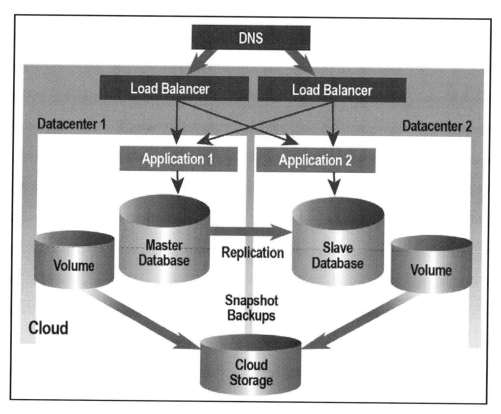

# Database resiliency

Primary-secondary or master-slave database relationships are common, but have some challenges when failures occur in high-transaction, heavy traffic environments. Databases are taking lots of requests and transactions are being written and read continuously. Backup processes can be taxing and time-consuming. Restoration and synchronization can take significant time. Heavy demand environments can benefit from an active-active database configuration with bi-direction replication to keep data synchronized on both database servers. This type of design does add more complexity but also adds greater levels of redundancy and resiliency within a single site, or across multiple sites, depending on configuration.

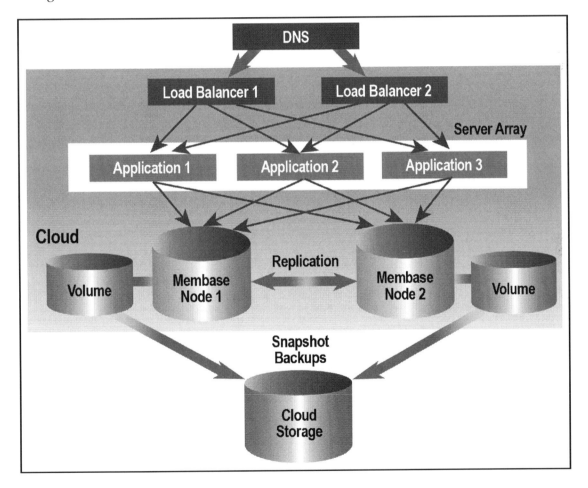

# Caching and databases

Content types can also affect architectures. As an example, caching techniques can change the load on database servers, load balancing design, database server sizing, storage type, storage speed, how storage is handled and replicated, as well as network connectivity, and bandwidth requirements. Current estimates place 80%-90% of enterprise data in unstructured categories.

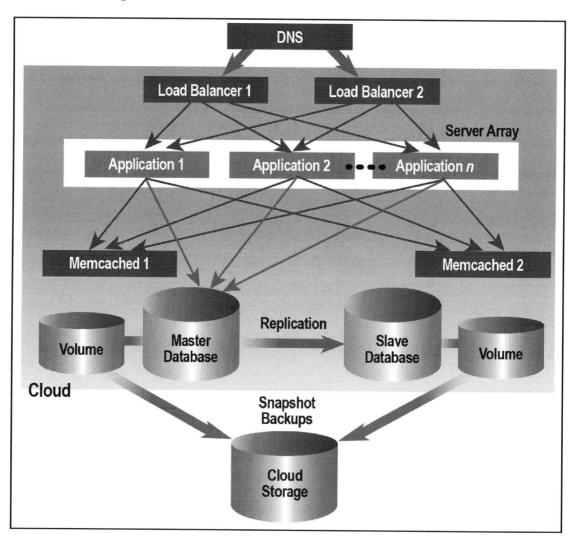

# Alert-based and queue-based scalable setup

Since multiple server arrays can be attached to the same deployment, a dual scalable architecture can be implemented. This delivers a scalable front-end and back-end server website array.

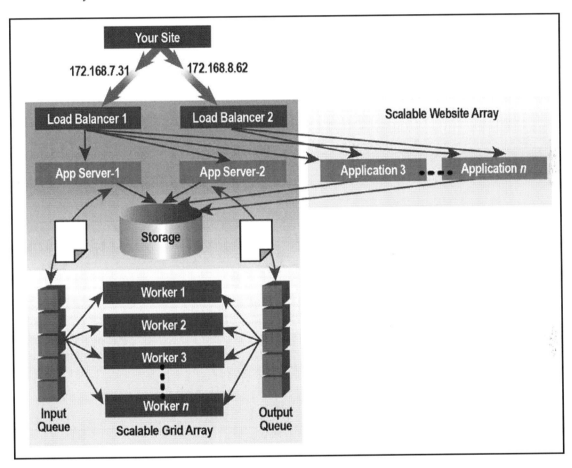

# Hybrid cloud site architectures

A hybrid cloud site architecture can protect your application or site redundancy by leveraging multiple public/private cloud infrastructures or dedicated hosted servers. This will require data and infrastructure portability between selected service providers. A hybrid approach requires an ability to launch identically functioning servers into multiple public/private clouds. This architecture can be used to avoid cloud service provider lock-in. It is also used to take advantage of multiple cloud resource pools. The hybrid approach can be used in both hybrid cloud and hybrid IT situations.

# Scalable multi-cloud architecture

A multi-cloud architecture, offers the flexibility of primarily hosting an application in a private cloud infrastructure, with the ability to cloudburst into a public cloud for additional capacity as necessary.

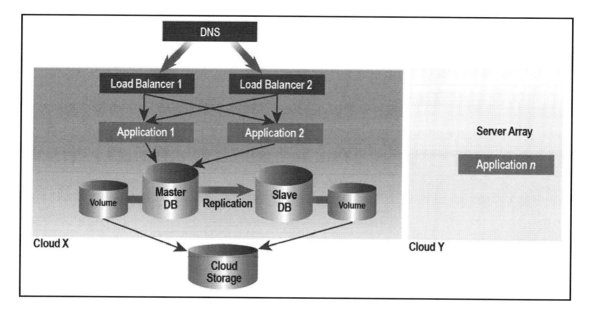

# Failover multi-cloud architecture

A second cloud service provider could be used to provide business continuity for a primary cloud provider if the same server templates and scripts could be used to configure and launch resources into either provider. Factors to be considered when using this option include public versus private IP addresses and provider service level agreements. If there is a problem or failure requires switching clouds, a multi-cloud architecture would make this a relatively easy migration.

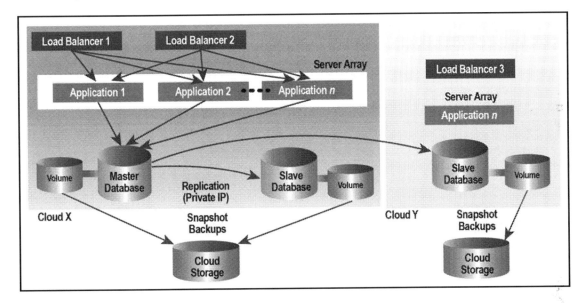

Sending and receiving data securely between servers on two different cloud service provider platforms can be done using a VPN wrapped around the public IP address. In this approach, any data transmitted between the various cloud infrastructures (except if used between private clouds) is sent over the public IP. In the following diagram, two different clouds are connected using an encrypted VPN:

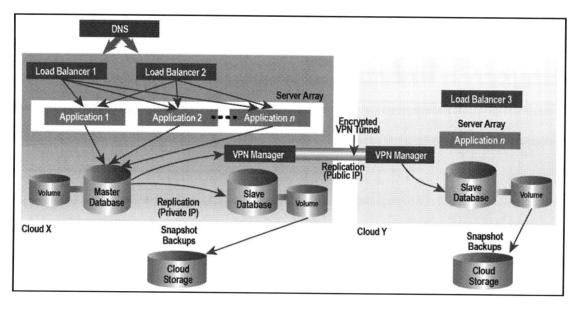

# Cloud and dedicated hosting architecture

Hybrid cloud solutions can use public and private cloud resources as a supplement for internal or external data center servers. This can be used to comply with data physical location requirements. If the database cannot be transitioned to a cloud computing platform, other application tiers may not have the same restrictions. In these situations, hybrid architecture can use a **virtual private network** (VPN) to implement an encrypted tunnel across a public IP between cloud and dedicated servers.

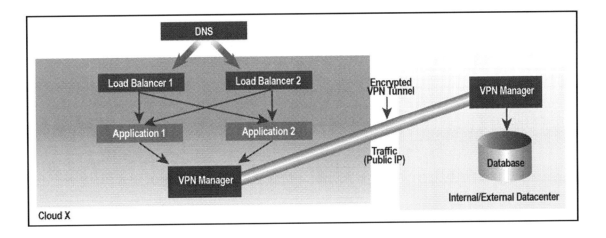

# Architecting for hybrid clouds

The various concepts of a hybrid cloud are explained in the following sections.

## Hybrid user interface

Varying user group workload interacts asynchronously with an application hosted in an elastic environment while the rest of the application resides in a static environment. An application responds to user groups with different workload behavior. One user group presents a static workload, while the other user group presents periodic, once-in-a-lifetime, unpredictable, or continuously changing workloads. Since user group size and workload behavior is unpredictable, this interface ensures that unexpected peak workloads do not affect application performance while each user group is handled by the most suitable environment. The user interface component serving varying workload users is hosted in an elastic cloud environment. Other application components that are in a static environment. The user interface in the elastic cloud is integrated with the rest of the application in a decoupled manner using messaging to ensure loose coupling.

# Hybrid processing

Processing functionality with the varying workload is in an elastic cloud while the remainder of the application is in a static environment. A distributed application provides processing functions with different workload behavior. The user group accessing the application is predictable in size but accesses the functions differently. Although most functions are used equally and experience static workload, some processing components experience periodic, unpredictable, or continuously changing workloads. The processing components with varying workloads are provisioned in an elastic cloud. Loose coupling is ensured by asynchronously exchanging information between the hosting environments via messages.

# Hybrid data

Data of varying size is in an elastic cloud while the rest of an application is in a static environment. A distributed application handles data with drastically varying size. Large amounts of data may be periodically generated and then deleted, data may increase and decrease randomly, or data may display a general increase or decrease. During these changes, the user number and application accesses can be static resulting in a static workload on the other application components. Elastic cloud storage offerings handle data with varying size that are unsuitable for static environment hosting. Data is accessed either by data access components hosted in the static environment or by data access components in the elastic environment.

# Hybrid backup

For disaster recovery, data is periodically extracted from an application and archived in an elastic cloud. Requirements regarding business resiliency and business continuity are challenging. There are also laws and regulations that make businesses liable to archive data for audits over very long periods of time. A distributed application is in a local static environment. Data handled by stateful components is extracted periodically and replicated to cloud storage.

# Hybrid backend

Backend functionality is made up of data-intensive processing and data storage with varying workloads is hosted in an elastic cloud while all other components reside in a static data center. A distributed application provides processing with different workload behaviors. Support for a mainly static workload needs to available, but some processing components experience periodic, unpredictable, or continuously changing workloads. Application components that have varying workloads should be in an elastic environment. These components, however, need to access large amounts of data during execution making them very dependent on availability and timely access to data. The processing components with varying workloads are in an elastic cloud together with the data accessed during operation. Asynchronous messages exchanged from the static environment are used to trigger the processing components in the elastic cloud through via message-oriented middleware message queues. A static environment data access component ensures that data required by elastic processing components is in storage offerings The data location may then be passed to the elastic processing components via messages. Data not required by the backend functionality may still be stored in stateful components in the static data center.

# Hybrid application functions

Some application functions provided by user interfaces, processing, and data handling is experienced varying workload and is in an elastic cloud while other application functions of the same type are in a static environment. Distributed application components experience varying workloads on all layers of the application stack: user interface, processing, and data access. All components provide functionality to the application user group, but user groups access functionality differently. In addition to the workload requirements, other issues may limit the environments to which an application component may be provisioned. Application components are grouped based on similar requirements and are deployed into the best fitting environments. Components interdependencies are reduced by exchanging data with asynchronous messaging to ensure loose coupling. Depending on the function accessed, a load balancer seamlessly redirects user accesses to the different environments.

# Hybrid multimedia web application

Website content is primarily provided from a static environment. Multimedia files that cannot be cached efficiently are provided from a large distributed elastic environment for high-performance access. A distributed application provides website access to a globally distributed user group. While most of the website has static content, there is a significant amount of multimedia content that needs to be streamed to users. Static website content is in a static environment where users access it. The streaming content is in an elastic cloud environment where it is accessed from a user interface component. Static content is delivered to users' client software which references the multimedia content. Streaming content retrieval is often handled directly by the users' browser software.

# Hybrid development environment

A runtime environment for production is replicated and mocked in an elastic environment for new applications development and testing. Applications have different runtime environment requirements during the development, testing, and production phases. During development, hardware requirements vary, so hardware resources need to be flexible and able to extend resources as necessary. During the test phase, diverse test systems are needed in order to verify proper application functionality on various operating systems or while being accessed with different client software. Large numbers of resources are also required for load tests. In production, other factors, such as security and availability are of greater importance than resource flexibility. The application production environment is simulated in the development and test environment using equivalent addressing, similar data, and equivalent functionality. Applications migration of is ensured through the transformation of application components or the compatibility of runtimes. Some testing resources are exclusively provided in the development environment to verify the application behavior under different circumstances.

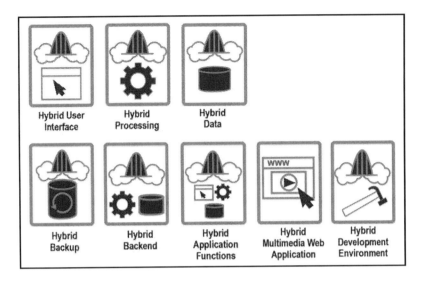

Each pattern employs certain characteristics and attributes. These help solution architects accurately visualize interoperability, and models, and compare the impact of economics, technology choices, and potential strategies. Pattern attributes and their associated metrics can also be used to models and test solutions using computing aided design tools. Aligning pattern characteristics, attributes, and metrics with organizational requirements and goals will normally lead to successful solution deployments.

# Summary

Successful design requires a simultaneous balance between desired strategic, economic, technical, and risk attributes. Complex designs are not necessarily better and can introduce additional risk rather than mitigate it. Defined requirements are where design starts, not where it finishes. As architectures are designed, evaluated, and compared, insight is revealed. Insight often provides a feedback loop for requirements to update or change. Updated requirements lead to new design scenarios and, potentially, more insight. When strategy, economics, technology, and risk align, objections will subside or will be negotiated away. Only add design complexity if non-negotiable requirements dictate it.

# 8
# Solution Reference Architectures

The reference architecture summaries presented in this chapter are meant to be starting points for your solution design. They outline the minimum components and processes to address the topic requirement but do not recommend specific technologies or cloud vendor solutions. They also cannot possibly address any unique organizational requirements or concerns. Real, deployable solutions require the addition of actual enterprise requirements, a solution architect's insight, modifications driven by the selected cloud service provider, and organizational team collaboration.

These summaries were created from complete reference architectures developed by the **Cloud Standards Customer Council (CSCC™)**. The CSCC™ is dedicated to accelerating the successful adoption of cloud computing. It provides users with the opportunity to drive requirements into standard development organizations and deliver materials that assist other enterprises. Complete reference architectures are available online for zero cost at `http://www.cloud-council.org/resource-hub.htm`.

In this chapter, we will cover the following topics:

- Application Security
- Web application hosting
- Public network
- API management
- E-commerce
- Big data and analytics
- Blockchain
- Architecture for IoT
- Architecture for hybrid integration

# Application security

This reference architecture summary presents the key components needed to secure any application or process in a cloud service provider's environment. Cloud service usage requires a clear understanding of security services, components, and options. This knowledge is paired with a clear architecture which covers development, deployment, and operations, as depicted in the following diagram:

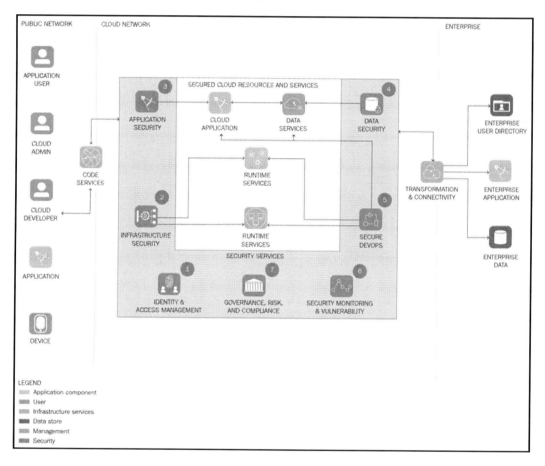

Figure 1: Architecture for the security of cloud service solutions

*Figure 1* is a high-level architecture for the roles and components needed in the security architecture for cloud service solutions. The solution is divided into three domains based on the applicable network. These networks are normally separately secured: public network, cloud provider network, and the enterprise network.

The public network (typically the internet) includes the parties that interact with the cloud solution, their end user devices, and the associated applications.

*Figure 1* also shows three main roles: application users, cloud administrators, and cloud developers.

The enterprise network contains the existing (non-cloud) enterprise components. These are usually required by the cloud solution and include the user directory, the applications, and the data systems.

The cloud provider network contains the major components of the cloud-based solution, running in cloud services—the cloud applications, the data services, the runtime services, and the infrastructure services. Security services are associated with these components (the numbers correspond to the numbers in *Figure 1*):

1. **Identity and access management**: Manage identity and access for your cloud administrators, application developers, and application users.
2. **Infrastructure security**: Handle network security, secure connectivity, and secure compute infrastructure.
3. **Application security**: Address application threats, security measures, and vulnerabilities.
4. **Data security**: Discover, categorize, and protect data and information assets, including protection of data at rest and in transit.
5. **Secure DevOps**: Securely acquire, develop, deploy, and maintain cloud services, applications, and infrastructure.
6. **Security monitoring and vulnerability**: Provide visibility into cloud infrastructure, data, and applications in real time and manage security incidents.
7. **Security governance, risk, and compliance**: Maintain security policy, audit, and compliance measures, meeting corporate policies, solution-specific regulations, and governing laws.

# Web application hosting

The web application-hosting architecture delivers web pages that contain static and dynamic content using HTTP or HTTPS. Static content uses standardized web page text with specialized content held in document, image, video, and sound clip files. Dynamic content is created in real time based on visitor input. The response is based on the request and content derived from linked databases. The core component is the web application server. Other components can include life cycle management, operations management, and governance:

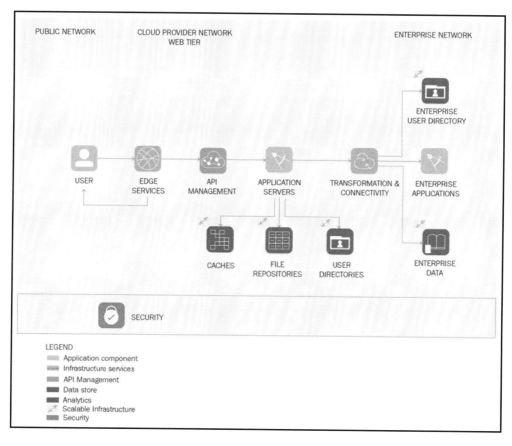

Figure 2: Web application hosting cloud architecture

# Public network

Public network components contain users and edge services. Users can interact with the web application using various devices and systems. Edge services have the capability to deliver application content and normally include the firewall, DNS server, load balancer, and **content delivery network (CDN)**.

# Cloud provider network components

The cloud provider network components are as follows:

## Web service tier

The CSP normally hosts the web services tier. This tier holds the program logic for generating dynamic web content. Web and application servers can also be deployed in a three-tiered design. This uses load balancers to connect separate pools of web and application servers. Other components include file repository, web application servers, user directory, and cache.

- **API management**: API management presents all available service endpoints needed for access to the application. Services can include security, scalability, composition, access, governance, analytics, deployment, and management.
- **Transformation and connectivity**: Transformation and connectivity ensures secure connection to legacy enterprise systems. It can also filter, aggregate, or modify data as it transitions between web components and legacy enterprise systems. In this reference architecture, the transformation and connectivity component are located between the web and enterprise tiers and can include enterprise data connectivity, data transformation, and enterprise secure connectivity.

# Enterprise network components

Enterprises normally host many applications that typically deliver critical business solutions. This is done in conjunction with providing infrastructure support. Applications also have data sources that are extracted and integrated with cloud-based services. Analysis is performed in the cloud, and output is delivered to on-premises systems.

# Service tier

The service tier holds the enterprise applications, enterprise user directory, and enterprise data. The enterprise user directory provides storage for and access to user information to support user access. Enterprise data includes metadata about the data as well as systems of record for enterprise application authentication, authorization, or profile data. Enterprise applications consume cloud provider data and analytics to produce results that address business goals and objectives.

# Security components

Security components include identity and access management, data and application protection, and security intelligence.

# API management

APIs are central to any cloud computing solution so they also must be managed. This function must not only address the multiple personas associated with API delivery and use, but all the different services, devices, and applications as well.

For in-depth information on API management, refer to: `https://slidelegend.com/cscc-cloud-customer-architecture-for-api-management_59fc74001723dd6ae4d97181.html`.

# E-commerce

The following diagram shows the e-commerce solution across three domains: public networks, cloud service provider, and enterprise networks. The public network domain contains commerce users and their e-commerce channel that supports user interaction. The edge services handle traffic between the pubic network and the CSP. The cloud service provider can host comprehensive e-commerce capabilities, such as merchandising, location awareness, B2B2C commerce, payment processing, customer care, distributed order management, supply chain management, and warehouse management.

The enterprise network domain represents existing enterprise systems. It includes organizational applications, data stores, and user directories. Results are delivered using transformation and connectivity components.

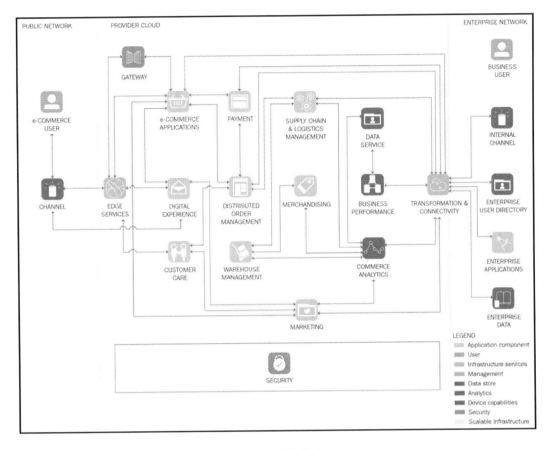

Figure 3: Cloud component relationships for e-commerce

# Public network components

The public network contains data sources and APIs, users, and the edge services. An e-commerce user accesses the commerce solutions via the cloud provider platform or organizational network. The channel provides a seamless, personalized experience independent of the customer access mode or channel. Key capabilities in this domain include the following:

- Website
- Mobile
- Connected devices

Edge services are needed to transfer data safely from the internet into the CSP and on to the enterprise. Edge services also support end user applications. Key capabilities include the following:

- Domain name system server
- CDNs
- Firewall
- Load balancers

# Cloud provider components

By allowing direct ordering from a manufacturer, ecommerce applications have extended the supplier's ability to tap into new markets and channels. Having a retailer participate as a delivery channel for a supplier has also provided convenience to customers and has allowed them to reach new customers and promote their brand. Key capabilities include the following:

- Mobile digital and store
- Product search and personalization
- Catalog
- Order capture
- Marketplace

A robust digital experience is the key to engaging customers, and the functional capabilities should include the following:

- Content
- Federated search
- Social engagement
- Digital messaging

A gateway is also critical because it allows smart devices to search, shop, and pay. Customer care assists the customer throughout the entire transaction life cycle and across all commerce channels. Online customer care should be offered in real time, often through chat facilities, cued by user behaviors such as abandoning a shopping cart or alternating between pages multiple times. Cognitive computing and natural-language processing have greatly enhanced customer care functions.

Key capabilities in this domain include the following:

- **Customer relationship management** (CRM)
- Loyalty management

Payment processing handles payment transactions that use credit cards or **electronic fund transfers (EFT)** from the following roles:

- Merchant
- Customer
- Merchant payment-processing service provider
- Merchant bank, if different than payment processor
- Customer's bank, or bank issuing credit or purchase card

The payment gateway, on the other hand, is the mediator between the e-commerce transaction and the payment-processing service. Security requirements prohibit the direct information transmission from the website to the payment processor. Payment gateways are offered by payment-processing vendors or contracted from vendors who only offer a gateway as a service.

Distributed order management orchestrates the workflow of orders from distribution centers and warehouses through direct fulfillment at stores. It can deliver superior customer experiences across an extended supply chain network and provide flexible order management across multiple channels. Key capabilities include the following:

- Order management and orchestration
- Global inventory visibility
- Returns management

Supply chain management is used to plan and manage product life cycle, supply network, inventory, distribution, and partner alliances. Logistics management addresses internal logistics for purchasing, production, warehousing, and transportation. Key capabilities in this domain include the following:

- Supply chain management
- **Product life cycle management** (**PLM**) and manufacturing
- Sourcing and procurement
- Supplier and partner data communications
- Transactional event ledgers
- Transportation management and optimization

Warehouse management enables efficient warehouse management operations. Modern organizations combine warehouse management wireless networks, mobile computers, **Radio Frequency Identification** (**RFID**) technology, voice-picking applications, and barcoding. This can fully extend an enterprise to the mobile worker, increase efficiency, and enhance customer service. Capabilities here include the following:

- Warehouse inventory management
- Inventory optimization
- Inventory

Merchandising planning is the management of merchandise or service-marketing rights. The goal is optimizing margin, gross revenue, or product shelf life. Domain key capabilities include the following:

- Assortment management
- Pricing management and optimization
- Product placement

Commerce analytics optimizes the shopper's journey to improve sales and business revenue. This component should drive the *next best action* at the right time and the best channel. Personalization is enabled through having a comprehensive customer view and predictive analytics. Key capabilities in this domain include the following:

- Digital analytics
- Cross-channel analytics
- Social commerce and sentiment analytics
- Merchandise analytics and optimization

The marketing domain supports the customer from product exploration through the purchase decision to transaction completion by delivering personalized offers, content, and product presentations. Understanding consumer consumption and shopping behavior is now key to building and growing market share. Key capabilities are the following:

- **Marketing resource management (MRM)**
- Campaign management
- Real-time recommendations

Data services deliver the ability to access, replicate, and synchronize data. These services aid in the management of merchandise inventory and distributing transportation. Other data services can also be used to generate and aggregate the reports from the enterprise data and applications.

The business performance component delivers important alerts, metrics, and **Key Performance Indicators** (**KPIs**) used to monitor commerce activities, tracking progress against goals, and adjusting offerings in response to market variations and demand. Data is usually displayed using dashboards that have been tailored for specific management roles. Commerce analytics and data services support real-time visibility of customer activity and provide the ability to drill down to individual transactions.

Retailers typically rely on a few fundamental metrics to provide an accurate view of their performance. These retail KPIs are as follows:

- Number of customers interacting in a store or via a website
- Conversion rates—how many store or website visitors actually make a purchase
- Average sales value of items purchased
- The size of a shopping basket
- Gross margin

The transformation and connectivity component provides secure connections to enterprise systems. It also provides the ability to filter, aggregate, modify, or reformat data. Key capabilities in this domain include the following:

- Enterprise secure connectivity
- Data transformations
- Enterprise data connectivity
- Extract, transform, and load

# Enterprise network components

Enterprise network components support on-premises systems and users. Key domain capabilities include the following:

- In-store
- Call center

Enterprise applications are important data sources in commerce solutions. Enterprise applications use cloud services and host legacy applications. Three key applications are the following:

- Finance
- Human resources
- Contract management

# Enterprise data

The enterprise data component hosts applications that deliver critical business solutions and their supporting infrastructure. These applications are key data sources that are extracted and integrated with analytics services. Key capabilities in this domain include the following:

- Reference data
- Transactional data
- Activity/big data
- Operation master data

The enterprise user directory provides user profile access for both the cloud and enterprise users. A user profile provides a login account and access control lists. The security services and edge services use this directory to control access to the enterprise network and services or to cloud provider services.

# Security

Security services enable identity and access management, protection of data and applications, and actionable security intelligence across cloud and enterprise environments. They use the catalog and user directory to understand the location and classification of the data they are protecting. Key capabilities in this domain include the following:

- Identity and access management
- Application and data protection
- Data encryption
- Infrastructure and network protection
- Application security
- Data activity monitoring
- Data lineage
- Security intelligence

# Mobile

The architectural elements described in this summary are used to instantiate mobile hosting environments with cloud service providers. Mobile applications have time-variable usage patterns that are well supported by the scalability and elasticity characteristics of cloud computing. Mobile applications also tend to make use of server-side data.

The frequency and volume of data access common with mobile apps can sometimes be difficult for traditional enterprise systems. Elastic provisioning and support of application-specific databases is an important and relevant cloud-computing capability. Using application-specific databases can also reduce the need to access enterprise systems and the associated resources.

# Mobile architecture components

*Figure 1* illustrates the high-level architecture of a mobile cloud solution. The architecture has four tiers:

- Mobile computing devices
- Public network that connects a device to the cloud services
- Provider cloud environment that hosts the necessary services

The following diagram depicts an enterprise network that contains legacy enterprise applications, services, and data:

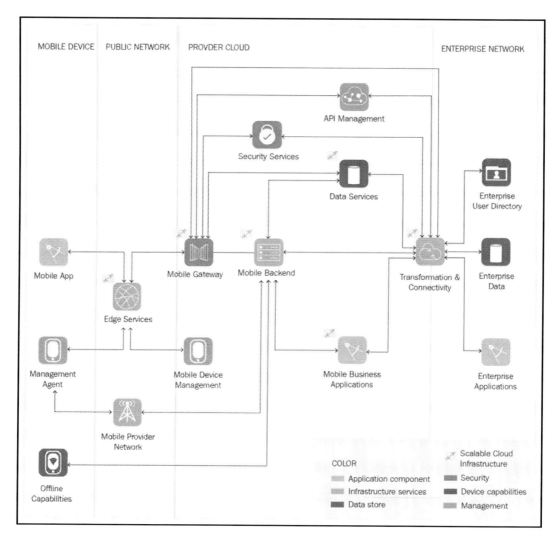

Figure 4: Cloud customer mobile architecture

# Mobile device components

Mobile applications are the core vehicle for user engagement with services on mobile devices. Mobile applications communicate with backend services via APIs, normally based on REST interfaces. The two key mobile app components are the following:

- Vendor frameworks
- Enterprise **software development kits (SDKs)**

Management agents apply enterprise policies. The agent is the SDK component that stores, enforces, and manages policies on the device. Offline capabilities give the application the ability to store and sync data securely on devices. A mobile app may use offline capabilities to access and store secure data.

# Public network Components

Edge services connect the mobile device and its applications to the mobile gateway using Wi-Fi or mobile provider networks. These include the following:

- Domain name system server
- Firewall
- Load balancers
- CDNs

The mobile provider network owns or controls the elements necessary to sell and deliver services to an end user. These typically include radio spectrum (http://en.wikipedia.org/wiki/Radio_spectrum) allocation, wireless network (http://en.wikipedia.org/wiki/Wireless_network) infrastructure, back haul (http://en.wikipedia.org/wiki/Backhaul_%28telecommunications%29) infrastructure, billing, customer care, provisioning (http://en.wikipedia.org/wiki/Provisioning) computer systems, and marketing and repair organizations.

# Provider cloud service components

The mobile gateway is the entry point from a mobile application to the mobile-specific solution services. It may also use data services and the enterprise user directory. A mobile gateway can be implemented using a common gateway across all channels into an API ecosystem. It provides the following:

- Authentication/authorization
- Policy enforcement
- API/invocation analytics
- API/reverse proxy

The mobile backend delivers runtime services to mobile applications in implementing server-side logic, maintaining data, and using mobile services. It provides an environment to run application logic and APIs. Here, application logic can communicate with the enterprise network and other applications that reside outside of the service provider. It provides the following:

- Application logic/API implementation
- Mobile app operational analytics
- Push notifications
- Location services
- Mobile data sync
- Mobile app security

**Mobile device management** (**MDM**) manages mobile devices and provides services to track enterprise-owned devices. It also manages devices that connect to corporate networks. MDM provides the following:

- Enterprise app distribution
- Mobile device security
- Device management
- Device analytics

Mobile business applications are the enterprise- or industry-specific capabilities needed to conduct business on the mobile devices. These can provide a gateway to enterprise applications and data, and may include analytics components that track usage. They can include the following:

- Proximity services and analytics
- Campaign management
- Business analytics and reporting
- Workflow/rules

API management advertises available service endpoints and provides API discovery, catalogs, APIs that connect to management capabilities, and service implementations, such as API versioning. The capabilities are the following:

- API discovery/documentation
- Management

Data services enable data to be stored and accessed in a form suitable for rapid access. This may include extracts of enterprise data. Data services can include the following:

- Mobile app data/NoSQL
- File repositories
- Caches

Security services ensure that only authorized users are able to access mobile cloud services. This also protects the data and enables the visibility required to have actionable security intelligence across all environments. Components include the following:

- Identity and access management
- Data and application protection
- Security intelligence
- Enterprise transformation and connectivity
- Enterprise security connectivity
- Transformation

# Enterprise network components

Enterprise network components provide backend connectivity to enterprise business services and include the following:

- Enterprise user directory
- Enterprise data
- Enterprise applications

# Enterprise social collaboration

The enterprise social collaboration architecture addresses services that support an enterprise social platform. This design also includes the internal and external extension points needed for data and services integration. These capabilities can be applied in modules. The interfaces between the social collaboration platform and on-premises systems are important when defining the final system architecture.

# Cloud customer reference architecture for enterprise social collaboration

The cloud customer reference architecture for enterprise social collaboration is explained in the following sections.

# Architecture Overview

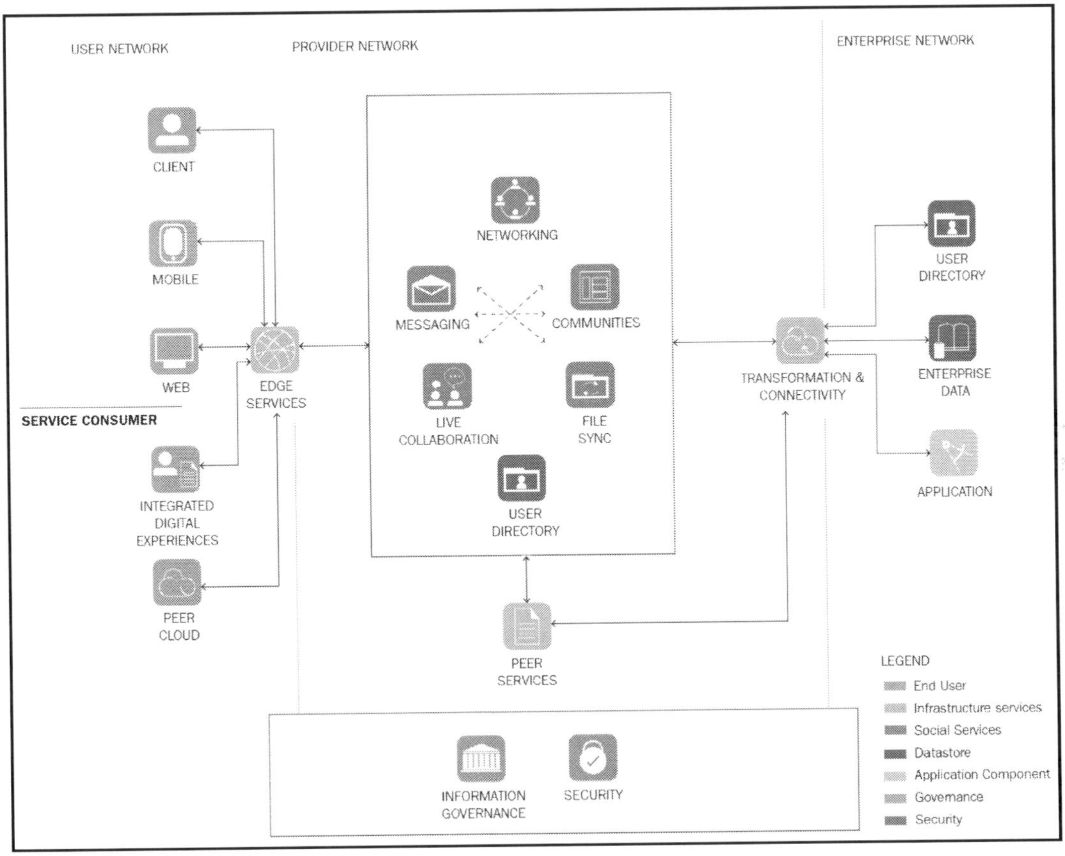

Figure5: Elements of enterprise social collaboration

# User network

The user network allows end users to interact with cloud provider services. These services are classified as desktop (client), mobile, and web applications. The end user enters requests for enterprise social collaboration services and receives results after processing has been completed. Services can also include end users' interactions. The key focus is social network interaction between the following:

- Web applications (via web browser)
- Mobile application
- Desktop rich client

# Service consumer

End users may not always interact directly with social services through the user network. They could also *consume a service* through other application interfaces. A service consumer describes this as a pattern where an end user consumes and contributes to the social services indirectly through the following patterns:

- Integrated digital experience, which is integrated capabilities that deliver an engaging, personalized, relevant, and meaningful digital presence to the user. Key capabilities may include the following:
  - Content
  - Digital messaging
  - Social engagement
  - Federated search
  - Personalization
  - Analytics
- Peer cloud services used for core business processes or to meet just-in-time requirements may also be required consume content, services, and interfaces from the social services that could include the following:
  - **Software-as-a-Service (SaaS)**
  - Cloud services (API)
  - **Platform-as-a-Service (PaaS)**

# Provider network

Provider cloud components include the following capabilities.

Edge services deliver connectivity options to end users and the capabilities needed to allow the safe flow of data between the internet, the provider cloud, and the enterprise. Capabilities in this domain include the following:

- **Domain Name System (DNS)**
- CDNs
- Firewall
- Load balancers

Enterprise social services represent a collaborative information exchange using secure social applications. This capability can blend an integrated user experience that is infused into business processes, integrated with other applications, and aggregated with other experiences. Key capabilities in this domain include the following:

- Networking
- Communities
- File sync
- Live collaboration
- Messaging
- User directory

As part of a social implementation, peer services may be consumed in order to deliver functionality provided by an external solution. These can also be integrated into social services and can be hosted within the service provider cloud. Peer services rely on the cloud service provider's cloud governance and security models and they can deliver the following:

- **Extended capabilities**: Functional experiences integrated into defined extension points of the enterprise social services experience
- **Enhanced experiences**: Additional tools and extensions to the existing enterprise social service
- **Foundation services**: Enhance the underlying functions of the social service

The information governance component assures enforcement of organizational policies by focusing on procedures that govern access to capabilities and information sharing. These typically include the following:

- Sign-on/on-boarding approval process
- Legal compliance
- Regulatory compliance (that is, PII, PCI, HIPPA, FINRA, FedRAMP, and so on)
- Audit reporting
- Data loss protection
- Corporate policies

# Security

As an integrated suite, the enterprise social collaboration may have some unique security considerations that need to be addressed. Some of the more prevalent of these are as follows.

Authentication to the service is needed to ensure that only authorized users have access to data, tools, and applications, while simultaneously blocking unauthorized access. Synchronizing enterprise user directories is beneficial in extending the on-premises environment to the cloud. The enterprise social services facilitate this by providing the following:

- On-/off-boarding of users
- User bulk provisioning and updates
- Provisioning of user through an administrative tool

Federated Identity Management uses **Single Sign-On (SSO)** to protect the transfer of user credentials across networks. Using SSO, authorized users can use different applications without additional authentication.

**Security Assertion Markup Language (SAML)** is used to facilitate SSO with other parties or enterprise directories. SAML is a widely used standard that leverages signed assertion documents instead of passwords as identity credentials. Customers maintain passwords internally for web application resources which help organizations do the following:

- Manage password requirements.
- Manage two-factor authentication requirements.
- Set password change intervals.
- Use **open authorization (OAUTH)**, which supports web applications, desktop applications, and third-party extensions. This is an open source methodology for API authorization.

Data security ensures only authorized users have secure access to customer data. This requires protection of the relevant data against service vulnerabilities and physical breach of data centers. Security requires the layered use of a combination of technology coupled with standard CSP processes and procedures. These can include the following:

- Platform and process
- Security checklist against every release
- Security compliance with ongoing automated health checks
- Data center
- Redundancy: Redundant systems to prevent a single point of failure in providing services, including application, power, network, and so on.
- Monitoring of the physical environment, which includes the logging of staff activities
- Access controls and fire-prevention systems
- Network and infrastructure defenses
- Layered firewall infrastructure
- Deployed network intrusion detection
- Process for people
- Separation of duty definitions
- Segregation of activities, including personnel with change access to the code base and those with operational configuration control
- Code reviews prior to deployment
- Regular ethical hacking penetration testing
- Audit logs and analysis of security-related events
- Data privacy and data ownership policies
- Encryption and email security
- Data in transit
- Data at rest
- Real-time antivirus at application and server levels
- Anti-spam protection on email messages

Transformation and connectivity ensures secure connections to backend enterprise systems. This also enables data filtering, aggregation, modification, or reformatting. Key capabilities in this domain include the following:

- Enterprise secure connectivity
- Transformations
- Enterprise data connectivity
- Extract, transform, and load

## Enterprise network

The enterprise network contains the on-premises systems components. While integration between the enterprise social services and enterprise applications may not be necessary, some use cases may need it. Services include the following:

- User directory
- Enterprise data

Enterprise applications are existing applications that accomplish business goals and objectives. These may also need to interact with cloud services. Organizational email is a common example.

# Big data and analytics

**Big data analytics (BDA)** is used to build competitive advantage, drive innovations, and enhance revenue. This capability offers a cost-effective cloud-based solution for data analytics. As big data grows in importance, organizations are striving to derive meaningful insight from this data. This is crucial to enabling an ability to respond to real business needs in a timely manner.

The following diagram illustrates a simplified enterprise cloud architecture for a BDA environment and contains three network zones: public, cloud service provider, and enterprise:

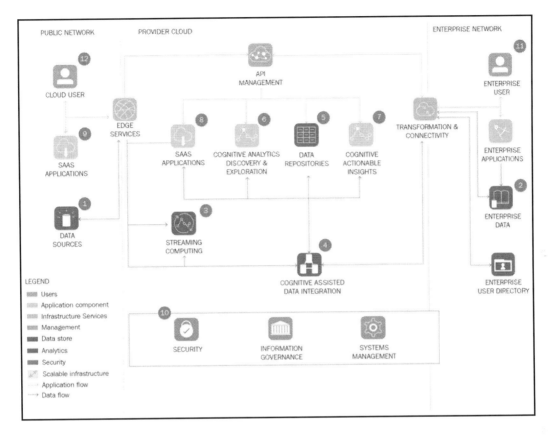

Figure 6: BDA solutions in the cloud

This architecture is similar to that of a data lake deployment. Both structured and non-structured data are used as sources. Data is then staged and transformed by data integration and stream computing engines, after which it is stored in various repositories. The data may also be augmented, transformed, correlated, and summarized until it is finally made available to consumers through APIs. Cognitive computing technologies such as machine learning and natural language processing can also be used to automate ingestion, integration, discovery, and exploration.

This architectural approach is applicable to the entire analytics life cycle and can be applied as a data lake solution for a DevOps environment. The latter is achieved by adding metadata and semantic definitions to the enterprise data repository descriptions that are stored in a service catalog. These catalog entries are then augmented with governance classifications, rules, and policies that automate data management as it flows in, out, and through the data lake. The following sections give a summary of each of the required components.

# Public network components

The public network contains cloud users, SaaS applications, data sources, and edge services.

A cloud user connects to the analytics cloud solution via the network. Human and non-human users may represent one or more of the following roles:

- Knowledge worker and citizen analyst
- Data scientist
- Application developer
- Data engineer
- **Chief Data Officer (CDO)**

All the different personas have the following common characteristics:

- Self-service is desired.
- They require access to sometime large volumes of data needed to accomplish an analytical task with associated data quality and provenance metrics.
- They require multiple tools and capabilities that may be open-source and consumed from on-demand services.
- Collaboration is required.

Data sources can be external, public, and varied, with multiple information sources contained within a typical big-data system. High velocity, volume, variety, and data inconsistency are often the norm. Edge analytics services may also be required. Data sources normally include the following:

- Machine and sensor
- Image and video
- Social
- Internet datasets
- Weather data
- Third party

Edge services allow data to flow safely and securely from the internet into the data analytics processing system. The data flow may also require **domain name system (DNS)** servers, CDNs, firewalls, and load balancer services before entering the cloud service provider's data integration or data-streaming service points.

# Provider cloud components

The cloud service provider delivers the analytics solution and hosts the required components. These functions are used to prepare data for analytics, storage, and results processing. Cloud service provider elements include the following:

- API management
- Data repositories
- Streaming computing
- SaaS applications
- Cognitive assisted data integration
- Cognitive analytics discovery and exploration
- Transformation and connectivity
- Cognitive actionable analytics

The data access component is used to express the many capabilities for interacting with the data repositories. This serves customer data access needs and includes the following services:

- Data access
- Data virtualization
- Data federation
- Open APIs

Stream processing is used to ingest and process large volumes of highly dynamic, time-sensitive, and continuous data streams from inputs such as sensors, messaging systems, and real-time feeds. The traditional *store-and-pull* data processing model is not usable for meeting low-latency or real-time streaming applications. Capabilities include the following:

- Streaming analytics
- **Complex Event Processing (CEP)**
- Data enrichment
- Real-time ingestion

The cognitive-assisted data integration component deals with the capture, qualification, processing, and movement of data into analytical data lake repositories. Here, it is shared with the discovery and exploration and actionable insights components using the data access component. Various cognitive technologies such as machine learning and natural language processing can be used to automate data ingestion and integration. Data integration capabilities include the following:

- Batch ingestion
- Change data capture
- Document interpretation and classification
- Data quality analysis

The data repositories are a set of secure locations used to store data prior to it being consumed by analytics tools and end users. The repositories are the core of the analytics environment. Operational and transactional data stores (such as OLTP, ECM, and so on) are not part of this component. They are help within the data sources component. Data repository types include the following:

- Landing zone and data archive
- History
- Deep and exploratory analytics
- Sandboxes
- Data warehouses and data marts
- Predictive analytics

Cognitive analytics discovery and exploration enables end users to collaborate about and easily interact with complicated data repositories using modern data science techniques. They also enable an ability to semantically search across both structured and unstructured content in order to glean new insights and obtain a complete data ontology view. Functionally, these provide the following:

- Data science
- Search and survey / shopping for data

The cognitive actionable insight component cohesively analyzes data from multiple sources in order to derive meaningful and actionable insight for the business. Techniques used within this function include the following:

- Visualization and storyboarding
- Reporting, analysis, and content analytics
- Decision management

- Predictive analytics and modeling
- Cognitive analytics
- Insight as a Service

Cloud service provider SaaS applications are often used to enable, manage or augment the following:

- Customer experience
- New business models
- Financial performance
- Risk
- Fraud and preparation
- IT economics

The transformation and connectivity component ensures secure connections to backend enterprise systems while also enabling data filtering, aggregation, modification, or re-formatting. Capabilities include the following:

- Enterprise security connectivity
- Transformations
- Enterprise data connectivity

# Enterprise network

The enterprise network is where the on-premises systems and users are located and includes users and applications. Enterprise data is also included and holds metadata on the data as well as systems of record for enterprise applications. It may flow directly to data integration or the data repositories and includes the following:

- Reference data
- Master data
- Transactional data
- Application data
- Log data
- Enterprise content data
- Historical data
- Archived data

The enterprise user directory contains the user profiles for both the cloud and enterprise users. A user profile provides a login account and access control lists. Security and edge services use this to manage data access.

Ubiquitous services that interact across the entire environment include the following.

Information management and governance components maintain a trusted, standardized, and accurate view of critical business data and include the following:

- Data life cycle management
- Master and entity data
- Reference data
- Data catalog
- Data models
- Data quality rules

# Security

The security component protects the data and delivers the ability to mask/hide data at a granular level and the following capabilities:

- Data security
- Identity and access management
- Infrastructure security
- Application security
- Secure DevOps
- Security monitoring and intelligence
- Security governance

System management refers to all activities performed to plan, design, deliver, operate, and control IT and cloud-based services typically addressed by **service level agreements (SLAs)**.

# Blockchain

Blockchain technology features an immutable distributed ledger accessed across a decentralized cryptographically secured network. This architecture allows for the sharing of an electronic ledger, through peer-to-peer replication. This ledger is updated every time a block of transactions is committed. This technology can radically alter the way business is conducted and how transactions are processed. With blockchain technology, participants can engage in transparent business transactions across geographical boundaries.

From a business perspective, a blockchain is an exchange network that facilitates transfer of value, assets, or other entities between willing and mutually agreeing participants, ensuring privacy and control of data to stakeholders.

From a legal perspective, blockchain ledger transactions are validated, indisputable transactions, which do not require intermediaries or trusted third-party legal entities.

From a technical perspective, a blockchain is a replicated, distributed ledger of transactions with ledger entries referencing other data stores. Cryptography ensures that network participants see only the parts of the ledger that are relevant to them, and that transactions are secure, authenticated, and verifiable, in the context of permissioned business blockchains.

# Blockchain Reference Architecture Capabilities

The following diagram presents the typical node capabilities needed to participate in a blockchain architecture and is depicted across three networks—public, cloud, and enterprise. The capability locations are representative of industry best practice, but any capability can be implemented in any network based on the solution needs:

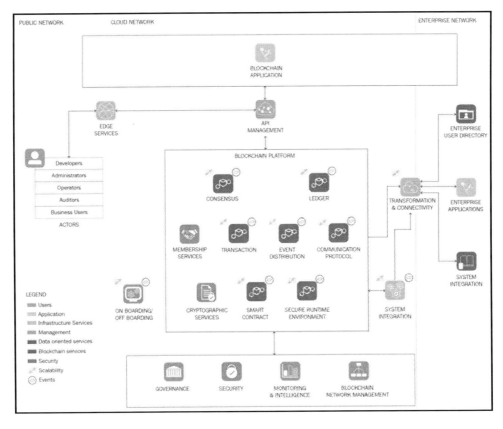

Figure 7: Blockchain reference architecture capabilities

# Public network

The public network contains the wide-area networks peer cloud systems, and edge services. Edge services allow data to flow securely and safely from the network into the cloud service provider and onto the enterprise. Edge services support end user applications and include the following:

- **Domain name system server (DNSS)**
- CDNs
- Firewall
- Load balancers

Users are the blockchain participants who create and distribute blockchain applications. Those performing operations using the blockchain may include the following:

- Developers
- Administrators
- Operators
- Auditors
- Business users

# Cloud network

Blockchain applications present business capabilities to blockchain system end users. Applications may also serve other users who have different roles. Blockchain applications can be web services or end user device(s) applications, or connected to server-side application services. These applications and services interface using the platform APIs. The applications may also have access to other resources such as databases if needed to implement capabilities.

API management capabilities publish catalogs and update APIs, enabling developers and end users to leverage discovery and reuse of existing data, analytics, and services to rapidly assemble solutions. Blockchain applications interface with the blockchain network by using the blockchain programming interfaces.

The blockchain platform supports essential capabilities via a blockchain network node or enterprise. Although each blockchain platform is implemented differently, core capabilities that should be considered are the following:

- Consensus
- Ledger
- Membership services
- Transactions
- Event distribution
- Communication protocol
- Cryptographic services
- Smart contract
- Secure runtime environment

Typical system integration methods include API adapters and an **Enterprise Service Bus (ESB)** connection between the blockchain platform and the organization's internal systems.

Transformation and connectivity capability enables secure connections to backend enterprise systems. It also provides filtering, aggregation, or data modification or data re-formatting as it moves between the cloud, blockchain components, and enterprise systems. This component includes the following capabilities:

- Enterprise secure connectivity
- Transformation

# Enterprise data connectivity

The enterprise network provides the enterprise user directory, enterprise applications, and enterprise data. Enterprise data includes metadata as well as systems of record for enterprise applications. Enterprise data relating to blockchain includes the following:

- Transactional data
- Application data
- Log data

# Blockchain services

Blockchain foundational services include the following:

- Governance
- Security
- Monitoring and intelligence

The blockchain network management component provides visibility across all blockchain network operations. This visibility includes business process, performance, and capacity data metrics. It also delivers the management interface for changing configurations and other parameters.

Other important blockchain concepts include permissions options:

- Permissionless networks are open to any participant. Transactions are verified against the pre-existing network rules. Any participant, even those that are anonymous, can view ledger transactions.
- Permissioned networks are limited to participants within a given business network. Participants are only allowed to view transactions relevant to them and can only perform operations for which they are permissioned.

When using blockchain, only a small amount of the transaction data is stored directly in the blockchain ledger. Other transaction is stored separately but is referenced by the entry. This approach avoids overwhelming the blockchain ledger with large data amounts. Storage options include the following:

- Ledger storage
- Data storage

Blockchain interaction options are varied and include the following:

- **Command line interface (CLI)**
- Client SDK
- **Software Development Kit (SDK)**

# Architecture for IoT

The IoT links physical entities (*things*) with information technology systems in order to derive information. This information is used to drive multiple applications and services. Since IoT covers applications that integrate systems from traditionally different communities, they must have architectures that are capable of accommodating many unique requirements.

IoT systems include sensors for gathering information about objects and human activities. They can also monitor actuators acting on other physical objects. Unique IoT architecture implementation aspects are shown in the following table:

| Architecture aspects | Description |
|---|---|
| Scalability | The numbers of sensors and actuators connected to the system, the networks which connect them together, the amount of data associated with the system, data speed of movement, and the amount of required processing power. |
| Big data | The ability to gather new insights from mining existing data. |
| Cloud computing | The use of large amounts of resources in terms of data storage and scalable processing. |
| Real time | Real-time data flow support and an ability to produce timely responses based on a continuous stream of events. There is also a parallel need to detected and avoid the use of corrupted data. |
| Highly distributed | Widely distributed devices, systems and data. |
| Heterogeneous systems | Heterogeneous set of devices that include sensors and actuators, types of networks, and variety of processing components. |
| Security and privacy | Data protection combined with significant data privacy protection. |
| Compliance | Regulatory compliance across specific industries, sectors, and verticals. |
| Integration | Ability to connect to existing operational technology systems such as factory systems, building control systems, and other physical management systems. |

The following diagram shows the capabilities and relationships for supporting IoT using cloud computing:

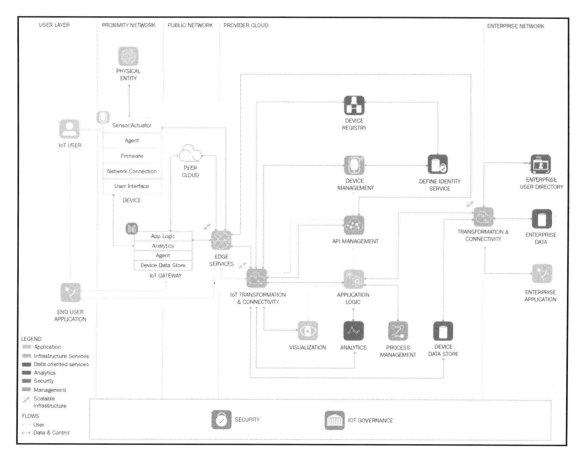

Figure 8: Cloud components for the IoT

The cloud components of IoT architecture are normally positioned in a three-tier architecture composed of edge, platform, and enterprise tiers.

# Edge tier

Proximity networks and public networks are in the edge tier. Here, data is received and transmitted to user devices. Data flows through the IoT gateway or through edge services into the CSP.

The cloud service provider in in the platform tier. The provider receives, processes, and analyzes data flows. The CSP also provides API management and visualization and can initiate control commands.

The enterprise network represents the enterprise tier, which is comprised of enterprise data, enterprise user directory, and enterprise applications.

An IoT system uses application logic and control logic across many locations, depending on timescales and datasets. Some code may actually execute directly on the IoT devices or in the gateways. *Edge computing* or *fog computing* is applied to the case where code executes in the IoT gateways or the devices.

IoT users and end user applications are in the user layer. The proximity network has all physical entities that interact with IoT system physical entities. The physical entity is the subject of sensor measurements or actuator behavior.

Devices contain sensor and actuator. The attached network connection enables interaction with the extended IoT system. The device may also be the physical entity being monitored by the sensors. Other important components include sensor/actuator, agent, and firmware.

The network connection provides connectivity from the device to the IoT system. This device often has low power and low range to reduce power requirements. Alternative communication mechanisms can include Bluetooth, **Bluetooth Low Energy (BTLE)**, Wi-Fi or wide area networking using 2G, 3G, and 4G LTE. The user interface supports user interaction with applications, agents, actuators, and sensors.

The IoT gateway connects devices to the public network. If the devices have limited network connectivity, the local IoT gateway enables the needed communications. The IoT gateway can also filter and react to data. The IoT gateway contains the following:

- App logic
- Analytics
- Agent
- Device data store

# Public network

The public network contains the wide area networks, other cloud systems, and edge services. Large IoT systems may combine a series of smaller IoT systems that each address a specific part of the solution. These *systems of systems* include connections between other clouds.

Edge services enable secure data flow into the CSP and onto the enterprise network. They include the following:

- Domain name system server
- CDNs
- Firewall
- Load balancers

# Cloud service provider

The CSP delivers core IoT applications and services. These can include data storage, analytics, IoT system process management, and data visualizations. IoT transformations and connectivity delivers secure connectivity between all IoT devices. This component must handle and transform high volumes of messages and route them to the correct solution components. The transformation and connectivity component includes the following:

- Secure connectivity
- Scalable messaging
- Scalable transformation

The application logic holds the core application components that co-ordinate the IoT device data handling and other services that support user applications. An event-based programming model is often used. Application logic can include workflow and control logic.

Visualization helps users explore and interact with. Visualization capabilities include the following:

- End user UI
- Admin UI
- Dashboard

Analytics is used to discover and communicate meaningful IoT data information patterns. These patterns are used to describe, predict, and improve business performance. IoT capabilities include the following:

- Analytics data repository
- Cognitive
- Actionable insight
- Streaming computing

A critical component is the device data store. This stores data from the IoT devices so that it can be integrated with other processes and applications. Devices can generate large amounts of real-time data which requires an elastic and scalable device data store. Device management is used to efficiently manage and connect devices securely and reliably to the cloud. Device management also contains provisioning, remote administration, software updating, device remote control, and device monitoring.

Transformation and connectivity enables secure connections to enterprise systems and the ability to filter, aggregate, or modify data or its format as it moves between the cloud and IoT system components. The transformation and connectivity component includes the following:

- Enterprise secure connectivity
- Transformation
- Enterprise data connectivity

# Enterprise network

The enterprise network hosts business-specific enterprise applications. These include enterprise data, user directory, and applications. Key IoT applications might include customer experience, financial performance, or operations and fraud.

# Security

Security and privacy in IoT deployments always need to address both **Information Technology (IT)**, security, and **Operations Technology (OT)** security elements. The level of attention to security varies based on the application environment, business pattern, and risk assessment.

There are many challenges in securing an IoT solution. Use of oversight and procedures is necessary to ensure that there is a means and mechanism for addressing new vulnerabilities and threats. An important difference in IoT systems is that exploits and failures have the potential to cause serious harm to humans, property, and the environment. Additionally, equipment is often installed in locations where change or replacement is not possible. IoT systems must, therefore, be designed and deployed with strong change/update/modification governance in mind. The cloud service provider components may also be subject to change over time. Appropriate governance must be in place to ensure that changes to these components are addressed as well.

# Architecture for hybrid integration

IT environments are now normally hybrid in nature. Integration across an ever-changing environment, delivered at the pace of modern digital innovation initiatives, is a significant challenge. This makes the hybrid integration platform is crucial. Hybrid cloud integration scenarios include the following:

- Viewing customer information between cloud-based CRM systems and on-premises **Enterprise Resource Planning (ERP)** applications
- Employee data integration between cloud-based human capital management systems and back-office applications

The hybrid integration reference architecture explores these and other common patterns observed in enterprises addressing these issues. It addresses the following considerations:

- **Connectivity**: Connecting systems and devices with other systems and devices. This integration may require low-level connectivity to **Systems of Record (SoR)** and the need to leverage cloud native systems as well.
- **Deployment**: Modern systems are deployed across a broad landscape so the accompanying integration components must have flexible deployment options. Components should also be able to run directly on bare metal, in virtual machines, or in containers.
- **Roles**: IT can be operated as bi-modal or multi-modal, where independent teams are working at different velocities. Integration needs to address these disparate velocities. Hybrid integration therefore expands beyond the IT organization business users and shadow IT departments that may be aligned with the line of business. Complex integrations are now collaborative, and APIs become the building blocks for collaboration between many different teams.

- **Styles**: Enterprise integration can be combined with APIs, events, and data to create seamless business processes and flows.

The hybrid integration architecture components are illustrated in the following diagram:

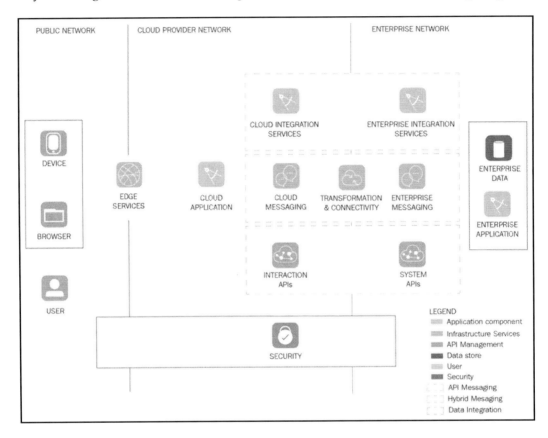

Figure 9: Cloud customer hybrid integration architecture

Hybrid integration delivers a seamless platform for applications to interchangeably consume services that, in turn, deliver end-to-end comprehensive mission-critical business capabilities. The reference architecture has three tiers:

- Public network
- Cloud service provider
- Enterprise network

Security is a cross-cutting theme that is applicable to all three tiers.

# Public network

The public network contains user access applications that reside on the cloud provider network. They are accessed using a browser or via a mobile native app. Edge services include capabilities needed to deliver function and content to the users via the internet. These include the following:

- DNS server
- CDN
- Firewall
- Load balancer

# Cloud provider network

The cloud provider network holds many of the key application and API services. The Cloud application component represents cloud-native applications that have been designed and developed within the cloud environment. These applications normally use modern techniques such as micro services architecture, lightweight run times, container technology, and DevOps methodologies. The application's services are often exposed using APIs and may need to access data from other systems via API calls, messaging, and data integration services.

Interaction APIs provide access to enterprise capabilities. They are maintained by the lines of business and are composed from lower-level system APIs. These APIs are business-led, may be exposed externally, and might even be *monetized* with a funding model based on their usage. This component is the API gateway into the enterprise network. The interaction APIs also advertises the available services endpoints to which the cloud application has access. This component provides API discovery, catalogs, and connection of offered APIs to service implementations and management capabilities, such as API versioning.

Cloud messaging gives fast, scalable, high throughput event delivery services with the enterprise network. This component should support multiple open event protocols. It should also abstract away any proprietary non-standard protocols of the enterprise messaging. This component is the event gateway into the enterprise network and should be able to do the following:

- Enable large-scale message processing
- Support a microservices framework and event-driven applications
- Enable hybrid messaging
- Perform batch and real-time analytics
- Accelerate applications and data integration

Cloud integration services deliver rapid, simple, and flexible integration capabilities. Unlike traditional **Enterprise Application Integration (EAI)** and ETL solutions, this component provides simple integration tooling with targeted capabilities. Customization is done performed via configuration and not by writing software code. This component is the gateway into SoR within the enterprise network and includes the following:

- Preparing/moving data to the cloud
- Extending business operations
- Accessing mainframe data and services
- Maintaining data consistency across applications
- Connecting on-premises apps and data to the cloud

The transformation and connectivity component enables secure enterprise connections. This component includes the following capabilities:

- Enterprise secure connectivity
- Transformation
- Enterprise data connectivity

# Enterprise network

The enterprise network holds legacy applications, data, and APIs.System APIs give access to enterprise applications and data. They are maintained by the corporate IT team and are normally lower-level, fine-grained APIs. Multiple interaction components might consume these APIs to compose higher-level capabilities. This component also provides API discovery, catalogs, and connection of offered APIs to service implementations and management capabilities.

Enterprise messaging is the enterprise messaging backbone. This is the primary messaging interface into the enterprise for the cloud messaging component and does the following:

- Provides secure and reliable messaging
- Supports heterogeneous application platforms
- Provides high-performance and scalable message transfer
- Provides simplified management and control

Enterprise integration services depict a broad variety of integration capabilities including enterprise data warehouse (ETL) systems, application integration components, and business process management systems. This is the primary integration interface into the enterprise for the cloud integration services component. Capabilities include the following:

- Preparing/moving data to the cloud
- Extending business operations
- Accessing mainframe data and services
- Maintaining data consistency across applications
- Connecting on-premises apps and data to the cloud

Enterprise applications are applications that run enterprise business processes and logic within existing enterprise systems, while enterprise data represents transactional data or data warehouses that represent the existing data in the enterprise.

Security for hybrid integration addresses the following needs:

- Data integrity
- Threat management
- Solution compliance

Capabilities include the following:

- Identity and access management
- Data and application protection
- Security intelligence

# Summary

This chapter provides the baseline architectures for some key modern business solutions. They are meant to serve as starting points for effective solutions the reader may be tasked to deploy. While the solutions are not readily deployable as documented, they do provide guidance and industry best practice recommendations for a solution delivery team. When used collaboratively across the solution delivery team, these reference architectures will accelerate and improve almost any solution design job.

# Cloud Environment Key Tenets and Virtualization

**9**

Designing cloud computing solutions is not about transplanting the same enterprise data center design onto another platform. To properly leverage the highly automated and dynamic cloud computing platform, an architect must use the environment's elasticity and scalability to improve operational efficiency or economics. The concepts in this section are essential tools for accomplishing that task and modifying the data center architecture design to leverage these approaches will be the key to a profitable cloud computing transition.

The following topics will be covered in this chapter:

- Elastic infrastructure
- Elastic platform
- Node-based availability
- Environment-based availability
- Technology service consumption model
- Design balance
- Virtualization

# Elastic infrastructure

Elastic infrastructures deliver preconfigured virtual machine servers, storage services, and network connectivity using a self-service interface. This type of infrastructure provides the proper amount of dynamically-adjusted IT resources necessary for a stated level of service. As the core capability of an IaaS service, this runtime infrastructure supports dynamic provisioning and de-provisioning of servers, disk storage, and network connectivity. Real-time monitoring of resource utilization is provided to enable traceable billing and automation of all associated management tasks.

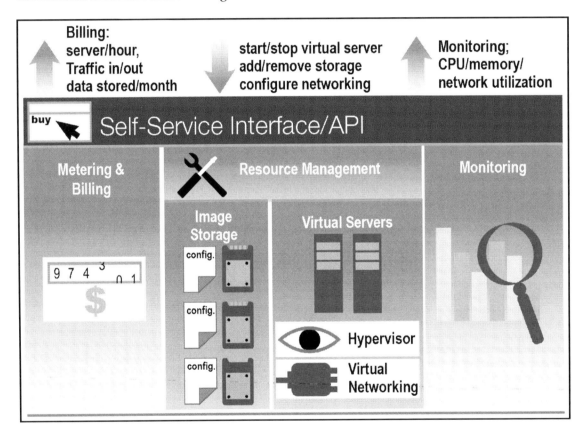

# Elastic platform

The provisioning of shared resources is an essential characteristic of cloud computing. Sharing enables economies of scale associated with the cloud. Elastic platforms extend resource sharing to the operating systems and middleware. The extension enhances economies of scale by increasing the utilization rates of these resources. This PaaS service delivers application components to various customers on a shared middleware platform. Maintained by the service provider, the environment is also referred to as an **integrated development environment** (IDE). Customers build and deploy custom application components to the middleware platform with a self-service interface. This enables resource sharing and automated middleware management.

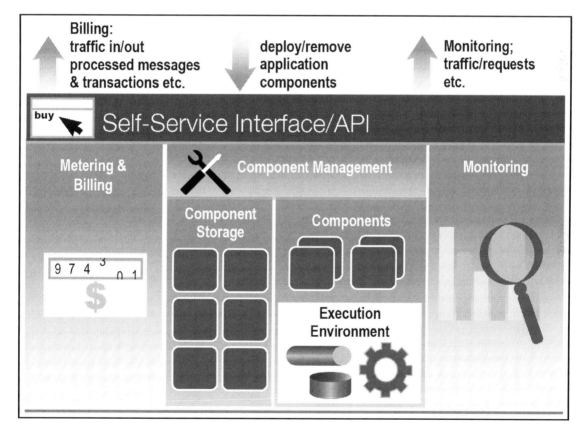

# Node-based availability

When either an elastic infrastructure or platform is offered by a provider, service availability is defined by the conditions that must be fulfilled by the offering and the time-frame within which service availability is assured. These two factors enable the computation of hosted application availability. With node-based availability, the service provider guarantees the availability of each application component.

Available is generally defined as being reachable and capable of performing its advertised function. This availability time-frame is expressed as a percentage. As an example, an availability of 99.95% means that a component will be available 99.95% of the time. The following figure depicts this example:

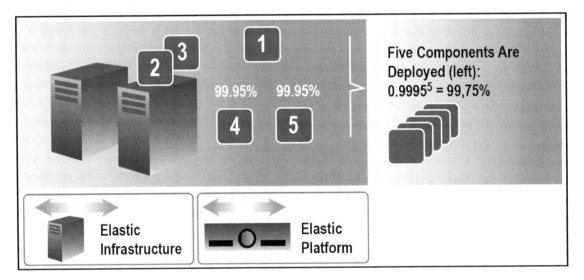

# Environment-based availability

When using environment-based availability, a cloud provider expresses the availability of an elastic infrastructure or platform as a whole. Availability of an individual application component using this type of expression is not defined. By communicating availability in this way, a customer is better able to match how end users commonly express availability. An example of this is expressing the availability of an at-least-once provisioned component or virtual server and the ability to provide a replacement if the first element fails. The following figure depicts this example:

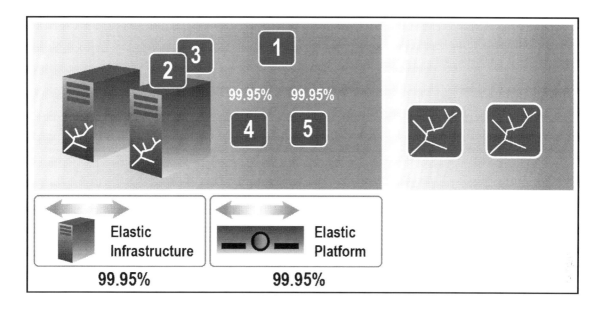

# Technology service consumption model

The IT service consumption is at the core of the industries embracing the OPEX expenditure economic model. It also highlights the intersection of rapidly-growing demands, ever-evolving technology, and the IT-enabled business model. IT is no longer just a cost center. It allows business processes and transactions that weren't possible before. This transformation from the traditional IT model to the pay-by-use contract avoids the direct purchase of equipment purchases and all expenses associated with operations and maintenance. Today, the equipment acquisition model is risky and costly due to rapid technology and consumer demand changes.

Companies now have many cloud computing options. They can adopt a full private cloud strategy, consume a single enterprise application from a public cloud, or take a hybrid route and source-specific service assets as a complement to traditional data center solutions. Successful IT organizations must cope with a dynamic cloud service vendor landscape that can deliver unprecedented choice.

IT and business leaders must team in the shaping of IT service consumption. When participating in this partnership, the IT organization must be both flexible and business model-aware. The previously ubiquitous approach of mandating technology equipment and use is no longer viable. In the face of this change, IT must still, however, maintain a central role across all stages of enterprise IT consumption. The IT team must become a trusted broker of technology services to the LOB. Their role will be as a critical intermediary and orchestrator, managing services, procurement, and delivery. They will also provide technical support and information technology security.

The consumption model shift requires the following:

- The consolidation of IT and corporate financial management strategies in a way that can also serve user needs through a consumption-based process across traditional infrastructure as well as public, private and hybrid clouds.
- Implementing an enterprise-wide set of financial and operational controls.
- Flexible IT planning and governance that measures and bundles usage into business-relevant IT service catalogs. This alignment will improve LOB resource visibility and selection.
- The use of a consistent and repeatable process for the timely capturing of consumption data.
- Data streamlines invoicing and revenue recognition.
- Link reporting views directly to resource usage and the transaction owner.
- The use of fixed, variable, tiered, scheduled, and resource state pricing features.
- The ability to track detailed usage and costs that also shows customer cost at a granular level.
- The establishment of alerts that capture and analyze data that compares allocated versus used capacity, usage trends, and forecasted usage across the entire enterprise.

# Design balance

When designing a cloud computing solution, the goal is balance across four specific organizational guidelines:

- Economics targets
- Operational goals
- Technological compatibility
- Enterprise governance (risks)

The solution architect must understand, respect, and document each of these limits. These guidelines will set the barriers, boundaries, and expectations of just about every conversation and meeting you will encounter. Everyone will want it all, but your toughest job will be the developing, presenting, and explaining the data in a way that leads to compromise and agreement.

# Virtualization

Virtualization enables the high utilization and high efficiencies associated with cloud computing. This technology approach is used through the computing stack. This section provides the background needed for the architect to understand how to use compute, network, data, and application virtualization.

# Compute virtualization

A hypervisor enables the sharing of common underlying physical hardware between different applications. The hypervisor will also reduce an application's dependency on a specific physical server by abstracting the hardware into virtualized instantiations. This allows various operating systems and middleware to be installed on the same physical server while maintaining isolation regarding the use of resources such as **central processing units** (CPUs), memory, disk storage, and networking.

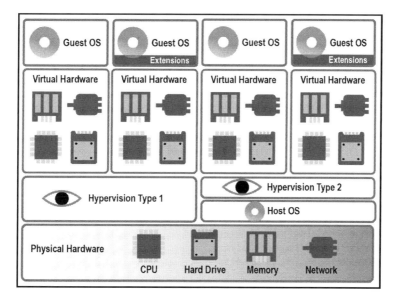

Also known as a **virtual machine monitor (VMM)**, the hypervisor may be software, firmware, or hardware. The hypervisor manages requests from virtual machines.

Hypervisors come in two types:

- The type 1 hypervisor runs directly on a bare-metal physical server. Sometimes referred to as a bare-metal, embedded, or native hypervisor, type 1 has direct access to the hardware. This type does not use a preloaded operating system. Completely independent from the operating system, the hypervisor is small and can monitor operating systems that run above it. Any problems manifesting in one virtual machine or guest operating system do not affect the other running operating systems.
- Examples include VMware vSphere/ESXi product, XenServer, **Red Hat Enterprise Virtualization (RHEV)**, open-source **KVM (Kernel-based Virtual Machine)**, and Microsoft Hyper-V.
- Type 2 hypervisors load inside an operating system like any other application. The OS manages them, and its virtual machines will be slower than on the type 1 variety. These are also known as hosted hypervisors and are entirely dependent on its host operating system for all operations. A type 2 installed on an operating system can also support other operating systems above it. Although the base operating system can allow better policy specification, any security vulnerabilities in the host operating system will affect the entire system, including the hypervisor running. Widely used type 2 hypervisors include VMware workstation, Microsoft Virtual PC, Oracle VirtualBox, and Parallels.

Type 1 hypervisors have dominated the server marketplace while type 2 hypervisors are mostly used on clients. Type 1 hypervisors running on client devices, however, are gaining market traction to support **virtual desktop infrastructure (VDI)** solutions).

# Network virtualization

There are three major approaches to the virtualization of network services:

- The first, referred to as **network virtualization** (**NV**), is a network tunnel. This version is used to create tunnels through an existing network to connect two separate domains. This is done as an alternative to physically connecting two network domains. Using tunnels is valuable because it avoids physical labor associated with physically installing new domain connection. This concept is even more critical when needed to connect virtual machines. NV also efficiently leverages capital investments in existing infrastructure thus avoiding additional capital outlays. When network virtualization is used with high-performance x86 platforms, movement of VMs can be done independently of any existing infrastructure connections, avoiding any physical network reconfiguration.

- The second network virtualization approach, **network functions virtualization** (**NFV**), uses best practices as initial policies and configurations for all network elements. One widespread use is adding firewalls and IDS/IPS systems. NFV enables the addition of functions on selected network tunnels, allowing the creation of virtual machine service profiles or flow. This approach avoids manual network provisioning and any associated training cost. It can also eliminate the need to practice network over provisioning of firewall or IDS/IPS services. By customizing these services for each instantiated network tunnel, initial CAPEX is reduced while simultaneously enhancing operational flexibility.

- The third option, **software defined networking** (**SDN**) is used to program network deployments through the use of a control plane and data plane. The control plane dictates what data packets should go to which destination. The data plane transports those packets and uses switches that are programmed using an SDN controller. One industry standard control protocol is OpenFlow.

NV and NFV both add virtual tunnels and functions to the physical network whereas SDN changes the physical network. That makes SDN an externally-driven method for provisioning and managing the network. Use cases include data flows to different ports (for example, from 1GE port to a 10GE port) or aggregating multiple small flows into a single port. SDN is implemented using network switches as opposed to using x86 servers for NV and NFV.

Network virtualization technologies address mobility and agility. NV and NFV are used on existing networks and reside on servers to interact with traffic directed to them. SDN is a new network construct that uses switches to implement separate data and control plane functions.

# Data virtualization

Data virtualization is used to retrieve and manipulate data without requiring the related technical data details like format or location (federated/heterogeneous data joins). Abstracted technical include API specifications and access language. This option can facilitate connections to heterogeneous data sources making all data accessible from a single location. Data federation can also be accomplished with data virtualization by using it to combine data result sets across multiple sources. When operational data and processed/cleansed data is needed to support of real-time data requirements, data virtualization software is used for data integration, business process integration, service-oriented architecture data services, and enterprise search is ideal.

In a cloud computing environment, data virtualization decouples data analytics and applications from physical data structures. This minimizes end-user impact if data infrastructure is changed. Another cloud use is linking between NoSQL sources and relational data sources.

Cloud solution architects should always architect with an enterprise view. With evolving organizational data virtualization requirements, these solutions can become less agile and deliver lower performance as more layers and objects are added. Duplicate business logic and dependencies may also affect performance. In mitigating these challenges, the cloud solution architect should design a layered view approach that isolates business logic. Always use consistent naming standards and common rules for reusability and layer isolation and push down processing requirements to the source as much as possible.

With data virtualization serving a gateway into corporate data assets, it should be governed as such. Data virtualization concepts and capabilities must also be implemented consistently across the enterprise. Data security will strongly impact data virtualization security management so data security managers should determine applicable regulatory guidance (such as HIPAA, SOX, and so on). In many situations, data virtualization should be used to limit access for specific users or user groups.

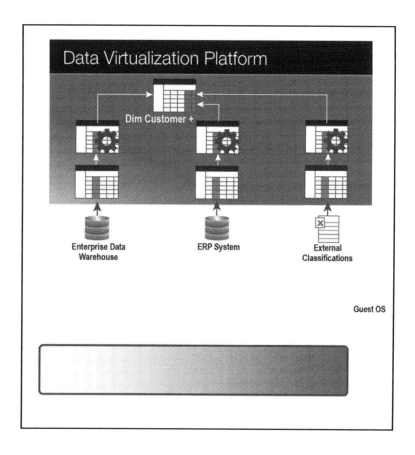

Many data virtualization tools can be used to display and export data lineage information. This forms an important component of business process metadata. This tool can can be used to analyze and resolve data quality issues. Data virtualization is a powerful technology, but enterprise governance that balances data management structure, data virtualization uptake, and innovation must be in place.

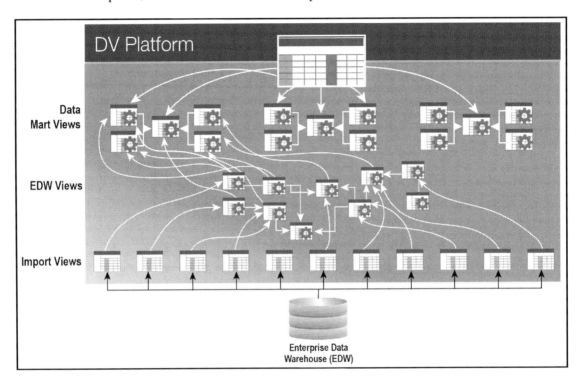

# Application virtualization

Application virtualization segregates computer programs from the underlying operating system. They do not install like a normal application, but execute as if they were. Contrary to how normal computing applications, when using application virtualization, each application sets its configurations at runtime. This leaves the host operating system and existing environments unaltered. The application will behave like it is interfacing directly with the operating system. Application virtualization is another technology that allows for the dynamic distribution of computing resources. Application virtualization allows applications to run in non-native environments.

# Summary

Successful cloud computing solutions align with the cloud environment key tenets outlined in this chapter. They also use compute, network, and application virtualization to delivery scalability and elasticity to the business or mission model. In the end, this is why cloud computing has revolutionized every industry vertical. The cloud solution architect must be intimately familiar with the purpose and tenor of every one of the environment tenets outlined in this chapter, because their job will depend on how they deliver value.

# 10
# Cloud Clients and Key Cloud Services

One of the five essential cloud computing characteristics is ubiquitous access. Network connectivity and the user's device client are necessary to enable this capability. Client selection typically depends on a decision between using a native application or a web app.

In this chapter, we will cover the following topics:

- Cloud computing clients
- IaaS
- Communications services
- Auditing

## Cloud computing clients

Native applications are built and designed for specific mobile devices. They install directly on the hardware after being downloaded from app stores or marketplaces. These applications are designed to be compatible with native features of the target device hardware and can work as standalone entities. An important drawback, however, is that users need to continually update the app.

Web apps are accessible via the mobile device web browser and are not downloaded onto the user's device. They can only access a limited number of the device's native features and update themselves without user intervention. This development option uses languages such as JavaScript, HTML 5, or CSS3 but no standardization or SDK is available. Web apps may also lead to higher maintenance cost across multiple mobile platforms.

From a user point of view, both options look and operate in similar manners. The choice is normally between deploying a user-centric app or an application-centric app. Sometimes, both native and web apps are developed to expand user reach and provide a better overall user experience. Client developers must also choose between using a thin or thick client. The following table shows the difference between a thin and a thick client:

| Thin Client vs. Thick Client | | |
|---|---|---|
| | **Thin Client** | **Thick Client** |
| Definition | The software relies on a remote server for its features typically through a web browser. | Software that primarily runs directly on a specified device. |
| Offline | Functions mostly don't work | Functions mostly work |
| Local Resources | Mostly consumes remote resources | Mostly consumes local resources |
| Network Latency | Functions typically depend on a fast network connection | Functions typically work without a network connection |
| Data | Data typically stored on remote servers | Data typically stored locally |

A terminal emulator emulates a video terminal within another display architecture. Usually synonymous with a shell or text terminal, the term refers to all remote terminals. A terminal emulator that resides inside a **graphical user interface** (GUI) is called a terminal window. It allows user access to text terminal applications like **command-line interfaces** (CLI) and **text-user interface** (TUI).

Rapidly growing in popularity as a cloud computing concept is the **Internet of Things** (**IoT**). A customer does not buy an IoT, but customers purchase solutions that use IoT components. An IoT solution will typically tap into an ecosystem of partners that span a value chain from sensors to the application.

The genesis of an IoT solution is making things smart by combining sensors, connectivity, and software. Machine-to-machine (M2M) solutions focus on connectivity, where the goal is to deliver intelligence by connecting items. Reporting data from these devices provided historical business intelligence versus real-time insight. IoT solutions focus on smart versus connected and near real-time analysis. The goal here is insight and action rather than reporting.

When designing IoT solutions, the architect should identify a precise problem that has a quantifiable response. Early IoT solutions used instrumented devices that sent data back to the cloud for processing. This approached proved impractical because physical-world solutions required a certain amount of processing at the edge for various reasons. Data needed to be processed and acted upon immediately using new concepts, such as fog computing. It could also be difficult to send large volumes of data over the network.

IoT solutions also need to be able to do correlation and analytics at the edge. Therefore, architects need to develop strategies that define when and where to process data. They must also select equipment with this type of edge processing in mind. The most valuable systems will offer machine learning that identifies patterns quickly and delivers timely and relevant information to its users.

Make sure the solution also preserves sensor battery life. Hardwiring an electrical line to each sensor is cost-prohibitive, but battery-powered sensing is useless if you need to expend labor to replace batteries too often. End sensing devices must, therefore, have software that optimizes battery life when processing and delivering data. IoT security can also be more challenging. Encryption is widely used and identity and authentication should provide additional protections. The network, hardware, and people accessing the data should all be trusted entities. IoT solutions must also be field-upgradable.

# IaaS

Infrastructure-as-a-Service delivers compute, storage, communications (which includes network services), metering/monitoring, and auditing services.

# Compute services

Compute combines CPUs, memory, and disks virtual equipment to create virtual machines. This is done by virtualizing physical servers and storage devices shared by multiple users.

A virtual machine is a computer software file, called an image, that acts like a real computer. It runs in a segregated environment, just like any other software program, and gives the end user the same experience as they would have on a traditional host operating system. The software inside a virtual machine is sandboxed and cannot escape or tamper with the physical computer. Multiple virtual machines can operate simultaneously on the same physical computer. This is called a multi-tenant environment, Multiple operating systems run side-by-side on the hypervisor, which manages them. Each virtual machine independently provides its virtual hardware. The virtual hardware is mapped to the actual hardware on the physical machine. This mapping saves costs by reducing physical hardware quantities, associated maintenance costs, power consumption, and cooling demands. Virtual servers scale quickly but may have reduced performance when compared to bare-metal servers.

A bare-metal server is a single tenant physical server that is dedicated to one customer. This prevents server performance from being impacted by other workloads. This service is typically used for latency-sensitive workloads that require a significant amount of raw processing power. Bare-metal clouds provision bare-metal servers with on-demand access, high scalability, and pay-as-you-go features. Bare-metal cloud economics can be compelling if the solution architect is faced with high load factors. They can be cheaper on a per-workload basis in environments where the virtual machines are large and continually heavily loaded.

Cloud service providers typically provide a choice of operating systems to their customers. Usually, this involves different versions of Linux (RHEL, Ubuntu, CENTOS, Freebird) or Microsoft Windows, Solaris, or IoS. The architect should poll organizational users and requirements to select the most appropriate OS. CSPs will package their compute offering with variations on the number of computing cores, amount of RAM, IOPs, and available ephemeral storage. Autoscaling is used to automatically change the number of computational resources deployed to a server farm. This is usually measured in the number of active servers. This number rises or falls automatically based on the farm workload.

# Storage services

IaaS storage services are either ephemeral or persistent. Ephemeral storage persists only when a specific virtual machine is live. If that machine is de-provisioned, any data in its ephemeral data store is lost. The **random access memory (RAM)** and cache are typically non-persistent storage technologies.

Transfer all ephemeral data to a persistent data store to prevent data loss. Persistent storage, as its name implies, persists after a virtual machine is de-provisioned and is sometimes referred to as non-volatile storage. This storage type is typically backed by mechanical hard disk drives or solid state drives in either a **storage area networks (SANs)** or **network attached storage (NAS)** schema. This can be in the form of file, block, or object storage.

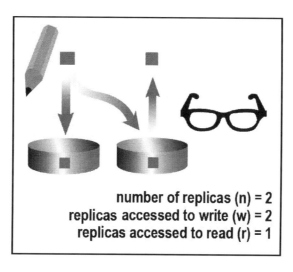

Failure tolerance in a storage offering duplicates data across multiple copies. These copies store the same set of data. If one of these copied versions is lost, data is still recoverable from the other copies. Storage consistency is a fundamental concept in cloud computing and describes the time it takes for all data copies to be the same. Strict consistency ensures that all copies of the data have been duplicated among all relevant copies to increase availability. A subset of the data copies is accessed by read and write operations. The ratio of replicas versus the number of replicas accessed during read and write operations can guarantee consistency across all copies. In eventual consistency, the consistency of data is relaxed.

This reduces the number of replicas that have to be accessed during read and write operations and reduces the overhead required to maintain strict consistency. With eventual consistency, data changes are eventually transferred to all data copies through the asynchronous propagation via the network.

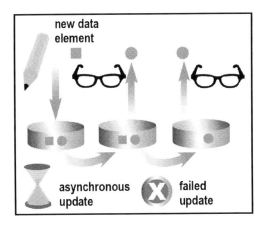

## Volume/block storage

Virtual and physical servers can be managed more efficiently if they don't store state information locally. This makes provisioning, de-provisioning, and failure handling much more manageable. Volume/block device storage is centralized storage that is accessed by servers as if it was a local hard drive.

## Object/blob storage

Distributed cloud applications are widely used to handle large data elements. Also referred to as **binary large objects (blobs)**, some examples include virtual server images, pictures, or videos.

These types of data elements are organized in a folder hierarchy where each data element has a unique identifier that includes its location and a file name. This globally unique identifier is passed to the storage offerings to retrieve data over the network.

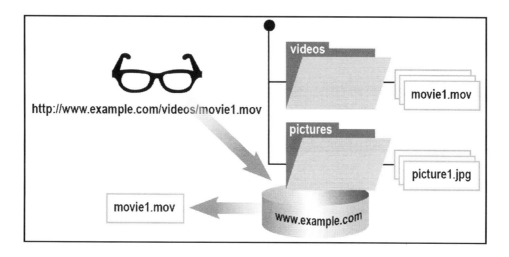

# Key-value storage

For higher availability and performance, storage offerings distributed data across different IT resources and locations. This can change storage requirements and increase the demand for a more flexible data structure. In these situations, data structure validation during queries may require high-performance connectivity between the distributed resources. Performance issues are avoided by storing identifiers (keys) and associated data (values) pairs and not enforcing data structure. Data query complexities are reduced significantly while simultaneously enhancing scalability and configurability. Semi-structured and unstructured data can also be scaled out among many IT resources without needing to access them in order to evaluate expressive queries.

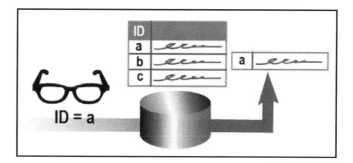

## Archival storage

Archival storage is very long-term data storage that uses SAN, optical, or magnetic tape technologies. This service is used to meet regulatory or legal retention requirements and is used to store data that does not require quick access.

# Communications services

Communication services encompass all of the functions normally associated with the network. These services are metered, based on the amount of data throughput or the number of input/output operations.

# Virtual networks

Virtual networks support application components deployed on elastic infrastructures and platforms. These virtual communications resources rely on physical network hardware to communicate. Customers are, however, isolated from each other on this networking layer.

Physical resources, such as **networking interface cards** (**NICs**), switches, and routers, are abstracted into virtualized equivalents that can be managed by service provider customers. Using the self-service interface and CSP applications, customers can design, implement, and configure virtual circuits, firewalls, load balancers, **network address translations** (**NAT**), and network cross-connects.

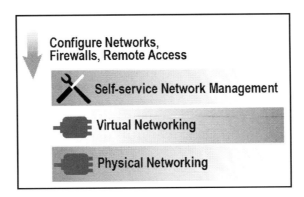

# Message oriented middleware

With distributed applications, application components hosted on different cloud resources need to exchange information. Often, this also requires integration with other cloud and non-cloud applications. Using message-oriented middleware, communication partners can exchange information asynchronously using messages. This service handles addressing, the availability of communication partners, and message format transformation.

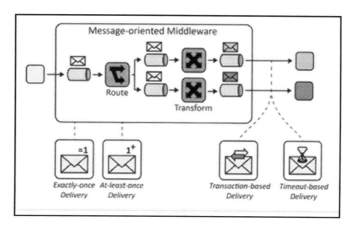

# Exactly-once delivery

This service is used for systems in which duplicate messages are unacceptable. For these cases, the messaging system ensures delivery of each message only once by automatically filtering all possible duplicates. When created, each message is tagged with a unique identifier. This identifier filters out message duplicates during transmission from sender to receiver.

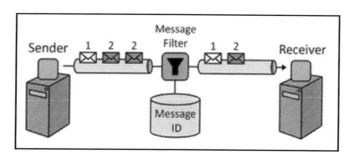

# At-least-once delivery

In some solutions, message-oriented middleware handles message duplicity. The system still, however, needs assurances that the message is received. With at-once-delivery, a service acknowledgment is sent back to the message sender for each message retrieved by a receiver. If this response is not received within a specific time frame, the message is resent.

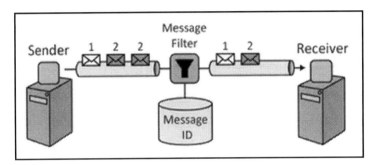

# Transaction-based delivery

Although message-oriented middleware can manage message traversal, an assurance that transmissions are received may also be required. With a transaction-based delivery service, both the message-oriented middleware and the receiving client participate in the transaction. All message communications operations are, therefore, performed under a single transactional context guaranteeing **ACID** (short for **Atomic, Consistent, Isolated, Durable**) behavior.

# Timeout-based delivery

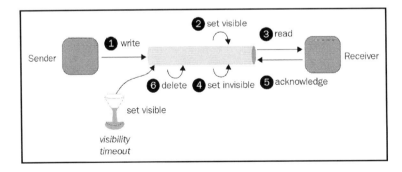

Timeout-based delivery service assures that a client receives a message before being deleted from a message queue. This is done by not deleting the message immediately after a client has read it, but only marking is as being invisible. After the client has read a message, it sends an acknowledgment to the message queue and the message is deleted.

# Metering/monitoring

The dynamic nature of the cloud and its pay-by-use economic model makes monitoring a crucial architectural component. Monitoring also forms the basis for metering which measures how use resources are used to support the charges levied. Metering also enables the automation of variable service quantities to support large variances in customer requirements.

Metrics used in metering services include the following:

- Per-unit of time for services
- Per-unit of data
- Per-transaction
- Per-user
- One-time charges

Services are monitored and metered across the operating system, network, and application categories. The operating system is fundamental to all monitoring and some of the fundamental tools are as follows:

- **Syslog**: Access to log entries that contain a description of the application that generated the message, severity level, time stamp, and the message
- **Vmstat**: Virtual memory statistics
- **Mpstat**: Processor-related statistics, activities of each available processor, and global averages
- **Top**: Linux tasks and a system summary

Well known open source tools include:

- **Nagios**: Availability, CPU load, memory, disk use, users logged in, and processes
- **Munin**: Performance monitoring tool that provides detailed graphs of system performance over a web interface

The primary network metering tool is Netstat, which provides data on network configurations, connection activity, and usage statistics.

Application monitoring needs to identify when a problem occurs, while analysis will locate related application structure issues. This is primarily an operations team responsibility while performance analysis is a development team responsibility. Performance analysis includes profiling, which requires insight into the application structure. Analysis tools should be able to capture output over time for use as input to monitoring applications.

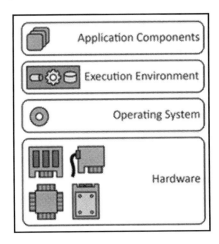

Monitoring results need to be actionable, but limited control over the production system might not afford the capability to reproduce problems or to do in-depth analysis. Tools that enable profiling can, however, significantly reduce application performance.

# Auditing

Information technology audits fall into either the internal or external categories. Internal audits address work done by the organization employees. These look at organizational processes and primarily focus on process optimization and risk management. External audits look at an organization's ability to meet legal and regulatory requirements from an outside perspective. Audits can also evaluate data availability, integrity, and confidentiality issues. A cloud solution requires a three-way negotiation among service organizations, **cloud service providers** (CSPs), and end users. The goal is to ensure productivity while maintaining an acceptable degree of security.

Cloud security audits look at whether security-relevant data is transparent to CSP customers, data encryption policies, and protections that address the co-located customer environment. The scale, scope, and complexity of cloud computing audits are also significantly different than a traditional enterprise equivalent. A significant challenge, however, lies in an auditor's cloud computing knowledge. Cloud security auditors must know cloud computing terminology and have a working knowledge of a cloud system's service design and delivery method.

Cloud security audits must make sure that all security-relevant data is available to CSP customers. Transparency enables rapid identification of potential security risks and threats. It also helps in the creation and development of appropriate enterprise countermeasures and recommendations. Access to accurate information reduces the risk of cyber security threats.

Data should be encrypted at rest, in motion, and, if possible, when in use. Encryption may not always be the most efficient solution and encryption key management options aren't always acceptable. Encryption and decryption performance shortcomings may make encryption at rest non-viable. Data in motion is usually encrypted using transport layer technologies like secure socket layer. Homomorphic encryption or encryption in use can allow encrypted queries to search encrypted texts without search engine decryption. It has the potential to solve the security issue of encrypted data at rest in both traditional IT and cloud infrastructures, but performance is still lacking.

While co-location enables the economic advantages of the multi-tenant environment, it also introduces some significant security concerns. An audit must ensure that the CSP hypervisors can reliably insulate **virtual machines** (**VMs**) from the physical computing hardware. A CSP must balance the multiple ways to build and manage cloud infrastructure hypervisors each with business needs and relevant security issues. In spite of the need to establish standardize cloud computing structures and multi-tenant security, no official standard exists.

With cloud computing, a single physical machine will typically host many virtual machines. Hosting multiple VMs can drastically increase the number of hosts that need to be audited. This increase can make the scale, scope, and complexity of cloud audits overwhelming. Standardization can dramatically assist in making the auditing process smoother and faster despite the larger scale of cloud computing. Another critical factor to consider is an adjustment of the audit scope.

While increased numbers of IT elements requiring audit drive scale issues, new technology types cause scope increases. An example is the examination of hypervisor security in the multi-tenant environment. Also, many cloud environments include intangible and logical elements that also require an audit. Auditors must be aware of these differences and take this complexity into account.

| Table 2. Standards applicable to cloud security auditing. | | | |
|---|---|---|---|
| **Standard** | **Type** | **Strength** | **Sponsoring organization** |
| Service Organization Control (SOC) 2 | Audit for outsourced services | Technology neutral | American Institute of CPAs |
| ISO 27001 and 27002 | Traditional security audit | Technology neutral | ISO |
| NIST 800-53 rev. 4 | Federal government audit | Technology neutral | National Institute of Standards and Technology |
| Cloud Security Alliance (CSA) | Cloud-specific audit | Dedicated to cloud security auditing | CSA |
| Payment Card Industry (PCI) Data Security Standard (DSS) | PCI Qualified Security Assessor cloud supplement | Cloud specific and provides guidance | PCI DSS |

Cloud service performance can vary based on the specific CSP. Within the same CSP, performance can also be dependent on service configuration, time (time of day, the day of the week, week of the month, and so on) and geographic location. Performance variance of over 1000% in compute services alone has been observed. Since pricing is typically a fixed rate tied to a specific metric, this will often lead to widely-differing price/performance values

Compute metrics recommended for auditing are CPU and input/output (I/O) performance. Network metrics such as latency and bandwidth allocation should also be measured from multiple CSP locations

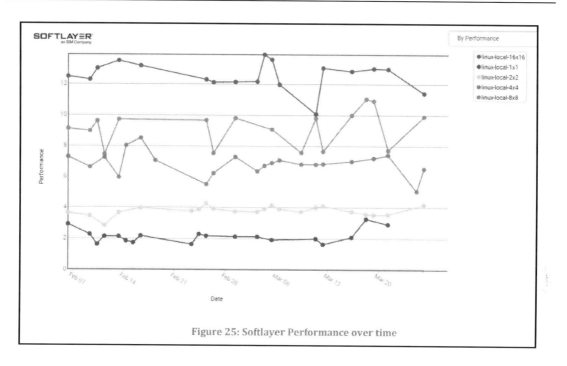

Figure 25: Softlayer Performance over time

# Service level agreement

The **service level agreement** (**SLA**) serves as both the blueprint and warranty for cloud computing services. Its purpose is to document specific parameters minimum service levels and remedies for any failure to meet the specified requirements. It should also affirm data ownership and specify data return and destruction details. Other important SLA points to consider include the following:

- Cloud system infrastructure details and security standards
- Customer right to audit legal and regulatory compliance by the CSP
- Rights and cost associated with continuing and discontinuing service use
- Other important criteria
- Service availability
- Service performance
- Data security and privacy

- Disaster recovery processes
- Data location
- Data access
- Data portability
- Problems identification and resolution expectations
- Change management processes
- Dispute mediation processes
- Exit strategy

Customers should read the cloud provider's SLA very carefully and validate them against common outage scenarios. Organizations should also have contingency plans in place to support worse case scenarios.

# PaaS

**Platform-as-a-Service (PaaS)** is an execution runtime environments offered in a multi-tenant environment. The underlying assumption is that applications often use similar functions and that these components can be shared with other applications. Sharing this common functionality should also result in higher environment utilization rates.

Common application functionality is offered in an execution environment that delivers platform libraries for custom application implementations using middleware solutions. The most common of these are databases and **integrated development environments (IDEs)**.

# Database

Database PaaS services typically align as either a SQL/relational form or NoSQL/non-relational type.

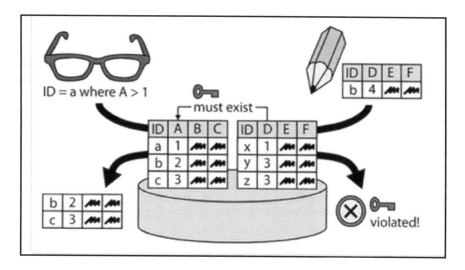

SQL/relational databases handled data comprising large numbers of similar data elements. These elements have identifiable dependencies among each other. When this structured data is queried, users make certain assumptions about the data structure and the relationship consistency between the retrieved data elements.

Data elements are recorded in tables, where each column represents a data element attribute. Table columns may also embed dependencies for how entries in one table column relate to a corresponding column in a different table. These dependencies are strictly enforced during any data manipulation.

In No-SQL/non-relational databases (Mongo, Map Reduce, and so on), an enforced database structure does not exist. This is useful when processing large data sets and the process is split up and mapped to multiple application components. This is often the case with cloud applications, usually handle enormous amounts of data, which need to be processed efficiently. As distributed applications are scaled out, data processing is similarly distributed among multiple components.

The data processing components simultaneously execute the query to be performed on the assigned data chunks. Afterwards, the processing results are consolidated or reduced into one result data set. During this reduction, additional functions (sums, average values, and so on) can also be applied.

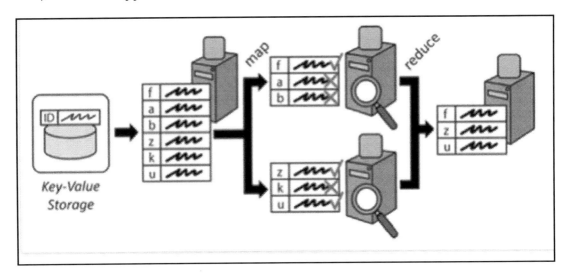

# Integrated Development Environment

An IDE provides an application development environment for developers that is managed by a cloud service provider. This eliminates the complexities associated with maintaining and operating the application development infrastructure. Developers can access and administer PaaS services via a web browser or IDE plugin. Some common PaaS IDEs include:

- Elastic Beanstalk, native to **Amazon Web Services** (**AWS**). The code is uploaded and the PaaS automatically deploys the WAR file to one or more EC2.
- Heroku, which uses standard libraries with application servers (such as Tomcat and Jetty) but is extensible and natively supports Ruby, Node, Python, Java, Clojure, Go, Groovy, Scala, and PHP.
- Red Hat OpenShift, which supports Java, Ruby, Node, Python, PHP, and Perl.
- IBM Bluemix, which is based on CloudFoundry, is extensible, and natively supports Java, Node.js, PHP, and Python.

- **Google App Engine (GAE)** which runs applications in a sandboxed environment and requests are distributed across multiple servers. This is specifically used for the building and deployment of applications onto Google's infrastructure.

# SaaS

Software-as-a-Service provides a fully managed application. The consuming organization manages the user base, access to the service, and the governance of the data inputted by organizational users. The CSP has full responsibility for the architecture, security, and availability of the service. Some of the most popular SaaS service offering categories are as follows:

- **CRM software**: Customer information management, marketing automation, and sales pipeline tracking.
- **ERP software**: Improved process efficiency and organizational information sharing combined with improved management insight into workflow and productivity.
- **Accounting software**: Improved financial organization and tracking
- **Project management software**: Project/program scope, requirements, and progress management. The tracking of changes, communications, and deadlines in a way that meets stakeholder requirements.
- **Email marketing software**: Automate email marketing and relationship building, while optimizing message delivery.
- **Billing and invoicing software**: Billing and invoicing automation. Implementing customer self-service payment options. The reduction of data entry costs, and elimination of billing errors.
- **Collaboration software**: Improved organizational communications that empower employees to more easily follow complex interactions. More efficient communications and enhanced enterprise productivity.
- **Web hosting and e-commerce**: Web hosting, content management systems, message boards, shopping carts, and so on.
- **HR software**: Employee time tracking. Improved recruiting and hiring. Automate payroll and more efficient management of human resources.
- **Transaction processing**: Credit cards and bank transfer processing. Publish and track coupons, in support of loyalty rewards programs.

# Summary

Delivering the desired cloud service through the appropriate client device is the desired result of any cloud computing solution. This chapter reviewed the basics needed to achieve that goal. Clients must seamlessly align with the expected end user consumption requirements while the services, as always, must align with the business or mission model. The services reviewed in this chapter are the essential solution building blocks.

# 11
# Operational Requirements

Until recently, enterprises designed data centers with the mindset of supplying hosting, compute, storage, or other services with typical or standard organization types in mind. This mindset is a problem when considering modern-day data centers and cloud service offerings. As cloud-based application development continues to gain popularity and widespread adoption, it is important for us to recognize the benefits and efficiencies, along with the challenges and complexities. Cloud development typically includes integrated development environments, application lifecycle management components, along with application security testing. Unlike traditional deployments within a data center or even a hosted solution where network controls are ubiquitous and compensating perimeter controls are sometimes depended upon to offer application security, cloud applications often run in a comparatively unprotected fashion.

In this chapter, we will cover the following topics:

- Application programming interface
- Common infrastructure file formats – VMs
- Data and application federation
- Deployment
- Federated identity
- Identity management
- Portability and interoperability
- Lifecycle management
- Location awareness
- Metering and monitoring
- Open client
- Availability
- Privacy
- Resiliency
- Auditability

- Performance
- Management and governance
- Transaction and concurrency across clouds
- SLAs and benchmarks
- Provider exit
- Security
- Security controls
- Distributed computing reference model

# Application programming interface

Organizations and practitioners alike need to understand and appreciate that cloud-based development and applications can vary from traditional or on-premise development. When considering an application for cloud deployment, one must remember that applications can be broken down into the following sub-components:

- Data
- Functions
- Processes

These components can be further broken up, so that portions that have sensitive data run in a traditional data center and less sensitive data runs in a cloud computing environment. It is also important for developers to understand that, in many cloud environments, access is acquired through the means of an **application programming interface (API)**. These APIs will consume tokens rather than traditional usernames and passwords. APIs can be broken down into two formats:

- **Representational state transfer (REST)**
- **Simple object access protocol (SOAP)**

REST defines a set of constraints and properties based on HTTP. These are referred to as RESTful web services and conform to the REST architectural style. By doing this they provide interoperability when computers communicate across the Internet. REST-compliant services allow the requesting systems to access and manipulate textual representations of web resources by using a standard set of stateless operations. SOAP, also referred to as simple object access protocol, is a more structured messaging protocol specification used predominately for exchanging structured information through web services across computer networks. The purpose of SOAP is to deliver extensibility, neutrality, and independence. It uses the XML information set for its message format and relies on application layer protocols, usually **Hypertext Transfer Protocol (HTTP)** or **Simple Mail Transfer Protocol (SMTP)**, for message negotiation and transmission.

The **application programming interfaces (APIs)** are a means for a company to expose functionality to applications. Some benefits of APIs include the following:

- Programmatic control and access
- Automation
- Integration with third-party tools

Consumption of APIs can lead to the use of insecure products by a company. Organizations must also consider the security of software (and APIs) outside of their corporate boundaries. Consumption of external APIs should go through the same approval process used for all other software being consumed by the organization. When leveraging APIs, ensure that API access is secured. This requires the use of SSL (REST) or message-level crypto (SOAP), access authentication, and logging of API usage.

# API levels and categories

There are four levels of APIs that developers must work with. For more information refer to: `http://www.jasongaudreau.com/2012/08/cloud-computing-use-case-part-3.html???history=0amp;pfid=1amp;sample=25amp;ref=1.`

# Common APIs for cloud storage

Data is central to operations so establishing standard APIs for accessing cloud storage services, databases, and other middleware services is a must. The use of custom code within a solution locks the enterprise into a proprietary design, eliminating portability, and eliminating the financial benefits and flexibility afforded by cloud computing.

# Common cloud middleware API

APIs needed to support creating and dropping databases and tables, connecting to message queues and other middleware operations should be consistent across the enterprise. Embedded restrictions in a database vendor product can significantly increase processing resource requirements when dealing with large datasets. Examples include restrictions on joins across tables and an inability to support a valid database schema. Such restrictions create significant challenges when contemplating a move to a different database. Limitations are especially applicable for applications built on a relational model. Middleware services such as message queues are more straightforward and will typically not present such a significant challenge.

## Additional concerns

A cloud solution architect must focus on meeting an organization's operational requirements. Lessons learned from previous cloud deployments have highlighted the criticality of addressing each of the requirements listed in this section adequately.

# Common infrastructure file formats – VMs

Virtual machine portability is a significant concern in a cloud computing environment. Concerns are especially valid in a hybrid IT deployment. Any enterprise solution should address possible differences in both the VM file format and the process for attaching storage to VMs.

# Data and application federation

When combining data from multiple cloud-based sources, enterprise applications need to coordinate the applications activities that may span multiple platforms; cloud managed service provider and traditional data centers. Hybrid environments require implementing data federation and virtualization techniques across the various environments.

# Deployment

Cloud application deployment involves both programming interfaces and cloud-specific packaging technologies. This operational requirement may include traditional packaging mechanisms like EAR/WAR files and .Net assemblies.

Building and deploying a VM image should be simple and portable between different hybrid infrastructure environments. Any required compensations should be well known and mechanisms for attaching storage to VMs well understood.

# Federated identity

When operating in a hybrid environment, the idea is to have the user maintain responsibility for a single ID with the infrastructure federating all other required identities. This federation would include the primary identity needed by an end user and all associated enterprise roles that the user is likely to hold within the enterprise.

# Identity management

Most cloud computing solutions can leverage industry-specific identity management standards and protocols, such as SAML and OAuth. These may also need to interact with traditional standards such as RosettaNet or OASIS. Although the specific standard may vary between applications, the solution must be able to handle all access and data authorization scenarios efficiently.

# Portability and interoperability

The cloud computing era brings with it the need to design, build, and manage a business-focused ecosystem. Efficient communication and interaction across such an ecosystem require interoperability between the enterprise and its ecosystem partners. Since a universal set of standards does not exist and most likely won't exist shortly, these ecosystems can encounter a significant risk of vendor lock-in. An ecosystem's ability to use reusable components to build systems that work together out of the box depends on the enforcement of portability and interoperability governance. A particular concern for in-cloud computing this is critical during the deployment or migration of systems to a cloud service provider. A typical scenario is an inability to migrate some components to the cloud due to data management or data sovereignty regulations. Cloud migration requires portability of all migrating components as well as interoperability of those components with systems that remain on-premise.

Specific technology categories where portability and interoperability standards should be specified include the following:

- **Data**: Enabling the reuse of data components across different applications. Since data interoperability interfaces do not currently exist, this may require the use of data virtualization techniques.
- **Applications**: This focuses on interoperability between application components. These have SaaS deployed components, application modules leveraged in a PaaS, or infrastructure components consumed as IaaS. Similar issues arise in a hybrid environment when interfacing with a traditional enterprise IT environment or with client endpoint devices. Application portability enables the re-use of all application components across the entire hybrid IT environment.
- **Platforms**: This category addresses the re-use of service bundles that may contain infrastructure, middleware, or application components along with any associated data.

- **Infrastructure**: Interoperability and portability associated with various hardware virtualization technologies and architectures.
- **Management**: Management interoperability is interoperability between cloud services (SaaS, PaaS, or IaaS) and programs concerned with the implementation of on-demand self-service. Management may also include application programs concerned with the deployment, configuration, provisioning, and operation of cloud resources.
- **Publication and acquisition**: The self-service aspect of cloud computing gives end users the ability to acquire software, data, infrastructure and various other cloud services. Developers can also publish applications, data, and cloud services via online marketplaces. This category addresses interoperability between platforms and cloud service marketplaces, including app stores.

# Lifecycle management

Lifecycle management of applications and documentation is a continuous challenge to all organizations. Tasks that fall within this requirement include versioning, data retention, and destruction and information discovery. Legal liabilities can be substantial if due diligence is not effective in identifying regulatory and legal restriction in this area.

# Location awareness

National data sovereignty laws are expanding globally. These new requirements not only apply to how an organization handles data but it also equally apply to data managed on the organization's behalf. The associated requirement may include legal restrictions on the location of the physical server when organizational data is present. Meeting location-dependent legal requirements may require the use of APIs that determine the location of the physical hardware associated with the delivery of all cloud services.

# Metering and monitoring

The pay-as-you-go cloud computing model requires consistent and ubiquitous metering and monitoring of all cloud services. This capability is essential to an effective cost control, internal charge-backs, and service provisioning process.

# Open client

Ubiquitous access to cloud services levies a requirement for the use of open clients and endpoint devices. The use of vendor-specific endpoints violates this essential requirement as cloud services should not require the use of vendor-specific platforms or technologies.

# Availability

Cloud service availability describes the degree to which a specific service is in a specified operable and committable state if a provisioning a request at a random time. Availability is usually expressed as a percentage and stated in the CSP service level agreement. The CSP sets availability, but additional payments can enhance this value. The solution architect should be aware of all service availability rates and advise mission/business owners on the service's ability to meet organizational goals.

# Privacy

Privacy addresses the condition of being free from observation or disturbance by others. Cloud computing has led to the establishment and strict enforcement of many new data privacy laws. One of the most evasive of these is the **General Data Protection Regulation (GDPR)**. Approved by the EU parliament on 14 April 2016, its enforcement date is 25 May 2018. A non-compliant organization can face hefty fines. GDPR invalidates the Data Protection Directive 95/46/EC and has a goal of harmonizing European data privacy laws, protecting and empowering all EU citizens' data privacy, and reshaping the how regional organizations approach data privacy. It applies to all personal data processing of EU residents, regardless of the company's location. It also covers data processed outside of the territorial limits of the EU and to the processing of personal data for EU citizens by non-EU companies when selling goods or services to an EU citizens. Penalties can be up to 4% of annual global revenue or €20 million, whichever is greater.

# Resiliency

Resiliency refers to the ability of a cloud service to recover from service delivery difficulties or failure. The CSP sets resiliency levels, but additional payments can enhance the property. The solution architect should be aware of all service resiliency specifics and advise mission/business owners on the service's ability to meet organizational goals.

# Auditability

Auditability describes the extent to which a cloud service consumer can conduct a thorough and accurate assessment of the cloud service provider's ability to deliver and appropriately account for the cost of delivering a cloud service. This sort of data is typically driven by legal or regulatory requirements and is often foundational to an organization's ability to use a service at all. The solution architect should be aware of all audit requirements and advise mission/business owners on the service's ability to meet them.

# Performance

While the service level agreement outlines the minimum level of service expected from a provider, performance may still vary widely across any specified parameter set. Service components that lie entirely outside the provider or consumer's control may drive variability. Things like network bandwidth limitations or abnormally large service provisioning request can dramatically affect the cost or availability of a service. Performance variability and auditing should, therefore, be directly addressed by the cloud solution architect.

# Management and governance

The ease of use associated with to opening an account and using cloud services creates the risk of abuse in the provisioning and consumption of cloud-based services. Cloud industry leaders often highlight this risk as a significant security risk. Organizations must, therefore, establish strict management and governance procedures. Recommendations are to include tracking for initiation and use of cloud services like storage, databases, and message queue volumes. Establishment and enforcement of governance are critical to successfully following government regulations, as well as industry and geography-specific policies.

# Transaction and concurrency across clouds

When operating across a cloud ecosystem, the sharing of applications and data drives the requirement for ACID transactions and concurrency. Any changes made by any member of the ecosystem must be visible, auditable and reliable. Specific to this requirement is an expanding use of blockchain and related technologies across the cloud computing industry.

# SLAs and benchmarks

Companies that sign SLA-backed contracts should also establish a standard way of benchmarking CSP performance. SLA should not only specify minimum requirement and variability expectations, but it should also specify appropriate remedies to the consumer should the CSP fail to meet a service level or restore services to the appropriate level within a specified period. Service definitions and metrics should be unambiguous.

# Provider exit

The cloud solution architect should prioritize risk mitigation as part of any solution design. Setting this as a priority dictates a carefully designed provider exit strategy plan before consuming any cloud service. Risk mitigation requires the identification and verification of secondary, and in some cases, a tertiary, supplier for all cloud service deemed crucial to the enterprise.

# Security

Cloud computing security is always a significant concern but focuses primarily on user data privacy. When using cloud services, end users do not have control of storage location. Apart from SLA-specified limitations, they also lack specific knowledge of storage location.

# Security controls

A security control acts as a tool to restrict a list of possible actions down to those that are allowed or permitted. An industry group, called the The Cloud Security Alliance, has documented a complete list of data security controls in a reference called the Cloud Control Matrix. This matrix is an important tool and is designed to help the security professional identify and selected data security controls, based on the applicable industry regulations or security governance environment.

Controls are generally described as being within one of three categories:

- **Administrative**: regulations, policies, laws, guidelines, and practices governing the overall information security requirements and controls
- **Logical**: Virtual technical and application controls such as firewalls, encryption, anti-virus software, and maker/checker routines
- **Physical**: used to manage physical access like a key to a door. Other physical controls include gates and barricades, video surveillance systems, the use of guards, and remote backup facilities

These three elements are crucial to an effective control environment but do not give clear guidance on the degree to which a risk is mitigated.

Data management controls can be classified as directive or deterrent.

- Directive controls cause or encourage a desirable event to occur, such as employees meeting objectives effectively. Formally written procedure manuals would be a directive control in this case because they would encourage employees to carry out particular functions in an effective manner.
- Deterrent controls are designed to discourage potential attackers by sending the message that it is better not to attack, but even if you do, the target can defend itself. Examples of deterrent controls include notices of monitoring and logging as well as the visible practice of sound information security management.

Controls that could be considered as mitigating controls include the following:

- Preventive controls which prevent data loss or harm from occurring
- Detective controls that monitor activity in order to identify where practices or procedures are not properly followed
- Corrective controls which restore the process or system back to a prior pre-incident state

Controls that extend data protection include:

- Recovery controls, which restore lost computing resources or capabilities and help the organization to return to normal operations and recover monetary loss caused by a security violation or incident.
- Compensating controls, which reinforce or replace normal controls that are unavailable for any reason. These are typically back-up controls and usually involve higher levels of supervision and/or contingency plans.

Controls should also be identified as manual or automated.

| | | | | Control Types | | |
|---|---|---|---|---|---|---|
| | | | | Administrative | Technical | Physical |
| Control Groups | Management Controls | Control Categories | Directive | Policy | Warning Banner | "Do Not Enter" Signs |
| | | | Deterrent | Demotion | Violation Report | "Bewre of Dog" Signs |
| | Mitigating Controls | | Preventative | User Registration | Passwords, Tokens | Fences, Bollards |
| | | | Detective | Report Reviews | Audit Logs, Intrusion Detection Systems | Sensors, CCTV |
| | | | Corrective | Employee termination | Connection Management | Fire Exinguisher |
| | Extended Controls | | Recovery | Disaster Recovery Planning (DRP) | Backups | Reconstruct, Rebuild |
| | | | Compensating | Supervision, Job Rotation | Keystroke Logging | Layered Defenses |

Since security is a critical operational element, the solution architect should also take all of the following aspects into account when developing a comprehensive enterprise solution. It should also be noted that many of these components actually fall under corporate governance and, as such, fall outside of the technical solution design. A failure to address these elements, however, could prevent the deployment and success of any cloud computing solution. As stated before, cultural change is an essential part of any transition to cloud. Effective IT governance is foundational to cultural change.

The Cloud Security Alliance has categorized these controls into industry standard control groups. Control group descriptions are provided in the following documentation: `https://downloads.cloudsecurityalliance. org/initiatives/ccm/CSA_CCM_v3.0.xlsx`.

# Distributed computing reference model

The various cloud service models expose applications, platform and infrastructure components in many different and unique ways. The different interfaces between the various components create a foundation for the distributed computing reference model. The open group created the model as a means for identifying and managing the interoperability and portability of cloud computing solutions. In offering the DCRM as a vital cloud solution architect tool, this chapter describes its components and processes. The architect should also note that the execution of all interactions is through industry standards, user-developed or vendor-specific APIs, or web services.

You can find more information at: `http://www.opengroup.org/cloud/cloud_iop/p5.htm`.

# Summary

Cloud computing represents a new operational model for delivering information technology services. This brings with it a number of unique operational requirements. This chapter explains each of those within an operational context so that they can be appropriately included in every architected cloud solution. Security controls are equally crucial due to the importance associated with managing and controlling access to all data.

The DCRM is presented in here, in this chapter, as a communicative tool. While the other models presented in this text are specific to cloud computing, this one represents a more generalized approach more suitable when evaluating portability and interoperability when operating across different cloud computing and traditional designs.

# 12
# CSP Performance

**Cloud service providers** (**CSPs**) are not all the same. Service performance from the same service provider can vary from day to day. From a consumer point of view, critical performance characteristics vary based on the cloud service model. For end users, SaaS performance measures are perceived as business transaction response times and throughput, technical service reliability and availability, and application scalability. PaaS performance measures, on the other hand, are indirectly perceived by users and defined as throughput, transaction response times, technical service reliability, availability, and the scalability of the middleware. Infrastructure performance, capacity, reliability, availability, and scalability typically define IaaS performance.

In this chapter, we will cover the following topics:

- CSP performance metrics
- CSP benchmarks

## CSP performance metrics

In general, performance measures characteristics of the higher service layers depend on those of the underlying technology components. Since consumers typically have no visibility into technology specifics, they can be clueless concerning performance expectations.

The typical user operational metrics used to evaluate cloud service providers are the following:

- **Service response time (delay)**: The latency time between service request and service completion
- **Service throughput**: The number of jobs processed by the service provider within a set time unit
- **Service availability**: The probability that the service provider accepts a customer service request at any time
- **System utilization**: The percentage of system resources being used for service provisioning
- **System resilience**: The stability of system performance over time, especially under bursty loads
- **System scalability**: The ability of a system to perform well with size or volume changes
- **System elasticity**: The ability of a system to adapt to changes in its loads

The interplay between multiple CSP performance drivers determines these metrics. One of the most important is the user's geographic proximity to the provisioning CSP data center. The relative geographic location affects the following:

- **Service response time (delay)**: Affected by the physical distance between the data center and the number of consuming customers
- **Service throughput**: Dependent on the nature of the network topology and network technology between the data center and the consuming customer
- **Service availability**: Dependent on the service capacity and the number of consuming customers from that location

Non-geographic performance drivers, mostly driven by data center physical and logical design choices, include the following:

- **System utilization**: The usage rate as a percentage of a system's maximum IT service capabilities
- **System resilience**: System's capacity to recover quickly from a failure
- **System scalability**: Ability to increase or decrease resources applied to a specific customer's request

- **System elasticity**: System responsiveness to a customer's request to increase or decrease applied resources
- **Underlying technology variability**: Level of technology consistency across a provider's global system
- **Rate limiting**: Overt action by the service provider to limit the amount, quality, or responsiveness of a requested service
- **Latency**: Service delay incurred following an instruction for its consumption or execution

# CSP benchmarks

As the number and variety of cloud service providers continue to expand, consumers face a growing information disparity concerning the level of service they should expect. This challenge is especially perplexing when the consumer tackles the complexity of selecting cloud services and service configurations that best meet the price and performance requirements of applications selected for cloud deployment.

For a cloud solution architect, this challenge is managed by comparing prospective CSP service levels and capabilities against industry benchmarks for those services. Challenges to being able to establish useful cloud computing industry benchmarks include the following:

- The sheer number of cloud service providers and the variety of cloud services in the market
- The broad geographic expanse of CSP platforms that typically span many different locations
- Geopolitical requirements and restrictions
- Wide area networking performance
- Variety of CSP business, pricing, and service models
- Multiplicity of service price changes
- Variability of performance within the same service at different times and from different locations

Additionally, services can be consumed by the hour, month, annually, or through a spot market. New products are introduced on an almost daily basis, and pricing changes weekly. Amazon, for instance, is known to make price changes monthly. One of the best industry benchmark studies was a collaboration between Rice University and Burstorm Inc., the result of which was the industry's first comprehensive and continuous price-performance benchmark:

| Provider | # Instance Types | # Locations | # Products |
|----------|------------------|-------------|------------|
| AWS | 30 | 3 | 90 |
| Google | 14 | 3 | 42 |
| Rackspace | 9 | 3 | 27 |
| Azure | 18 | 3 | 54 |
| Linode | 9 | 3 | 27 |
| HP | 11 | 1 | 11 |
| Softlayer | 5 | 3 | 15 |
| | | | |
| Selected total | 96 | 19 | 266 |

Table 1: Testing Scope

| Provider | North America (NA) | Europe (EMEA) | Asia (APAC) |
|----------|--------------------|--------------|-------------|
| AWS | Ashburn US | Dublin IE | Singapore SG |
| Google | Council Bluffs US | Saint-Ghislain BE | Changhua County TW |
| Rackspace | Grapevine US | Slough GB | Hong Kong HK |
| Azure | California, CA | Omeath IE | Singapore SG |
| Linode | Fremont US | London GB | Singapore SG |
| HP | Tulsa US | N/A | N/A |
| Softlayer | San Jose US | Amsterdam NL | Singapore SG |

Table 2: Locations by provider

Using a highly automated process, the first benchmark was across seven suppliers (Amazon, Rackspace, Google, Microsoft, HP, IBM, and Linode), across three continents (North America, Asia, and Europe) , as shown in the preceding tables, with a total of 266 compute products spread over three locations per vendor. The benchmark was executed every day, for 15 days. The results were normalized to a 720-hour, monthly pricing model to establish the price-performance metrics. These results showed the following:

- The range of performance within a single provider can vary widely:

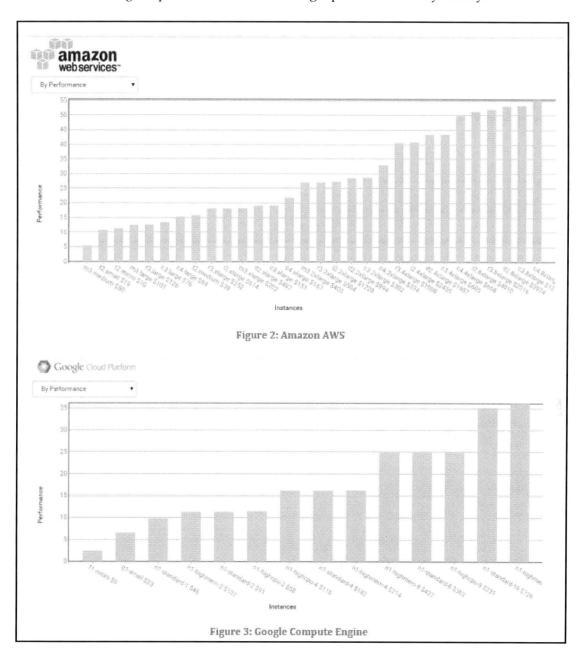

Figure 2: Amazon AWS

Figure 3: Google Compute Engine

- The diversity of platforms and solutions offered by different CSPs can result in a 1-core instance performance variance of as much as 622%:

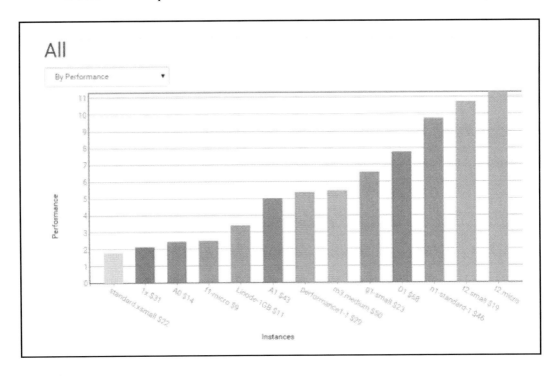

- There is a 4-core compute price performance variation of 1,000%:

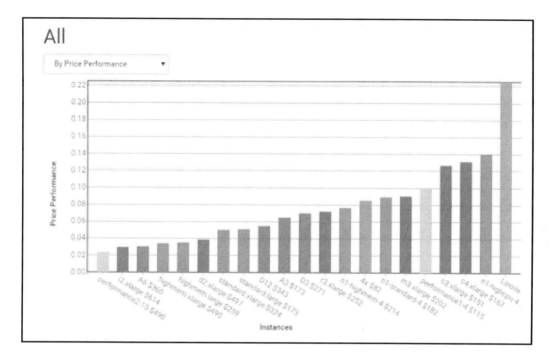

- There can be instance performance fluctuations of as much as 60% over time:

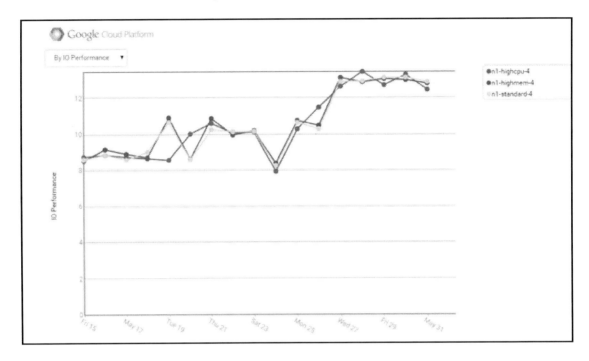

- There is a wide variance in the availability and performance of instance types when measured at different locations.

Rapid changes over time in instance types, pricing, performance, and availability of services by location demonstrates that benchmarking of a small set of instance types in a unique event is not sufficient for cloud computing. Even within the short span of this study, Google updated their infrastructure and pricing:

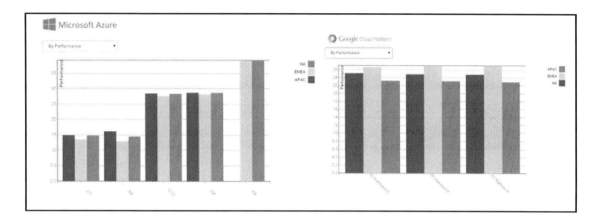

# Service level agreements

The Cloud Standards Customer Council has developed industry best practices for the design and enforcement of cloud service level agreements. You can find a convenient summary of these recommendations at `http://www.cloud-council.org/deliverables/practical-guide-to-cloud-service-agreements.htm`.

# Summary

Performance metrics are often overlooked when designing and deploying cloud computing solutions. This is especially troubling because service level agreements should be used to define and track these.

As the number and variety of cloud service providers continue to expand, consumers must be proactive in how they identify and select performance metrics, as these should form the basis for the service level agreement. Cloud solution architects must also be able to compare prospective CSP service level metrics and capabilities against industry benchmarks for those services.

# Cloud Application Development 13

The adoption of the cloud computing model invariably leads to changes in an organization's application development process. Changes are due to the cloud service consumer's inability to have any real control over the cloud application's underlying infrastructure. In the traditional software development life cycle, application developers can exert direction and sometimes complete control over the hardware used. When an application is destined for deployment to a CSP, neither control nor even visibility into the underlying infrastructure is possible. Critical aspects of security, including responsibility for executing and monitoring required security controls, is left to the service provider. Data security is the primary reason for adherence to the fundamental design principle for cloud application development.

We will cover the following topics in this chapter:

- Core application characteristics
- Cloud application components
- DevOps
- Microservices and serverless architectures
- Application migration planning

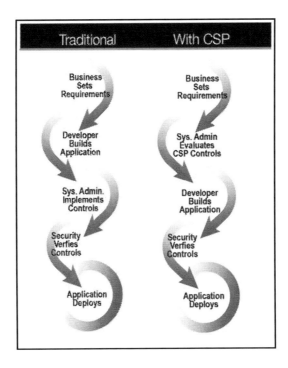

# Core application characteristics

All cloud computing applications should adhere to the following basic characteristics.

# Loose coupling

The loose coupling of application components operating in the cloud maximizes the ability for each component to be individually self-contained. This approach logically separates components and leads to more straightforward and less numerous interactions, which improves application resiliency and portability. Interactions should not be time-critical as communication latency between cloud-based components cannot be reliably predicted.

# Service orientation

Service orientation is a design approach that focuses on the linkage between services and service-based development and the outcomes of those services. It is referred to as **service-oriented architecture (SOA)**. A service does the following:

- Logically represents a repeatable business activity that has a specified outcome (for example, check customer credit, provide weather data, consolidate drilling reports)
- Is designed to be self-contained
- Is often composed of multiple different services
- Has its technical details abstracted from the service consumer

Cloud applications are organized as a service, or a set of services, and may use other services. Their most common characteristics include the following:

- **Stable interfaces**: Cloud application interfaces should not vary over time. Any variations should be backward-compatible. Component interface changes could require significant re-integration with other components, which could negatively affect lifetime cost.
- **Described interfaces**: Cloud application interfaces must be human- and machine-readable and describable. Human-readability is needed to support component acquisition and integration. Machine-readability is needed for dynamic service discovery and composition.
- **Use of marketplaces**: Application marketplaces afford easy and rapid access to cloud-based products and services. Using a marketplace, high product quality and consistent device compatibility are assured. They also provide user freedom of choice between competing products and reinforce application and data portability and interoperability.
- **REST: Representational State Transfer (REST)** uses uniform interfaces to provide cacheable, stateless, and layered client-server interactions. Using REST, every client-to-server request contains all the information needed to execute the request. It also enables robust, scalable, and loosely coupled services that contain stable interfaces.

- **Base transactions**: Cloud applications are usually designed to perform transactions with **BASE** properties: basic availability, soft-state, and eventually consistent. Traditional transactions follow ACID properties: atomicity, consistency, isolation, and durability. This means that transactions are reliable, but consistency is not possible without sacrificing availability. With BASE, replicated resources are allowed and at least one copy is available but other copies are temporarily in different states. Synchronization will, however, drive them eventually into consistency. Some applications require ACID transactionality. In others, components providing parts of the transaction can use BASE transactionality for interoperability with other components:

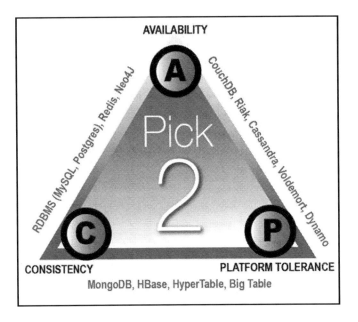

# Cloud application components

Cloud applications consist of the software and programming language combinations used to create a web or mobile application. Software application components, client-side and server-side, are also known as frontend and backend. Each application layer builds on the features of the one below it, creating an application development stack. The following figure shows the major building blocks of a typical stack:

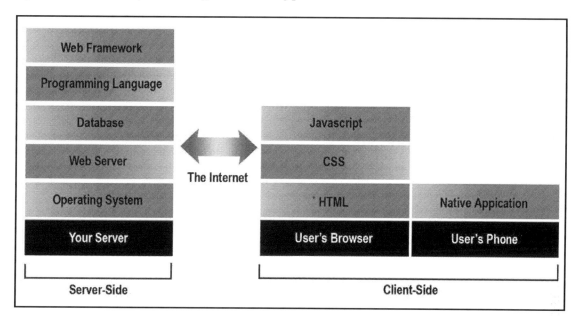

# Server side

On the server side, three development models, or stacks, are widely used in the cloud computing industry:

- LAMP stack (Linux/Apache/MySQL/PHP)
- WISA stack (Windows/IIS/SQL Server/ASP.NET)
- Java web application stack (Linux or Solaris/Tomcat/MySQL/JSP)

# LAMP

LAMP is considered an open source development stack. Usually, there is no direct cost associated with licensing, installation, setup, or deployment open source software, but the process does require expertise, and without it, could be very time-consuming. There are many LAMP variations in the market. When deployed, LAMP stack products work together straightforwardly. Linux has fast performance, but the PHP layer does present some limitations. Since PHP is an interpreted language, the server interprets each PHP script, every time it runs. While this provides benefit by not needing compilation and gaining some language perks, the downside is performance. **Alternative PHP Cache (APC)** or other accelerators can enhance performance.

# WISA stack

The WISA stack core is the .NET Framework. It is a widely deployed standard and the marketplace has an abundance of certified professionals. This can be very appealing for enterprises that enforce Microsoft standards. Benefits include clustering, failover, security, automated administration, and business intelligence features. The .NET framework is compiled **just-in-time (JIT)**, which enables code hiding and increased performance. Although compiling the .NET architecture only once provides significant performance benefits, it does bring with it a lack of portability. The **integrated development environment (IDE)** for WISA is Visual Studio.

# Java

The largest Java stack market shares are held by Red Hat and JBoss. Although stack components vary, the use of Java code is consistent. Performance and development differ drastically, however. Red Hat stack uses the Linux Tomcat server and is fully configurable using XML configuration files. Because servlets are compiled into JARs, they offer information hiding and a performance benefit that scripted technologies don't have. MySQL works well in a web application. MySQL scales well for particular (that is, read-only) web applications, but lacks DBMS functionality.

JBoss web server blends an **enterprise application resource (EAR)** server and a web server into a single product. It also uses the Tomcat server but the database is not specified. JBoss applications use the Hibernate persistence manager. Applications are written once and deployed anywhere. The J2EE standard provides many enterprise-level components such as transactions and pooling.

# Client side

Client-side scripting options are many and varied. Device capability and developer skill set dictate selection and use. Some of the more common options are the following:

- JavaScript client-side scripting language
- REXX, which is an IBM mainframes scripting language
- **Tool Command Language** (**TCL**), which processes strings and passes commands to interactive programs
- **Active Server Pages** (**ASP**) by Microsoft, which uses scripted pages on the web server and acts as an interpreted interface between the backend application and browser
- **Java Server Pages** (**JSP**) from by Sun Microsystems, which uses scripted pages that are compiled to run on the server as small programs called servlets
- PHP, an open source server scripting language embedded into HTML
- **Asynchronous JavaScript And XML** (**AJAX**), which is not a programming language but uses XM and HTTP to request data from a web server
- HTML5—the current version of the HTML standard used for structuring and presenting web content

# DevOps

DevOps combines cultural philosophies, practices, and tools to increase an organization's ability to deliver applications and services at high velocity. Accelerated velocity is accomplished by evolving and improving products at a faster pace than organizations using traditional software development and infrastructure management processes. DevOps uses a concept referred to as *Infrastructure as a Code* where scripting is used to instantiate cloud-based infrastructure through the use of APIs. The primary tools for configuration management are the following:

- **Chef**: Uses Ruby, a **domain-specific language** (**DSL**), to write system configuration recipes. Chef installation uses a workstation to control the master. Agents are installed using the knife tool with SSH. Managed nodes authenticate with the master using certificates.
- **Puppet**: Used to manage data center orchestration. It works with many operating systems and provides operational support tools for major OSes. Setup requires a master server and client agents on each managed system. Modules and configurations use a Puppet-specific language based on Ruby.

- **Ansible**: Ansible requires no node agent installation to manage configurations. It uses Python with an installation through a GIT repository clone. All functions use SSH. Ansible node management requires appending SSH authorized keys to each node.
- **Salt**: A **command-line interface (CLI)** tool that uses a push method for client communication. It is installed on Git or the package management system. Salt communicates through general SSH. It also includes an asynchronous file server for speeding up file serving. Python or PyDSL are used to write custom modules.

# Microservices and serverless architectures

As cloud computing advances, application design techniques are also advancing. One significant development is the microservice architectural style. Applications are structured an as a collection of loosely coupled services that combine to implement business capabilities. The microservice architecture is used to support the continuous delivery/deployment of large, complex applications. It also enables an organization to evolve its technology stack. Another important new approach is the exclusive use of third-party services that provide ephemeral containers using a just-in-time infrastructure provisioning model, called serverless computing. With this execution model, the cloud provider dynamically manages the allocation of machine resources. Pricing is based on the actual amount of resources consumed by an application, rather than on pre-purchased units of capacity.

# Application migration planning

While developing applications for the cloud is an essential area for the architect to understand, most large enterprises have some existing applications targeted for migration to the cloud environment. The cloud solution architect is intimately involved in these activities as well. Application migrations typically go through four distinct phases:

- Organizational assessment
- Solution definition and design
- Application migration
- Application operations

During the assessment phase, the migration team assesses the organization's infrastructure and targeted applications for readiness to transition to a cloud computing environment. Systems and applications owner interviews are core to this assessment. Application owners answer questions about their current application state as a prerequisite. Cloud adoption itself is an application portfolio activity. Interactions and dependencies between business applications may be more important than the data or application itself. Dependencies make the upfront screening, analysis, and hybrid infrastructure design crucial to the cloud readiness prescreening. This screening process captures as-is the application architecture and current sustainment costs. It also should provide the baseline data for migration option cost-benefit analysis to support the stakeholder's decision process. Migrating applications are typically targeted for one of four transition processes:

- **Lift and shift**: Required infrastructure is rebuilt using appropriate CSP services, and the application is transitioned as-is with no modifications.
- **Refactor**: Applications designed to operate on customized infrastructure are modified to leverage available cloud services before migrating.
- **Rebuild**: Applications that are still required by the organization but cannot be modified to use available cloud-based services. These applications are redesigned and rebuilt before transitioning the process to the cloud.
- **Retire**: Applications that are no longer operationally or economically viable to the organizations. Associated processes are either eliminated or replaced with available SaaS.

In the solution definition and design phase, organizational requirements and associated metrics are used to define, design, and compare candidate solutions. A **multi-cloud analysis platform** (**MCAP**) is typically used to support this stage. An MCAP enables enterprises, service providers, and systems integrators to model, design, benchmark, and optimizes information technology infrastructures. They are also used to design and model prospective system architecture alternatives. During this phase, *to-be* architecture options are reviewed to gain insight into mission suitability and an understanding of how migration impacts application performance, security, and scalability. This phase also encompasses finalizing all data security control requirements. Operational needs, laws, or industry regulatory dictates drive security requirements. Since security is a shared responsibility between the organization and selected cloud service providers, this activity identifies all required security controls and their application within the solution design.

In the application migration phase, applications first migrate into a sandboxed environment to complete functional and security testing. After verifying functional capabilities and security controls, they are promoted into the production environment.

In the application operations phase, the final operational entity starts managing the infrastructure and application. Users must continually monitor CSP adherence to **service level agreements (SLA)** throughout this phase. Continuous monitoring of all cloud-based resources is also necessary. The organization should continually recalibrate cost by comparing planned versus actual and should recommends policies to streamline cloud usage. As requirements and available market services improve, the transition to other service providers may be a more optimal choice.

# Summary

Cloud applications consist of the software and programming language combinations used to create a web or mobile application. These applications should also adhere to cloud-friendly characteristics such as loose coupling, stable and described interfaces, marketplaces, and REST. The most prevalent server-side stacks include LAMP, WISA, and Java. Many enterprises have accelerated the application development process by adopting DevOps. It uses a concept referred to as *Infrastructure as a Code*, where scripting is used to instantiate cloud-based infrastructure through the use of APIs. While developing applications for the cloud is an essential area for the architect to understand, most large enterprises have some existing applications targeted for migration to the cloud environment. Cloud solution architects should use organizational requirements and associated metrics to define, design, and compare candidate solutions.

# 14
# Data Security

The explosion of cloud computing and consumer IT means that your data, as well as data about you, can be virtually anywhere. This expanding concept of data mobility means that traditional security concepts, which focus in depth on infrastructure defense, no longer apply. Implementing security requirements associated with transitioning from an infrastructure-centric data security model to the data-centric cloud computing security model are challenging to every modern organization. As the cloud solution architect, however, your job focuses on how to address this issue without disrupting your end users' workflows. A data-centric security model ensures that the most important asset of the business—the data—is always protected.Having your data everywhere is also critical to the success of the cloud computing business model. A data-centric security solution must target the direct protection of the data, not the endpoint devices. Device protection requirements invariably mean additional fortification of the corporate security measures that are currently in place. Cloud solutions focus on protecting data, files, documents, and folders stored and used by the user community throughout its life cycle. They should also protect the data in motion and distributed to employees internally, externally, and to partner organizations. By embracing public clouds such as Box, Dropbox, OneDrive, and Google Drive, enterprises are embracing these services as opportunities to work smarter, faster, collaboratively, and efficiently. The data itself is an essential component of this digital commerce because it holds intellectual property, employee information, and customer data. Developing a comprehensive data-centric security program, including data discovery, classification, encryption, and file protection, can uniquely position your organization to protect its data, and make security move with your data to comply with global regulations such as **General Data Protection Regulation (GDPR)**.

In this chapter, we will cover the following topics:

- Data classification
- Data privacy

# Data security life cycle

The secure data life cycle has six phases:

- **Create**: The generation or acquisition of new digital content, or the alteration/updating of existing content. Creation can happen internally in the cloud or externally after the data is imported into the cloud. The creation phase is the preferred time to classify content according to its sensitivity and value to the organization. Careful classification is necessary because weak security controls could be implemented if the content is classified incorrectly.
- **Store**: Committing digital data to a storage repository; typically occurs nearly simultaneously with creation. When storing data, protection should align with its classification level and controls, such as encryption, access policy, monitoring, and logging, and backups should be implemented to avoid data threats. Content can be vulnerable to attackers if **access control lists (ACLs)** are not well implemented, or files are not scanned for threats or classified incorrectly.
- **Use**: Viewing or processing, or otherwise used in some activity, not including modification. Data in use is most vulnerable because it might be transported to unsecured locations such as workstations.
- **Share**: Information made accessible to others, such as between users, to customers, and to partners. Since shared data is no longer under the organization's control, maintaining security can be difficult. Data loss prevention technologies can be used to detect unauthorized sharing, and data rights management technologies can be used to maintain control over the information.
- **Archive**: Data leaves active use and enters long-term storage. Considerations of cost versus availability can affect data access procedures. Data placed in an archive must still be protected according to its classification. Regulatory requirements must also be addressed, and different tools and providers might be part of this phase.
- **Destroy**: The permanent destruction of data using physical or digital means (for example, crypto-shredding). The destroy phase can have different technical meanings according to usage, data content, and applications used. Data can be destroyed through the logical erasure of pointers or via permanent data destruction using physical or digital means. Consideration should be given according to regulation, type of cloud being used (IaaS versus SaaS), and the classification of the data:

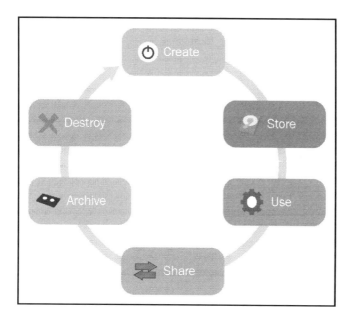

Although this life cycle addresses the phases data passes through, as shown in the previous figure, it does not address data location, how the data is accessed (device or channel), the functions that can be performed with the data, or the process of authorizing a given actor (person or system) to have access to the data. A secure cloud solution must address all these aspects.The data security life cycle should be managed as a series of smaller life cycles running in different operating environments. Data can, and does, constantly move into, out of, and between these environments. Regulatory, legal, contractual, and other jurisdictional issues make keeping track of the physical and logical locations of data a high-priority issue. These aspects also control who is authorized to use the data and, often, the device and communications channel that can be used. Devices and channels have different security characteristics and may use different applications or clients.When accessed, a given datum can be acted upon through three specific functions:

- **Access**: View/access the data. Access includes creating, copying, dissemination, and file transfers.
- **Process**: Performing a transaction on data. This includes updating it or using it in a business processing transaction.
- **Store**: Store the data for future use (that is, in a file or database).

Functions are performed in a location, by an actor (person, application, or system/process, as opposed to the access device). Protecting the datum requires the selection, implementation, and enforcement of security controls. Controls restrict a list of possible actions down to those who are allowed. The appropriate governance regime typically drives control selection. Applicable governance regimes include the following:

- **GDPR**: The General Data Protection Regulation (Regulation (EU) 2016/679) is a regulation by which the European Parliament, the Council of the European Union, and the European Commission have unified and strengthened data protection for all European Union (EU) individuals.
- **SOX**: The Sarbanes-Oxley Act of 2002 controls data access to reduce corporate fraud.
- **HIPPA**: The Health Insurance Portability and Accountability Act of 1996 is United States legislation that provides data privacy and security provisions for safeguarding medical information.
- **FedRAMP**: The Federal Risk and Authorization Management Program is a United States government-wide program that provides a standardized approach to security assessment.
- **PCI DSS**: The Payment Card Industry Data Security Standard is a set of policies and procedures designed to optimize credit, debit, and cash card transactions security. It protects cardholders against misuse of their personal information.
- **FERPA**: The Family Educational Rights and Privacy Act is a United States federal privacy law that protects parents and their children's education records (that is, report cards, transcripts, disciplinary records, contact and family information, and class schedules).

The Cloud Security Alliance provides a reference known as the *Cloud Control Matrix* (`https://cloudsecurityalliance.org/download/cloud-controls-matrix-v3-0-1/`) that lists required data security controls for these and many other industry governance regimes. The cloud solution architect is responsible for identifying all required data controls and ensuring that the implemented solution enforces the required control on the data, no matter where the data is located or what actor attempts to access it.

# Data classification

Given the importance of protecting data at all times and in all places, the most critical data management task is data classification. Ideally, data is classified immediately upon creation by the entity that creates the data. If this is not done, data needs to be reviewed and classified by others based on the organization's information governance guidelines. Information governance represents the policies and procedures for managing all data and should include the following:

- **Information classification**: High-level descriptions of critical information categories. The goal is to define high-level categories to determine appropriate security controls.
- **Information management policies**: Policies that define allowed activities for different data types.
- **Location and jurisdictional policies**: Where data can be located geographically. Legal and regulatory restrictions drive this.
- **Authorizations**: Define which employee/user types are allowed to use or access which types of information.
- **Ownership**: The ultimately responsible party for the protection of information.
- **Custodianship**: Who is responsible for managing the information, at the direction of the owner.

When classifying data, best practice suggests that the schema used should, at a minimum, address the following eight key areas:

- Data type (format, structure)
- Information context
- Jurisdiction and other legal constraints
- Data ownership
- Trust levels and source of origin
- Contractual obligations or business constraints
- Value, sensitivity, and criticality of data to the organization
- Obligation for retention and preservation

The classification categories should match the data controls used.

# Data privacy

Compliance with the relevant **privacy and data protection (P & DP)** laws (by geography) represents, both for customers and service providers, an essential factor for the success of any cloud computing services implementation. Cloud service customers and cloud service providers must work together to find viable solutions by implementing appropriate agreements and controls. The outcome should focus on ensuring defined roles and the attribution of due care and due diligence responsibilities. The P & DP regulations affect not just those whose personal data is processed in the cloud (the data subjects), but also those (the cloud service customers) using cloud computing to process others' data, and those providing cloud services used to process that data (the cloud service providers). Key data privacy roles are the following:

- **Data subject**: An identifiable subject is one who can be identified, directly or indirectly, in particular by reference to an identification number or one or more factors specific to his physical, physiological, mental, economic, cultural, or social identity [telephone number, IP address].
- **Controller**: The entity which alone, or jointly with others, determines the purposes and means of the processing of personal data. When national or community laws or regulations determine the purposes and means of processing data, the controller may be designated by national or community law.
- **Processor**: A natural or legal person, public authority, agency, or any other body that processes personal data on behalf of the controller.
- **Data owner**: An entity that can authorize or deny access to data and is the authority responsible for its accuracy, integrity, and timeliness.

In a cloud deployment, your organization may play any or all of these roles. Your data security controls must protect all data as dictated by the data owner. Meeting privacy and data protection laws may require addressing the following data classification aspects:

- P & DP law for any relevant countries or jurisdictions
- Scope and purpose of the processing
- Categories of the personal data to be processed
- Categories of the processing to be performed
- Data location allowed
- Categories of user allowed

- Data retention constraints
- Security measures to be ensured
- Data breach constraints
- Status

# Personally Identifiable Information – PII

The **personally Identifiable Information (PII)** is data that can be used singularly or with other data to identify, contact, or locate a single person. The classification of any specific datum as PII is dictated by laws or regulations of the relevant government or jurisdiction. PII can be divided into two categories: linked information and linkable information. Linked information can be used to identify an individual and includes the following:

- Full name
- Home address
- Email address
- Social security number
- Passport number
- Driver's license number
- Credit card numbers
- Date of birth
- Telephone number
- Login details

Linkable information is information that, by itself, cannot be used to identify a person but that when combined with another piece of information, could identify, trace, or locate a person. Examples include the following:

- Country, state, city, postcode
- First or last name
- Gender
- Non-specific age
- Race
- Job position and workplace

**Non-personally identifiable information (non-PII)** is data that cannot be used on its own to identify, trace, or identify a person. Examples of this are the following:

- Device IDs
- IP addresses
- Cookies

# Summary

Data security is the core of cloud security. The solution architect must establish and maintain that mindset across the entire organization. Having your data everywhere is also critical to the success of the cloud computing business model and the most critical data management task is data classification. An ever changing aspect of data classification is the fluid nature of global **privacy and data protection (P&DP)** laws. Every solution must recognize the multiple data protection roles and ensure that all required security controls, for whatever role the organization plays, are in place.

# 15
# Application Security

In this chapter, we will cover the following topics:

- The application security management process
- Application security risks
- Cloud computing threats

# The application security management process

The ISO 27034-1 standard provides a very valuable framework for implementing cloud application security. The standard's underlying principles include the following:

- Security requirements are defined and analyzed throughout the application's life cycle and managed continually.
- Application risks are influenced by security requirement type and scope, which are driven by (1) business; (2) regulatory; and (3) technological domains.
- Application security controls and audit measurements costs should align with the targeted level of trust.
- Auditing process should verify that implemented controls are delivering management's targeted level of trust.

ISO 27034-1 also lays out the components, processes, and frameworks to help organizations acquire, implement, and use trustworthy applications, at an acceptable (or tolerable) security cost. These components, processes, and frameworks provide verifiable evidence that applications have reached and maintained a targeted level of trust. The recommended top-level processes are as follows:

- The **Organization Normative Framework (ONF) management process**, used for managing the application security-related aspects of the ONF.
- The **Application Security Management Process (ASMP)**, used for managing security for each application used by an organization. This process is performed in five steps, shown in the following diagram:

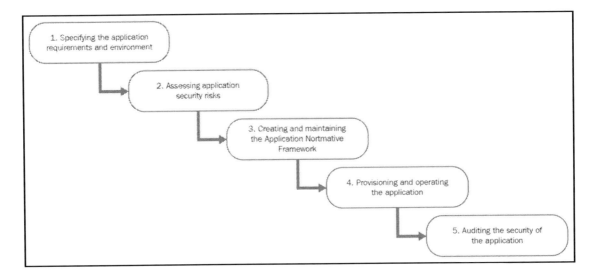

The ONF stores all the organization's application security best practices, or those from which they will be refined or derived. It comprises essential components, processes that utilize these components, and processes for managing the ONF itself. It will contains regulations, laws, best practices, and roles and responsibilities accepted by the organization. The ONF is a bidirectional process meant to create a continuous improvement loop. Innovations that result from securing a single application are returned to the ONF to strengthen all organization application security in the future. Its specific IT governance components include the following:

- **Business context**: Includes all application security policies, standards, and best practices adopted by the organization.
- **Regulatory context**: Includes all standards, laws, and regulations that affect application security.
- **Technical context**: Includes required and available technologies that apply to application security.
- **Specifications**: Documents the organization's IT functional requirements and the solutions that are appropriate to address these requirements.
- **Roles, responsibilities, and qualifications**: Documents the actors within an organization who are related to IT applications. Includes processes related to application security.
- **Application security control library**: Contains the approved controls that are required to protect an application based on the identified threats, the context, and the targeted level of trust.

The application security risk assessment, the second step in the risk management process, applies the risk assessment process at the application level. Its primary purpose is to obtain the organization's approval for a target level of trust through specific application-oriented risk analysis.

As the third step of the process, the **Application Normative Framework (ANF)** is a subset of the ONF that contains the information required for a specific application to match the required targeted level of trust as set by the application owner. It identifies the relevant elements from the ONF which are applicable to the target business project.

The ONF to ANF is a one-to-many relationship, where one ONF will be used as the basis to create multiple ANFs:

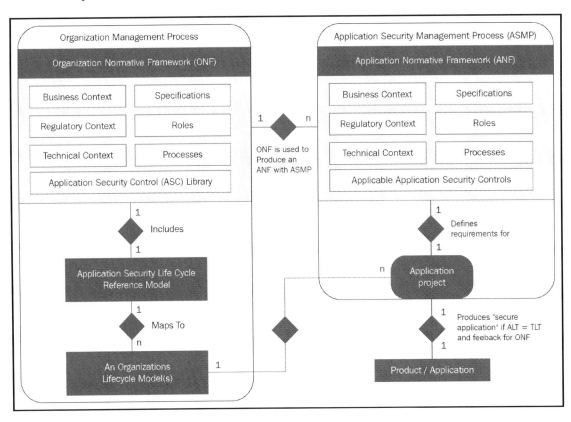

Provisioning and operating the application is the fourth step of the ASMP, which involves the deployment and follow-up within the application project. It actually implements the security activities contained in the ANF. Application Security Audit is the ASMP fifth step and deals with the verification and recording of the supporting evidence regarding whether a specific application has attained its targeted level of Trust.

A descriptive graphic of the entire ASMP is provided as follows:

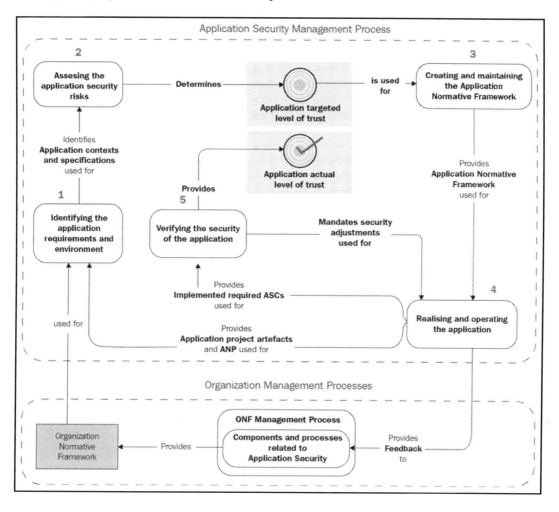

# Application security risks

After all appropriate data controls are identified and designed into the cloud computing solution, applications themselves need to be hardened against attack. The best guidance for this hardening process is the OWASP top 10, which lists the 10 most critical web application security risks. Refer to `https://www.owasp.org/images/7/72/OWASP_Top_10-2017_%28en%29.pdf.pdf` for a detailed list along with the description of each risk.

# Cloud computing threats

The most critical threats to cloud-based applications have been enumerated by the Cloud Security Alliance. Referred to as the **Treacherous Twelve**, a secure cloud solution must protect all applications and processes against these attack vectors. Refer to `https://downloads.cloudsecurityalliance.org/assets/research/top-threats/Treacherous-12_Cloud-Computing_Top-Threats.pdf` for a detailed description of each of these critical threats.

# Summary

Application security requires data security supported by a standardized and consistent application development process. The ONF and ANF provide the standardization and the ASMP delivers the consistency. Cloud computing is often referred to as the *industrialization of IT,* but that value can be irretrievably damaged by a flawed application development process. Applications are key to an ability to deliver value with any solution so the architect should definitely drive toward the ideals presented in this chapter.

# 16
# Risk Management and Business Continuity

Cloud computing solutions balance the risk of data and information loss against the business and mission value of using the cloud. This chapter gives you the tools needed to present both sides of the equation to management so that they can make the many complex decisions embedded throughout the cloud solution architecting process.

In this chapter, we will be covering the following topics:

- Framing risk
- Assessing risk
- Monitoring risk
- Business continuity and disaster recovery

## Framing risk

The risk in cloud computing is multifaceted and involves multiple participants. The entire model relies, in fact, on a shared risk model between the providers and the consumers. Enterprises using cloud assume risks as part of an interrelated service ecosystem that may not be controlled by the internal IT department. Traditional risk management design is targeted for low uncertainty environments that have few interconnections. The risk in today's networked world, however, is managed in an environment of high uncertainty and dynamically changing, interconnected systems. Key cloud computing risks include the following:

- Failure to meet financial objectives
- Inability to work within the context of corporate organization and culture

- Unsurmountable difficulties in integrating the cloud services involved
- Inability to comply with legal, contractual, and moral obligations
- Inability to recover from a disaster
- Technically inadequate cloud service
- Inadequate solution quality

A definition for each of your organization's specific risks should be developed and agreed upon at the start of any transition to cloud computing.

# Assessing risk

The first step in managing an organization's risk of adopting cloud computing is an assessment. The assessment should evaluate financial, culture, service integration, regulatory compliance, business continuity, and business or mission system quality.

The impact of financial risk is always critical as it directly drives the return on all investments associated with a cloud computing transition. When using cloud services, costs are directly related to workload and revenue. While this model does reduce some financial risk, it affects other factors differently. The critical assessment factors for cloud ROI risk probability are the following:

- Utilization
- Speed
- Scale
- Quality

These four factors drive ROI directly because they affect revenue, cost, and the time required to realize any investment return. Differences between actual and projected values indicate a likely failure to achieve the desired ROI.

| RISK | Manageability | | |
|---|---|---|---|
| Extreme/High Risk 7 – 9 | High Alert | High Alert | Caution |
| Medium Risk 4 – 5 | High Alert | Caution | Safe |
| Low Risk 2 – 3 | Caution | Safe | Safe |
| LIKELIHOOD | Probable | Possible | Unlikely |

Managing the cultural impact of a cloud transition is, in many ways, the most challenging aspect of deploying a cloud computing solution. When adopting any cloud-enabled business processes, organizational executives must project clear vision, direction, and support for all associated business transformations. Establishing a precise procurement and implementation roadmap is imperative and may require significant training of the acquisition and legal team. Stakeholder coordination and reconciliation between competing strategies are needed to build internal consensus for storage, computing, and networking services. Tasks associated with migrating applications require a thorough understanding of customer demand. Pilots and demonstrations should be used to create confidence and to build buy-in and cloud service usage in the user community. They also help in building required transition skills and cloud technology knowledge. The organization's financial governance and acquisition processes may need to be modified to effectively and efficiently leverage the cloud computing economic model.

Organizations of any size typically consume services from three or more cloud service providers. This Service integration risk requires both process and technology integration efforts. There is a risk that this integration does not deliver the expected results. An assessment of service integration risk consists of an evaluation of technical interface details, the organization's ability to modify the existing system, and the skill sets available within the team. Interface details provide data to support integration costs. Solution architects can obtain an initial qualitative estimate by classifying all interface points as required using one of the following:

- Syntactic conversion, which is relatively straightforward
- Semantic compatibility modification, characterized as possible but expensive
- Process model changes, which would be required if the services have radically different process models

A similar triage process is used when evaluating the organization's ability to change the existing system. Risks are high in any redevelopment effort.

A significant source of regulatory compliance risks is mandatory or required interfaces with external services or systems. Driven by regulations or company policy, these usually restrict data to particular geographical areas or legal jurisdictions. There may also be a minimum set of security, integrity, or confidentiality controls. Online or offline retention periods are also often dictated. These types of restriction are particularly applicable to personal and financial data. While the impact of failing to meet such regulations varies, it typically includes financial penalties and operationally detrimental enforcement actions. External cloud supplier dependencies can increase the probability of non-compliance, even if compensating contracts clauses are in place, because force majeure may prevent the supplier from honoring them.

Business continuity management risk can arise from external services, internal systems, or physical disasters. Business events such as mergers and acquisitions of suppliers, unforeseen bankruptcy, or contract cancellations could also affect operational continuity. Cloud computing models can make it harder to respond to these types of changes due to the reduced level of direct control. As part of a risk analysis, assess the probabilities and impact of unplanned events that could harm the enterprise. Also make general provision for unforeseen events that disrupt the cloud services that are used, or damage their data. Having first identified the risks, build into the solution design elements that reduce their probability or mitigate their effects.

This is always a risk that the solution fails to live up to the end user's expectations. Classified as system quality risk, the impact can be seen in reduced margin and loss of ROI. Specific quality areas of concern are the following:

- **Functionality**: Risk associated with the use of external cloud-based systems, or non-cloud-related factors such as the quality of the solution specification.
- **Performance**: Failure to meet required operational or technical metrics.
- **Availability and reliability**: Insufficient reliability as measured by **mean time between failure (MTBF)** and the **mean time to repair (MTTR)**.
- **Fault tolerance**: Excessive availability risk caused by a **single point of failure (SPOF)** or an inability to accommodate multiple failures within a specified service window.
- **Recoverability**: Inability to recover from a failure or excessive data loss should a failure occur.
- **Responsiveness**: Solution that is not sufficiently responsive as measured by user response times and response variability specifications, primarily if the degraded response is due to throughput overload.

- **Manageability**: Factors of configurability, reporting, and fault management, mainly when associated with the provisioning of cloud services.
- **Security**: Risk associated with internet accessibility and the shared security control model. Failure to meet security requirements can result in financial loss, data unavailability, sensitive information leakage, reputational damage, and failure to meet privacy regulations. The use of multiple CSPs can also lead to elaborate security arrangements, introducing the possibility of gaps in the data security defenses.

# Monitoring risk

Risk management is an integral part of the solution architecture development. Risk assessments should, therefore, be repeated at every significant decision stage of the architecture development process. This ensures that the levels of risk exposure continue to be acceptable. Since cloud service procurement is an operational expenditure and not a capital expenditure, cloud solutions must include a continuous service monitoring component.

Cloud service risk assessment for suitability is completed at the start and throughout the solution's lifetime. Services should also be reevaluated if the service provider introduces changes or if alternative service options are made available in the broader marketplace. This requirement is the basis for maintaining and updating industry benchmarks for every critical cloud solution service. Industry benchmark data is also an important input to CSP **service level agreement (SLA)** negotiations.

# Business continuity and disaster recovery

A solution is worthless if it cannot deliver service to its intended consumers. This is why business continuity and disaster recovery should always be included when architecting a cloud computing solution. Although the solution architect may exert minimal influence on a solution's operational deployment, the good solution architect considers the following key BCDR questions before presenting a recommended solution:

- Can the recommended cloud service provider deliver the required service elasticity if BCDR is invoked?
- Are any other CSPs capable of delivering all the required services under a similar SLA?

- Does the recommended CSP have available network bandwidth for timely replication of data?
- Will there be available bandwidth between the impacted user base and the BCDR locations?
- Are there any legal or licensing constraints that prohibit the data or functionality to be present in any CSP data center location?

Cloud solution disaster recovery options fit into three broad categories:

- On-premises data center uses a CSP to support BCDR requirements
- Cloud service consumer depends on the CSPs redundant infrastructure to support BCDR requirements
- The cloud service consumer moves from the primary CSP to a secondary CSP to support BCDR requirements

The cloud solution architect should recommend the most practical of these options as the BCDR path for any recommended cloud solution. The impact of a BCDR scenario on all critical risk elements should be considered as supporting data in consideration of the following planning factors:

- Enumeration of the importance and priority of data and critical organizational process assets
- The current locations of these assets
- Network bandwidth and transport cost between data assets and all relevant processing sites
- Actual and potential location of enterprise workforce and business partners
- Enumeration and prioritization of anticipated disaster events and scenarios
- Process for initiating BCDR activities for each anticipated event or scenario
- Return to normal process for each event or scenario

# Summary

Cloud computing brings risk management to the forefront of information technology. The risk-averse reflexive management decisions of the past will result in rapid business failure in today's world. The smart use of other people's infrastructure, also known as cloud service providers, demands a robust risk management process, with continuous monitoring and rapid reaction. BCDR itself is a risk management process that should also leverage CSP capabilities.

# 17
# Hands-On Lab 1 – Basic Cloud Design (Single Server)

Cloud architecture can be difficult; at times, we make it more difficult than we need to. Cloud is shifting everything because it is an economic innovation, not a technical one. Cloud is driven by economics rather than technology. Each new service continues to drive progression via economics by enabling the realignment of strategy, technology, and economics. Containers and serverless are using new economic models to change the way infrastructure and software are deployed. Because the cloud is primarily economics and strategy, it requires updates to skill sets and additional data for decisions.

The cloud is an answer, but not the answer to everything. Cloud does not make bad decisions better. The cloud is a tool. The cloud is a philosophy, a strategy, a mindset, and an attitude. Above all, cloud is a process. A single aggressive move from CAPEX to OPEX is likely to be expensive; it will probably fail, and probably will not solve much. Fork-lifting the same design from an on-premises data center to an off-premises service provider will move the problem, but not solve it. Cloud success requires research, change management, governance, and comparative design. Every design choice affects economics, strategy, technology, and risk.

## Hands-on labs and exercises

The next three chapters will discuss the impact of design choices at increasing levels of complexity. These chapters are meant to be used as a step-by-step hands-on guide that will navigate through designs and design choices, yielding real-time insight each step of the way.

This chapter will start with a single-server infrastructure, then we will accelerate into more complex insight and scenarios in Chapter 19, *Hands-On Lab – Advanced Cloud Design Insight* and Chapter 20, *Hands-On Lab 3 – Optimizing Current State (12 Months Later)*. It is suggested to navigate these example chapters in order, as each one builds on the previous. Complexity with each example grows, adding considerations for applications, application stacking, utilization, and general market and current trends. The examples and exercises in the book will also be accessible via the Burstorm platform, with unlimited use for 30 days.

# Complexity

Cloud is typically associated with outcomes such as lower cost, speed, and simplicity, yet cloud can be very complex even in its most basic form. For example, a single server can have many attributes that must be considered. How many cores? How much RAM? How much storage? Is it a virtual server or a physical one? What operating system? What type of connectivity? Is the server on a shared or dedicated environment? What about going serverless? What about containers?

The answers to these seemingly simple questions have a drastically different economic impact and a huge effect on strategy. Each attribute feels somewhat technical in nature, yet they are more about economics and how economics affect strategy. Why would virtual servers be chosen over physical? Better utilization? Isn't utilization really about maximizing the use of an expensive resource? Virtualization allows for the acquisition of only what is needed for as long as needed. Not really. Virtualization has been around since the 1960s. Recent billing innovations are what allow partial resources to be consumed in very short increments of time. Virtual servers can be deployed faster. True, but why does that matter? Physical deployments are very manual, expensive, time-consuming, and potentially filled with human error. Virtual machines can be deployed very quickly and programmatically, eliminating much of the expense, time, and effort associated with deployments.

Virtualization and its benefits are well known. Designs using virtualization have been around for several years now. What is so different? For the first time, we see economic models driving design decisions, for example, reserve instance versus current market rate. Reserve instances require a large upfront fee with a very low monthly fee. What situations are better suited for a longer-term commitment with significant money up front? What strategy does this line up with? How does this affect risk? With the high fees up front and longer commitment requirements, reserve instances are better suited for persistent workloads with fairly flat traffic patterns. Cyclical or seasonal traffic patterns do not fit here, as resources would be paid for when they were not being utilized fully. A major change, as mentioned earlier, is that designs can now be created for the low point with burst or up-cycle moves to support increases in the traffic pattern.

# Eliminating the noise

Successful next-generation designers are able to quickly triage true requirements from wants and wishes. Much of the truth is drowned by emotions, agendas, hype, marketing, and other forms of distracting noise. Simplify, then build. Quickly get to the lowest and simplest common denominator and add where truly needed. Every server and GB of storage requires monitoring, administration, management, and all other care-and-feeding type activities. Poor choices at basic infrastructure levels can dramatically affect economics as all of the other requirements are piled on.

A single server is not as simple as it sounds. The following diagram shows a set of basic options that can be applied to any server. There are a number of options for each attribute, of which one is chosen. The chart shows almost 6.3 billion potential combinations for this single server. Considerations for other attributes, such as external storage, port configuration, software, patch level, and so on, have not been accounted for. The potential combinations can quickly reach into the trillions for a single server when all attributes are considered. Add in additional combinations when adding in additional servers, licensing options, additional devices, additional potential locations, potential providers, pricing options, business models, consumption rules, deployment rules, and the many other nuances that permeate every solution design.

In the following example, we see three different term options. This may equate to 12-, 24-, or 36-month terms, with only one term being chosen. We see that cores, in this example, can be any number between 1 and 12. RAM could be anything between 1 and 16. Obviously, there are many other options and add-ons, such as monitoring, management, licensing, and so on. But just basic server configuration choices already place this single server into the 6+ billion combination range:

| Server Attributes | # of Options | # Chosen |
|---|---|---|
| Term | 3 | 1 |
| Cores (1-12) | 12 | 1 |
| RAM (1-16) | 16 | 1 |
| Storage (40-400, 10GB) | 37 | 1 |
| OS Type | 8 | 1 |
| VM (Yes or No) | 2 | 1 |
| Shared (Yes or No) | 2 | 1 |
| Client Managed (Yes, No, Both) | 3 | 1 |
| # of Locations | 3 | 1 |
| Connectivity 1 | 8 | 1 |
| Connectivity 2 | 2 | 1 |
| Connectivity 3 | 2 | 1 |
| Connectivity 4 | 2 | 1 |
| Connectivity 5 | 2 | 1 |
| Connectivity 6 | 2 | 1 |
| Connectivity 7 | 2 | 1 |
| Connectivity 8 | 2 | 1 |
| Total Potential Combinations | 6,285,164,544.00 | |

# Burstorm lab 1 – background (NeBu Systems)

All of the hands-on exercises will be for a company named NeBu Systems. NeBu creates software for the automotive industry. New cars have almost as much processing power within them as full data centers in recent years. With all of the sensors gathering IoT data and the tremendous compute power available for processing, NeBu is trying to transition away from large monolithic legacy applications to highly flexible cloud-based modular functions aimed at changing the automotive experience. The goal is to be positioned to adapt as some functions become widely adopted while others are driven to satisfy certain niche markets. Ideally, functions are added as custom apps similar to adding apps to cell phones or picking car colors and upholstery types.

In this first lab, NeBu is developing a new application that will be engineered for the cloud from the beginning. No legacy code to deal with. No legacy dependencies or specific hardware requirements complicating things. The code will be written using modern languages, eliminating concern over hardware compatibility.

# Burstorm lab 1 – getting started

Please send an email to support@burstorm.com with the following:

- (Required) current email address (must work as initial password information will be sent to this address)
- (Required) full name
- Please include the following code within the subject of the email: **NeBu214495**

## Burstorm lab 1 – creating new model

1. Please go to http://app.burstorm.com/login and enter your email address and temporary password, which will need to be changed once you have logged in
2. From the dashboard/home screen, please click on **Design**:

3. Click on **New Project | Model**:

4. A dialog box will appear, asking for basic information to be entered:
    1. Please enter a **Model Name**
    2. Please change the **View** field from **My Organization** to **Myself**
    3. Scroll to the bottom and select **Create**:

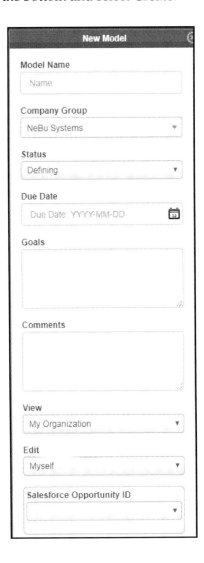

Congratulations, your model has been created. In this platform, a model is figuratively a scope or a problem that is trying to be solved. There may be multiple ways to solve a problem or series of problems. NeBu is trying to transform from large monolithic apps to smaller functional blocks of code and smaller targeted apps.

There are many ways to navigate that scope or problem. Should NeBu deploy on existing infrastructure? Should it be deployed on-premises or off-premises? Should NeBu deploy it within existing collocation environments? What about virtual machines as a cloud service? All are potential options. How do we start sorting it out?

As discussed in this book, there are many things to consider when assessing current cloud readiness, developing new applications using new styles of infrastructure consumption and deployment patterns, and recycling/up-cycling existing code bases. This book has discussed many approaches and frameworks that can be used. After several internal meetings, discovery sessions, and planning conversations, NeBu has determined a path forward. NeBu has chosen to develop new code that will be deployed on Linux servers and begin to embrace more of the open source community.

As code begins to navigate through the development lifecycle, resource requirements tend to increase with each stage. Initial development is handled by relatively few people, requiring minimal infrastructure when building and testing initial rounds of code. As the code progresses, more people and infrastructure are needed to perform logical and resource testing. During testing and each development stage, developers must determine infrastructure requirements for initial deployment and anticipated capacity plans. Responsible testing should yield logical and resource constraints that will determine initial deployment and growth increments. Wouldn't these answers change based on the provider and infrastructure chosen?

How can initial anticipated performance level and basic resource requirements be determined if the infrastructure options, pricing, and performance are unknown? Based on Burstorm ongoing benchmark data, the same instance type within the same provider, at two different locations, has shown up to 700% different in performance tests. These performance differences can dramatically change infrastructure requirements, deployment styles, and associated solution economics. In the next exercise, we will begin examining characteristics and attributes that will help determine a short list of potential providers and instance sizes that match up to technical, strategic, and economic requirements.

Return to the initial model created and verify. The model should appear as a blank drawing board as shown in the following screenshot. In the following screenshot, a model named **Single Server (Reference)** is shown. This model was created and shared as a follow-along model that can be viewed if you choose to do the configuration work later. The reference model is also meant to be used as a reference to check progress and see the results expected:

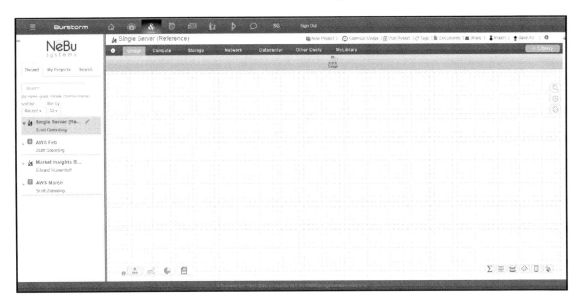

## Burstorm lab 1 – creating a design scenario

As mentioned, understanding available solution components, where they are available, what they cost, and how they can be combined with other services is very helpful when used from the very beginning. In this example, a single server design will be created to help identify potential providers, configurations, and services that may affect final solutions as development cycles move closer to production deployment at NeBu Systems:

1. Starting at the top center of the page, please click and drag the **Design** icon onto any blank space on the drawing board.
2. The application will create a new scenario as shown in the following screenshot:

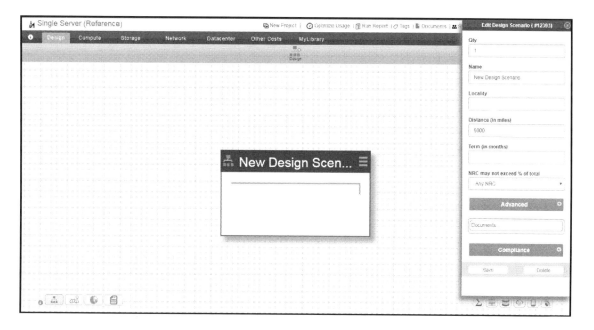

3. Please enter a name for the scenario. In this example, I have used `Single Server`. The name can be anything you choose that is helpful as you try to remember what it is for:

4. Service providers deploy products and services in specific locations. Services are not generally available anywhere, although some can be (for example, equipment deployed on client premises). In-house services are also only available in very specific locations. For this reason, one of the initial scenario defining characteristics is location. NeBu Systems has chosen to deploy the new application in a central location within the US. The Midwest has additional benefits, with lower risk factors than higher-profile, more densely populated cities such as New York and Los Angeles. The threat of natural disaster is much lower than California. Please enter the initial location as `Chicago, IL`, shown in the following screenshot. Chicago also has very good connectivity options as many of the carriers pass through in large telco hotels.

5. Please add `Chicago, IL` to the **Locality** field. This will set the general search epicenter for potential solution products and services:

```
Locality
Chicago, IL|
```

6. Not every product or service will be located in Chicago, IL. NeBu Systems does not have a firm requirement that forces it to locate within Chicago. Since other potential providers and locations may be available within an acceptable distance from Chicago, please enter `300` as the search radius to be used when mapping and matching acceptable providers, products, and services:

```
Distance (in miles)
300
```

7. Products and services not only have specific locations, but they also have predetermined business and consumption models. As an example, reserve instances from AWS have an economic and consumption model that requires a minimum commitment of a 12-month term with significant **non-recurring cost (NRC)** due up front. Once the upfront (NRC) costs have been paid, a smaller ongoing monthly payment is required for each month of the specified commitment term. NeBu systems have strategic interest and a financial policy that desires more emphasis on preserving capital favoring **operational expense (OpEx)** driven solutions.

8. Please leave the **Term** field blank. This will indicate that the minimum term is not specified and will allow economic models with no minimum term to respond. If a reserve instance model were required, a minimum of 12 months would be entered instead of leaving the field blank:

```
Term (in months)

```

9. Please leave the % NRC field set to the default of **Any NRC** as shown in the following screenshot. This example will not limit the NRC amount:

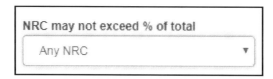

10. Please leave **Compliance** set as default and choose **Create** at the bottom.

11. The result should show a single design scenario on the board titled with the name previously entered:

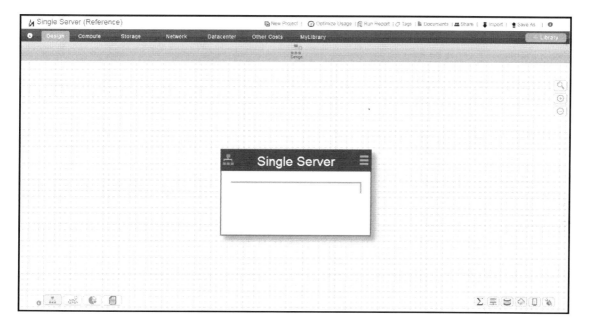

NeBu chose to deploy on Linux servers. Application and code design conversations have not been able to provide a consensus for a single provider, or shortlist of providers. Different stakeholders have their own agendas and priorities that are being brought to the table. One of the administrators wants it to be housed at Google because he has good relationships from engagements completed with Google Cloud at previous employers. NeBu developers like the idea of using AWS due to the scope of all available cutting-edge services. Sales likes the idea of using Azure as many of the clients are comfortable with Azure and like where the direction and progress Azure has made recently.

What is needed to resolve this debate? Data. Real-time analytics and performance data will help in many ways. Many people may consider RFP, RFI, or RFQ type processes. For this exercise, a Linux server can be pulled into the scenario and provide real-time data that may help navigate the dynamics of this internal debate as a provider, or set of providers, are chosen.

12. Please click on **Compute** near the top left of the design board as shown in the following screenshot:

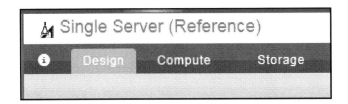

13. A series of preconfigured compute options will show across the grey ribbon, as shown in the following screenshot. Please click on the first icon, named **Linux**, and drag it into any empty space within the scenario box created earlier:

14. The Linux icon should now appear in the box with a dialog window open on the right side of the screen:

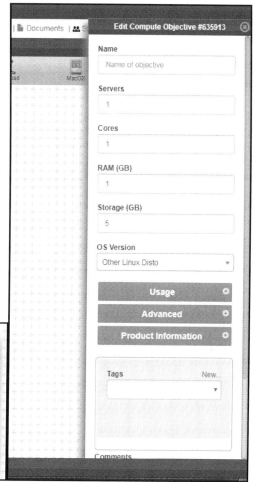

15. NeBu Systems anticipates the new application workloads, and workload types to utilize far less compute power when compared to RAM requirements. The current plan will utilize virtual servers on a shared platform to continue proving the concept, test code, and baseline initial performance characteristics. The initial configuration will start at 1 core and 8 GB of RAM. We will address storage at a later step.

16. Per the NeBu requirement, please update the RAM from 1 to 7 (yes, the earlier statement mentioned 8, please use 7). Also, please clear the storage amount from the storage line. Storage will be addressed in a later step. Please refer to the following screenshot to verify the configurations match:

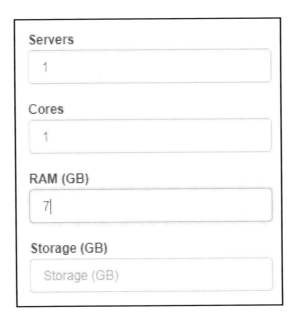

17. Please click the blue **Advanced** bar to drop down the additional options. Please verify that **Is VM?** and **Is Shared?** are set to **Yes**. NeBu's initial solution requires a virtual server from one of the shared IaaS providers available in the current market:

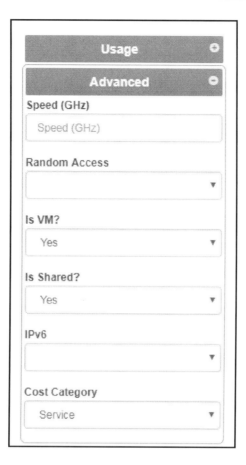

18. Please click the **Save** button at the bottom. The server configuration should update to match the following screenshot:

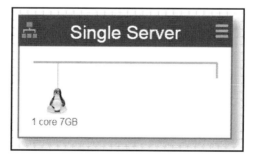

## Burstorm lab 1 – design scenario solution results

For NeBu to move forward most effectively, they have requirements to control cost while acquiring as much performance as possible per dollar spent. There are many providers in the world, with more arriving daily it seems. Each provider has their own personality, deployment style, consumption model, pricing model, and unique combination of available products and services. How can a shortlist of favored providers be assembled? Two requirements and prioritizing characteristics have been stated previously: cost and performance. We can start there:

1. Please click on the hamburger menu in the top-right corner of the design scenario box and choose **BurstormIQ** from the drop-down menu:

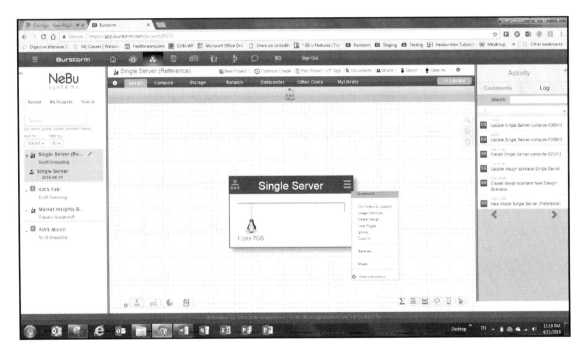

In real time, the platform will return a set of results based on real-time API connected providers, their available products, services, consumption rules, deployment rules, and pricing. Results may vary depending on when you access the real-time data. Data updates/changes often:

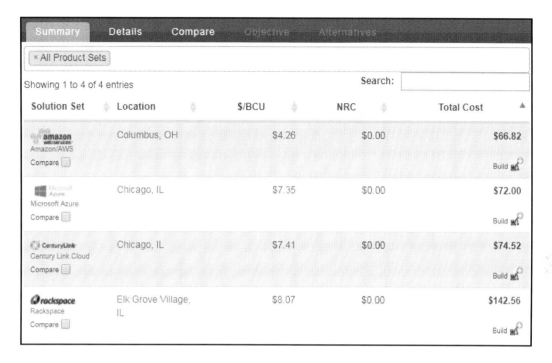

2. In order to choose a provider and technology partner as NeBu moves forward with testing and deploying the new functions and applications, NeBu would like to see more provider data from a wider set of providers. Please click on the blue bar with the scenario name in it. This will open the characteristics and attributes of the scenario itself. Please change the distance to 500 miles. Click **Save** at the bottom:

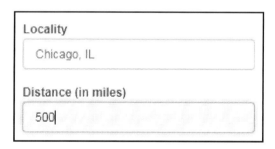

Instantly, NeBu has access to more providers and potential service options that match the stated requirements for strategy, technology, and economics:

## Burstorm lab 1 – high-level rapid insights

Successful cloud deployment requires not only good strategic, technical, and financial decisions; it also requires significant change management and governance. The real-time data presented in this single view contains solution options from multiple providers and some very interesting insight that NeBu Systems can use to not only support decisions but also help promote effective change management and establish governance.

NeBu expressed interest in being near Chicago, IL. Truly, it was a desire to be in the Midwest to avoid many of the potential disasters associated with the higher-profile cities and regions in the US. NeBu also required good connectivity options, as clients would be accessing from several locations across the country. Resiliency was important, along with controlling costs and gaining as much performance as possible for money invested.

Data shown within Bustorm has been automatically normalized so that it can be compared in real time. One of the largest challenges with architecting cloud solutions is gathering and normalizing relevant data. Designers, architects, strategists, and stakeholders must gather, normalize, and compare data for the current state in various forms. Current state billing data is a fairly common starting point. Billing data is compared against deployed information, which is then also compared to actual consumed detail and ultimately compared to potential future state options.

NeBu Systems chose to start greenfield as strategically there was not enough value in trying to repurpose or up-cycle what has already been deployed. Current state still needed to be considered, normalized, and compared. Starting with a new environment does not mean current state is completely ignored. In many cases, current state must be evaluated as an option until it is proven to be less than desirable.

Architecting cloud solutions is about alignment and balance. Successful solutions require risk to be offset by economics. Technology helps accomplish strategy requirements, with strategy influencing technology choices. At times, technology choices can also dramatically impact economics while economics can certainly influence technology choices. In the solution results side of the design board, a greater than 300% difference in price can be seen from low to high. There is a 50% difference that separates the three lowest-cost providers. The request was the same; why are the prices so different? Is it performance difference? Resiliency? Location? Size of infrastructure? Brand value? There are many factors that can affect cost. Many of these questions will be answered in the next chapter as we dive deeper into the insight needed for successful design and architecture.

Another interesting insight the data presents is that none of the three lowest-cost providers (Google, AWS, and Azure) are in Chicago. If NeBu Systems' requirement was to be in Chicago, CenturyLink and Rackspace become the only options available. Data also shows AWS to be the highest performing of the solutions available based on the components requested. Performance is a big requirement for NeBu Systems. Quickly spotting that detail is covered in depth in the next chapter.

# Summary

Solution design and architecture can be filled with lots of unnecessary noise and distractions. Much of the information can be misleading and is often misrepresented. Returning to the basics and starting with things that are non-negotiable to establish baseline requirements is the best way to begin. Start with a few high-level requirements and let the insight become the foundation, not the technology. Build upon the insight, which enables proper alignment and balance.

In this chapter, NeBu Systems has been able to start with a very basic set of requirements, quickly assess initial economic impact, identify a short list of providers to focus on, and quickly confirm some of the strategic and technical pieces. Beginning with non-negotiable requirements helps solution designers and architects avoid unnecessary complexity and scope-creep. This iterative method allows data to expose additional insights that may affect direction and choices that would have been otherwise missed.

The next chapter will explore deeper-level detail and additional insight that helps refine cloud solution design.

# 18
# Hands-On Lab 2 – Advanced Cloud Design Insight

Successful cloud design requires good data. Successful cloud design, more importantly, requires the effective communication of decision supporting data. Many transformation projects fail from poor communication, poor execution, and a lack of adoption, all potentially resolved with well-executed change management and communication plans. Successful solutions require real-time data; the same data that is very beneficial when used for change management and communication plans.

In this chapter, real-time data takes center stage. Additional scenario data and insights will be examined in greater depth. Additional infrastructure design options and ideas will be explored. Later in the chapter, additional services and application data will be factored into the options reviewed and decisions made.

We will learn about the following topics in this chapter:

- Data-driven design
- Burstorm lab 2

## Data-driven design

In the previous chapter, complexity was painted somewhat as a villain. Complexity itself is not the villain; complexity without data to support it is. While implementing *cool* features based on the data outlined in successful stories within popular blog posts and magazine articles could be considered data-driven, it is not really a data-driven approach that leads to success most often. Transformations are hard enough without trying to recreate someone else's story. Why are transformations so hard? Cloud is supposed to make things much easier to align and implement.

How tough can cloud transformation be? Choose the number of cores and RAM. Add storage. Pick a virtual server with the desired OS. Give it some bandwidth and start loading applications. Easy. Even easier: put it in a container. It spins up fast, is very portable and cheap. Awesome. Wait, better yet, go serverless. That removes the server, correct? (Insert laughing audio file here).

Transformations are difficult because of the data. Not necessarily a lack of data, but the challenges associated with identifying relevant data and making it useful. Today, it is assumed that excruciating amounts of data at mind-numbing levels of detail must be gathered to describe the current state accurately. Today, most also assume that equally excruciating amounts of mind-numbing potential future state details are required for credible solutions to be built and accurate decisions to be made. Today, most assume that results will fall short of expectations if sufficient levels of detail are not considered. These assumptions lead to another assumption: that these deep, drawn-out investigations require a lot of time and can be accelerated by throwing more people and expense at the problem. In other words, we dive way too deep, way too fast, and wrap ourselves around the axle and get completely stuck.

# All data is useful; maybe not

Cloud transitions fail most often because the data used is not the most relevant, both when designing the solution and managing change. What does relevant data mean? How do we know what data is relevant and what is not? How should data be triaged and prioritized? Relevance implies that there is a level of focus brought by comparing data to a set of criteria. The criteria used must eliminate extraneous *noise* and unwanted distractions. Throughout this book, it is often stated that the simultaneous alignment of strategy, economics, technology, and risk is critical to success. These four segments become the criteria for both filtering and communicating solution data. To correctly triage and prioritize information, the data must have a significant impact across all four segments. Any data that does not impact all four segments simultaneously should be addressed at a later stage or as part of implementation planning. An example of this may include NeBu Systems' interest in moving away from physical servers and monolithic apps to virtual servers with functions and services loaded. Can this be considered a strategic choice? Is this a technical choice? Does the use of virtual machines and outsourced services affect economics? Does the use of virtual machines provided by a service provider change the risk profile?

NeBu Systems made a few initial decisions based on a few non-negotiable concepts:

- Move away from monolithic applications and coding methods
- Move away from physical servers in favor of current virtualization methods
- Minimize risk associated with natural and man-made disasters by locating infrastructure in the midwest
- The application will likely be more RAM intensive than processor
- Economics impact is weighted the heaviest of all decision criteria if all others are equal
- Linux is a requirement with an emphasis placed on embracing open source when possible
- OpEx model is required
- The project will be greenfield with portions of the current state infrastructure subject to sunset after new deployment and go-live

In the last chapter, part I of the lab could quickly be created with incredible amounts of detail and relevant insights instantly revealed. The simple input data was enough to get enough relevant data that the project could move forward collaboratively without any additional delay while waiting for more potentially useful input data.

Two to three providers clearly showed promise, even with the limited input data used. The provider data is normalized, compared, and ranked, giving proper focus to where time and effort should be invested if any additional investigation is required. Based on results from the initial scenario, the following insights are shown:

- Google offers the lowest cost for the requirements provided
- AWS appeared to be the best performer (compute)
- Azure and AWS are virtually the same cost, making Azure a viable option as well
- None of the three lowest-cost options were in Chicago, but all were in the Midwest
- Responses show a 300% difference between low- and high-cost providers for the same request
- Virtually no difference in cost between AWS and Azure
- Price-to-performance cost is 50% different between AWS and Azure; this gets very interesting since the price was virtually the same.

# Burstorm lab 2 – advanced insight (NeBu Systems)

The second part of this lab is diving into additional data and insights that can help shape next-level decisions that may include the following:

- Infrastructure choices
- Application stacking
- Application layout
- Infrastructure footprint
- Various types of optimization that become interesting due to data and insight revealed

Based on the response data, next-level decisions can be made to quickly refine solution choices and turn them into building blocks for the final solution design. In the next series of steps, each change will continue to expose deeper-level details that can confirm choices or highlight potential alternatives that may provide a better fit with strategy, technology, and economic requirements.

# Burstorm lab 2 - accessing additional detail

1. Please click on **Details** in the gray ribbon above the results side of the window. Please use the following screenshot as a reference for where the tab is located:

Once clicked, additional solution detais will be shown based on the results returned from each provider. Please refer to the following screenshot:

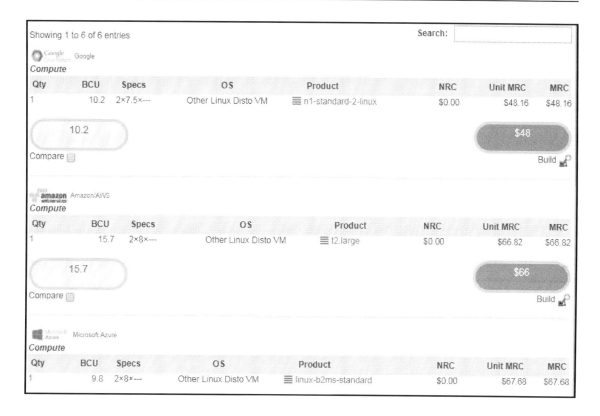

Showing 1 to 6 of 6 entries                                    Search:

**Google** Google
*Compute*

| Qty | BCU | Specs | OS | Product | NRC | Unit MRC | MRC |
|-----|-----|-------|----|---------|----|----------|-----|
| 1 | 10.2 | 2×7.5×--- | Other Linux Disto VM | n1-standard-2-linux | $0.00 | $48.16 | $48.16 |

10.2                                                                    $48

Compare ☐                                                             Build

**amazon** Amazon/AWS
*Compute*

| Qty | BCU | Specs | OS | Product | NRC | Unit MRC | MRC |
|-----|-----|-------|----|---------|----|----------|-----|
| 1 | 15.7 | 2×8×--- | Other Linux Disto VM | t2.large | $0.00 | $66.82 | $66.82 |

15.7                                                                    $66

Compare ☐                                                             Build

**Azure** Microsoft Azure
*Compute*

| Qty | BCU | Specs | OS | Product | NRC | Unit MRC | MRC |
|-----|-----|-------|----|---------|----|----------|-----|
| 1 | 9.8 | 2×8×--- | Other Linux Disto VM | linux-b2ms-standard | $0.00 | $67.68 | $67.68 |

# Overview of the Details tab

There is a lot of data shown in a very confined space. The layout allows for this data to be used for many types of comparisons quickly. The data is presented visually so interesting connections can be made by referencing consistent data locations.

Under the provider's name, a table of data for matching solution products and services shows actual product details in the middle, any pricing information on the right side of the tab, and any performance data shown to the left. The green ovals contain the total cost for the entire solution, accounting for the term length requested for that scenario. Since NeBu Systems did not specify the term, a standard of 720 hours is used as a standard month.

In this view, details can be compared visually for quick decision-making. The segmented view is Google's response to the design created in lab 1; details for quantity, pricing, specs, and performance are shown along with the total price and real-time benchmarked performance data. In this example, Google can be quickly identified as a less expensive alternative to AWS (for this solution combination) by comparing pricing in the green oval. AWS can be quickly identified as the faster alternative based on performance data. Google provides the smallest infrastructure size based on specs listed in the response (though not enough difference to truly impact performance related to the NeBu Systems use case).

# Burstorm lab 2 – selecting for direct comparison

Data by itself does not tell us much at all. Data is only helpful when it can be compared to something. The comparison then leads to insight. In this portion of the lab, comparisons will be made that will lead to insights that shape solution decisions:

1. Please check the **Compare** box for both AWS and Azure as shown in the following screenshot:

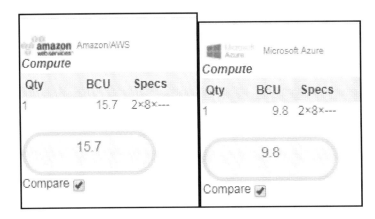

2. After checking the boxes for the solutions to be directly compared, please click on the **Compare** tab as shown in the following screenshot. The **Compare** tab is next to the **Details** tab described in the previous section:

The following view will help confirm that the first two steps have been completed correctly. The view should change to one comparing the two selected solutions side by side:

This view allows solutions to be aligned and compared, line by line. Each line matches exactly for each objective in the design scenario. In NeBu Systems' current design, there is only one objective defined. Imagine a solution with many lines that need to be mapped, matched, and compared. It takes a lot of time to normalize and compare data using manual methods today. The current NeBu Systems design and comparison only took a few clicks. Insightful data is shown in an instant, accelerating design and decision processes.

# Comparing by price

Cloud solutions require insightful data. Comparing on price alone leads to trouble quickly. Cheap solutions may not be the best fit strategically or have the right level of performance. Throughout this book, the economic impact has been mentioned as a requirement, but it is not the only requirement. In many places throughout the platform, a red number is shown. This number is a normalized number that takes pricing data and performance data and runs a calculation that normalizes the data and presents a consistent and dependable number that allows the viewer to compare the several performance and pricing metrics for solution and solution component decisions:

1. In the upper-right corner of the **Compare** window, there is a drop-down box. Please verify the box contains **By Price**. This drop-down menu is a selectable way to reorder and prioritize how the data is presented based on what is most important to the viewer at that moment. The default is set to **By Price**:

2. In the comparison just created for NeBu Systems, which provider is the lowest cost? Is the lower-cost provider on the left or the right? There are several visual clues to help quickly identify the optimal solution based on the prioritization method chosen. When comparing AWS and Azure, as shown below, the lowest-cost provider for the current solution requested is AWS. This insight is shown in a few ways. First, the green oval within the AWS response also shows **best** below the price as the optimization method chosen was by price. The optimal solution option is always shown on the left; again, in this situation, the optimal solution is from AWS based on price alone:

There are a few other indicators to help the viewer quickly find highly relevant insights. Within the green oval on the Azure side, there is a red number below the price. The red number, in this case, states that the price difference between the two solutions is 1% or less.

Another quick visual indicator is the red or green indicator at the end of each line item within each response. Within the AWS solution, it again says best, but using green text. In the Azure response, the red number indicates the difference in price for that line. Please see the following screenshot:

Based on the requirements and responses, pricing difference between the two providers is 1% or less. This difference is too close to make an informed provider choice. Additional data is needed to choose the right path forward.

# Comparing by performance

In this step, additional data points can be quickly added for consideration. In the previous step, 1% difference in cost is not enough to clearly choose which solution is optimal. In a later step, price distribution will also be considered:

Please click the drop-down box that currently shows **By Price** and change it to **By Performance**:

The view will change to now prioritize views based on normalized, real-time performance benchmark data. This additional data enables the comparison of multiple solutions based on performance as the priority data set to organize the views and calculate differences. Please confirm the current views match the following screenshot:

Some may have noticed that the view did not change. There are a couple of reasons for this. First, in the bottom-left oval, the performance numbers presented are pulled from Burstorm's ongoing cloud benchmark service that randomly and continuously tests cloud providers in real time. For this scenario, the performance number **15.7** for AWS is greater than the **9.8** for Azure. The AWS performance is greater than Azure and presented on the left. No change in view is needed. Second, there is only a single line item in the solution; none of the data needed to be changed or reordered since AWS is the lowest cost and the highest-performing in this scenario. Again, no change is needed. If Azure was higher-performing with AWS still the lowest cost, this view would have moved Azure to the left side, as it was the higher-performing solution, and prioritized the data based on performance, as indicated in the drop-down list at the top right.

With this additional data, AWS is slightly lower in terms of cost but appears to be significantly faster. The text in the bottom of each oval on the left side will again visually indicate which is best and what the difference between them is. Please see the following screenshot. In this scenario, the difference is 38%:

Pricing did not give much indication of which would be optimal. The infrastructure sizes also appear to be equal, with both showing as 2x8 machines.

Please note, in the scenario when created, the requested infrastructure size was one core and 7 GB of RAM (1x7). The platform automatically corrects to match how products and services are sold by the providers, how they are meant to be consumed, and how the products and services are deployed.

In this scenario, both AWS and Azure would deploy the requested compute resources as a two-core and 8 GB of RAM (2x8) virtual instance. See the following original request from the lab part 1:

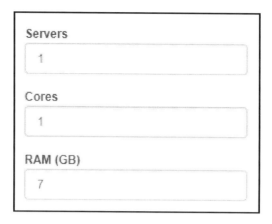

Please compare the requested details to the response details from each provider shown as follows:

# Comparing by price-to-performance

Infrastructure size has not provided any meaningful differentiation. Pricing has not shown any major benefit from one provider to the other. The performance looked to be significantly different, with AWS appearing more favorable. Another very helpful indicator when comparing potential cloud solutions is price-to-performance benchmarks. In many cases, the price may clearly indicate a provider or two are optimal with performance showing a different provider, or set of providers, as optimal. Price-to-performance benchmarks enable value-oriented comparisons that will clearly show which provider has the lowest cost for the highest level of performance. Of course, other factors may still influence final decisions, but the data can help build strong cases as solution designs progress:

1. Please go again to the top right, click the drop-down list, and choose **Price Performance** as the priority when viewing data:

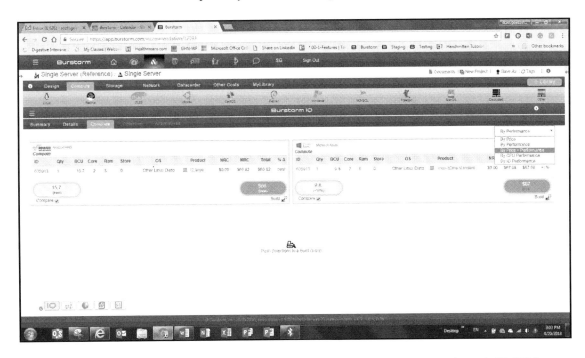

All red numbers should change to match the following screenshot. A **$BCU** is now shown within each line item. This is the normalized price per unit of performance for each line item. In the case of AWS, the cost for every unit of performance is $4.26. For Azure, it is $6.91, which is a 38% higher cost per unit of performance for the same size infrastructure than AWS:

Based on this additional data, it appears that AWS is likely the optimal answer based on the data points considered to this point. It takes very little to make the same comparison between AWS and Google. Google was the original low-cost provider based on the requirements included in the scenario to this point.

2. Please return to the **Details** tab and uncheck Azure, and check Google for the comparison. It is perfectly fine if you check the box for all three and compare them side by side. The only challenge is being able to see all the data as you must scroll left and right to see all the data when you select three or more for comparison. Please see the AWS and Google comparison in the following screenshot:

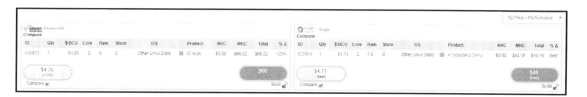

- Which provider is the lowest cost?
- Which provider has the highest performance?
- Which provider would be optimal based on price-to-performance data?

Google is 28% less expensive based on what was requested. By price alone, this would look optimal. AWS is higher-performing, with a 38% difference. It is an interesting side note that, if you felt that the difference was 50% or so, that calculation would be a margin number that is different than the amount of difference. Viewing the data based on price-performance shows AWS as a slight favorite (10%) even though Google was 28% lower cost in this scenario.

# Summary

There are many factors to consider as cloud solutions are built. In this section, several additional important data points were examined:

- Requested infrastructure sizing
- Updated infrastructure sizing based on provider deployment sizing
- Normalized infrastructure detail based on consumption and business models
- Normalized details based on updated pricing matching updated sizing based on deployment rules
- Performance data and analytics
- Price-to-performance data and analytics

Because price-to-performance is so important to the process of building cloud solution designs, an in-depth paper from Burstorm can be found at: `https://slidex.tips/download/cloud-computing-benchmark`. Many of the aspects of why and how are included in the paper. Price-to-performance is a critical dataset that must be included as solution options are evaluated.

There are many more details to consider as solutions are normalized, compared, and chosen. Based on very high-level details, a path can be chosen and focused on. Additional data points can then be added and compared to either confirm the right path is chosen or clearly illustrate that a different path is needed. This allows projects and decisions to progress quickly while reducing the level of effort to compare all data across all potential providers. Starting with infrastructure also allows for the creation of a solid foundation to build on. It can be very expensive to manage environments that sprawl and spread unnecessarily. It can also be very hard to change directions if a solution goes too far too fast in the wrong direction.

Based on the data to this point, NeBu Systems chooses to utilize AWS at this stage of the project. The next chapter will examine how NeBu Systems' choice to utilize AWS has progressed. How has their solution worked out strategically and technically, and how is it currently affecting the economics? Using the same concepts from this chapter, what can NeBu Systems do differently? What changes should be made? Are there better options that should be considered?

# 19
# Hands-On Lab 3 – Optimizing Current State (12 Months Later)

In the last chapters, data and insight quickly identified Google, AWS, and Azure as well-suited providers for the infrastructure and services NeBu Systems required in the very early stages of their transformation. Based on price, performance, and price-to-performance data, AWS was chosen as NeBu Systems' initial cloud service provider.

As with many transformations, NeBu Systems has had challenges with change management and governance, which, in turn, have slowed adoption. Many questions are being asked as infrastructure costs have escalated. NeBu Systems has chosen to examine the current state in a little more detail. NeBu has imported one of their most recent AWS billing files. The plan is to quickly identify ways to optimize current state and control costs.

In this chapter, real-time data and insight will continue to provide a solid foundation for evaluating next steps, options, and decisions.

# Visualizing current state data

Current state data is typically spread across different locations, several different tools, and often many curators. A couple of the many challenges with trying to work with current state data is that the data itself is not interactive or insightful. Collections of data do not really do anything helpful until comparisons are made. Comparing data is revealing and insightful. As an example, a lease can provide details regarding how much is being paid and the amount of time left on the lease. It would be much more helpful to compare the lease information to current market costs and other solution options. It may be beneficial to terminate the lease early and refresh technology through a more cost-effective current solution or better simply benefit from fast-moving markets and current market economics, as an example.

Visualizing data is the quickest path to insight. Many have stated that human perception is 75%-85% based on sight. If you ask a chef the same question, it would be 75%-85% through olfactory nerve (smell). If you ask someone practicing shiatsu massage, that same percentage would most likely come from touch. Humans are experts at making data match purpose. Science has proven that light travels much faster than sound; about 1 million times faster than sound. This supports the fact that sight is the fastest of the human senses. Our other senses in order from fastest to slowest are sound, touch, smell, and lastly, taste. In my rudimentary thinking, I know that I personally struggle with tasting and smelling current state data. The best way for me to process it and quickly identify insight is visual interaction. It has been well documented that data represented visually leads to accurate insight much quicker than any other method.

As mentioned previously, in this chapter, the lab will visualize data from an AWS bill. These different visualization steps will create many opportunities to make visual comparisons that will yield many insights that can be used to optimize or transform the current state. This lab section will focus on identifying insight that will help NeBu Systems optimize current state to better match up with the strategy, technology, economic impact, and risk profiles for the current project.

# Hands-on lab 3 – visualizing the data

For convenience, an AWS bill has already been imported for the lab. The import was done using the import function at the top right of the design board. Please see the following screenshot:

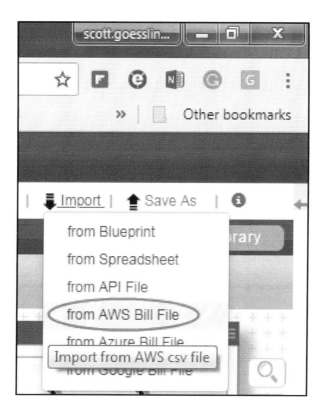

After the import, a new project will show in the left window. After a billing file is imported, it is added to the project list as an existing state project (green letters). Please confirm that **AWS Feb** and **AWS March** are within the list in the left window and accessible by your user. Please confirm your view matches the following screenshot:

Please click on the project name **AWS Feb** (green letters) in the left window pane, shown in the preceding screenshot. Clicking the name opens the project in the main drawing board window. The view should match the following screenshot:

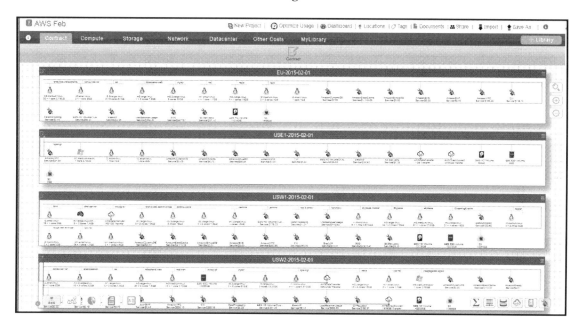

The imported billing data has created a visualization of the current state data included in the billing file. The visualization includes all infrastructure and services along with any AWS user-created tags that were included in the billing file details. The view is automatically split by location. US West 1 and 2, US East 1, and Europe were included in this file.

# Hands-on lab 3 – NeBu Systems' transformation progress update

NeBu Systems has made a lot of progress in a very short time. While things appear to be successful at first glance, rapid growth and transformation have many challenges. Adoption can be difficult. Proper change management and governance are critical to success but very hard to do well.

Initially, NeBu Systems did a very good job with change management. Unfortunately, people have moved on. As the transition has progressed, teams have been shuffled a bit to realign people with current strategy, technology, and economics. Change management has suffered for the last few months, slowing adoption significantly. People are gravitating back to old, comfortable methods rather than embracing the new processes, infrastructure, and updated services.

NeBu Systems saw significant early adoption, which led to rapid growth in the infrastructure supporting the growing user base. With rapid growth, details get missed. Costs have escalated beyond where initial budgets were set. Scope-creep has become a problem. Leaders want to re-examine where they are today, reset to align infrastructure with the current strategy, and do a better job of controlling costs.

# Hands-on lab 3 – Current billing file

What is in the current billing file? How can it be compared to the current market? Today, analyzing a cloud billing file is very difficult. Billing files are very detailed. They usually have many different services, with different locations, different billing methods, different terms, quantities, and very cryptic ways of identifying exactly what product or service is being referenced. Today, many try to download spreadsheets and CSV files to analyze them line by line. This is very time-consuming and prone to error. Most automated tools do not have the ability to compare and drive insight across the entire market. Many efforts take days and weeks to normalize and compare billing data. Cloud solutions have services that last fractions of a second, hours, and days. Taking weeks to analyze, compare, and design solutions is not acceptable in the cloud industry. Automation and enablement is a requirement.

1. In the bottom left of the design board, there are a few icons that can start leading us to visually-driven insight. The first icon should be currently selected. The first icon shows the logical visualization of everything in the file:

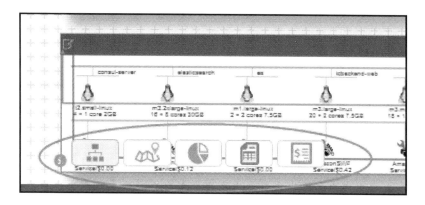

2. This billing file has four main locations as described earlier, three in the US and one in Europe. Please click on the icon located furthest to the right in that same row at the bottom left of the design board:

This view visualizes the billing file line by line with a total at the bottom. The following screenshot shows a partial view of the **Bill of Material (BOM)** view. Please confirm you have selected the correct tab by comparing to the following screenshot:

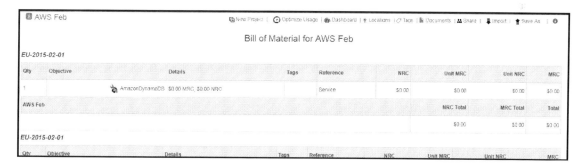

3.  Please scroll to the bottom of the page, using the small slider on the right side of the page or use the mouse wheel to scroll. At the bottom of the page, a green oval will hold the total for the billing term specified in the billing file loaded as well as a second green oval with the total **monthly recurring cost** (**MRC**). Since this is an AWS bill that has services for a term of one month or less, the monthly (MRC) will match the total. The oval labeled NRC has a total of $0.00. This confirms that no reserve instances are being consumed. Please confirm that views match up to the following screenshot:

The imported billing file shows a total of $65,337.13. This is the rolled-up total for all locations contained in the billing file. It is important to be able to understand the stories the data is telling. It is also very important to understand what questions still need to be asked and what answers still need to be found. For example, how much of this bill is allocated to each site? Which site is primary? What products and services are currently deployed at each site?

4.  Please click on the icon in the bottom left of the screen; this time, please choose the icon located second from the right:

This icon will bring up a list that can be searched and filtered, again enabling quick visual insight utilizing various ways to align and compare data. Please confirm views have changed to the correct location by comparing to the following screenshot:

5. The columns can be sorted by clicking the heading for each column. Please confirm which service has the highest MRC cost by clicking MRC twice. The first time will arrange it from low to high. The second click will reverse the order and arrange it from high to low. Please confirm via the following screenshot. Which service is the most expensive? Which site is it deployed in? What is the second highest and where is it deployed?

**AmazonElasticCache** appears to be the highest-cost line item in the bill. This service is currently deployed in USW1 (AWS San Jose). Some interesting questions regarding optimization surface now that we know caching is the highest-cost item in the entire billing file. Caching is typically a service that is employed to keep the cost of other services down:

- Is caching working as planned?
- Is it deployed correctly?
- Is it refreshing content and removing stale content working as planned?
- Does the caching service offset other more expensive services as intended?
- Should this much content in San Jose be caching this often?
- Is San Jose the primary location that should be serving a majority of the content?

Quickly visualizing data in this way enables attention, focus, and effort to be placed in the most effective way based on insight revealed. Cloud architecture requires a keen sense of utilizing only what is needed only when it is needed. Cloud architecture is being as mindful of economic impact as required for technical details.

The bill also has **AWSDirectConnect** as the second most expensive line item. This line item is deployed in a different location from the caching service. **AWSDirectConnect** is deployed from US East 1 (Northern Virginia), not US West 1. **AWSDirectConnect** is used to connect client locations directly to AWS. What types of questions surface knowing these details?

- How does the direct-connected location on the east coast relate to the west coast location that appears to be caching a lot of content?
- Is the US East 1 location the primary location or is the US West 1 location primary?
- There were four sites represented in the billing file. Is one of the other locations primary?
- Why is there 2445 GB of data being transferred in one month across the **AWSDirectConnect** link? Big transfer or backup job?
- 2445 GB transferred in less than 720 hours per month equates to a fully utilized 7 Mbps-8 Mbps line. Is there a more cost-effective solution for low bandwidth connectivity?
- What location does the AWS US East 1 location directly connect to?
- Can/should the services connecting to AWS be moved into a cloud service to eliminate the monthly cost associated with **AWSDirectConnect**?
- At current market pricing, direct-connect to a 10G port is $2.41/hour. If using 720 hours as a standard month, the monthly cost shown in the bill would equate to a total of three 10GE ports sending a total of 7 Mbps. What is the story that this is telling?
- The actual cost is for transfer out. AWS does not charge inbound. At an average of $0.02 currently per GB of outbound transfer, 2448 GB should account for less than $50.00 total for the month. Again, what is the story that is behind such an anomaly?

6. As great cloud architects, diving deeper is a must. There is more to this story. Please click on the **Contract** column header at the far left:

Showing 1 to 100 of 102 entries

| Contract | Objective |
|----------|-----------|
| USW1-2015-02-01 | AmazonElastiCache |
| USE1-2015-02-01 | AWSDirectConnect |
| USW1-2015-02-01 | RDS |
| USW2-2015-02-01 | EBS HD Volume |
| USW2-2015-02-01 | EBS SSD Volume |
| USW1-2015-02-01 | EBS SSD Volume |

By clicking this header, you can sort the table by this column using alphabetical order. Clicking one time will sort A-Z. Clicking a second time will sort Z-A. Please click one time only. Please scroll down to find USE1 for US East 1. Please confirm the view matches the following screenshot:

| EU-2015-02-01 | AmazonSWF | Service | $0.00 MRC, $0.00 NRC | | $0.00 | $0.00 |
|---|---|---|---|---|---|---|
| EU-2015-02-01 | AmazonSimpleDB | Service | $0.00 MRC, $0.00 NRC | | $0.00 | $0.00 |
| USE1-2015-02-01 | AWSDirectConnect | Transfer | 24450B Xfer | | $0.00 | $4,529.37 |
| USE1-2015-02-01 | m3.medium-mswin | VM on shared hypervisor | 1 Cores × 3.8 Ram × 4 HD Windows | | $0.00 | $88.38 |
| USE1-2015-02-01 | AmazonRoute53 | Service | $0.00 MRC, $0.00 NRC | | $0.00 | $29.99 |
| USE1-2015-02-01 | AmazonVPC | Service | $0.00 MRC, $0.00 NRC | cosmgt | $0.00 | $27.35 |
| USE1-2015-02-01 | ElasticIP | Service | $0.00 MRC, $0.00 NRC | | $0.00 | $24.93 |
| USE1-2015-02-01 | t2.small-linux | VM on shared hypervisor | 1 Cores × 2.0 Ram × 0 HD Linux | | $0.00 | $17.47 |
| USE1-2015-02-01 | t2.micro-linux | VM on shared hypervisor | 1 Cores × 1.0 Ram × 0 HD Linux | | $0.00 | $8.74 |
| USE1-2015-02-01 | AmazonKinesis | Service | $0.00 MRC, $0.00 NRC | | $0.00 | $8.73 |
| USE1-2015-02-01 | EBS HD Volume | Disk | 63 GB HD | | $0.00 | $3.60 |
| USE1-2015-02-01 | AmazonDynamoDB | Service | $0.00 MRC, $0.00 NRC | | $0.00 | $2.05 |
| USE1-2015-02-01 | S3 Requests | Service | $0.00 MRC, $0.00 NRC | | $0.00 | $1.09 |
| USE1-2015-02-01 | S3 | Storage | 3 GB HD | | $0.00 | $0.06 |
| USE1-2015-02-01 | AWSDataTransfer | Transfer | 1GB Xfer | | $0.00 | $0.02 |
| USE1-2015-02-01 | EBS HD VolumeIOUsage | Service | $0.00 MRC, $0.00 NRC | | $0.00 | $0.02 |
| USE1-2015-02-01 | EBS SSD Volume | SSD | 0 GB SSD | | $0.00 | $0.01 |
| USE1-2015-02-01 | CW | Service | $0.00 MRC, $0.00 NRC | | $0.00 | $0.00 |
| USE1-2015-02-01 | AmazonSNS | Service | $0.00 MRC, $0.00 NRC | | $0.00 | $0.00 |
| USW1-2015-02-01 | AmazonElastiCache | Service | $0.00 MRC, $0.00 NRC | | $0.00 | $4,779.26 |
| USW1-2015-02-01 | RDS | Service | $0.00 MRC, $0.00 NRC | | $0.00 | $2,978.47 |

More very interesting data points rise in this view. Unfortunately, at this time, we appear to be finding more questions than answers. Please look at the types of services (second column) and the monthly costs (last column on the right). What stands out? What is the story being told?

- Fairly normal infrastructure is deployed that could be used in either primary or backup locations including DB, block storage, compute, S3, DNS, and so on
- Costs are minimal and in some cases $0.00
- It appears that this site would be set up as a redundant site; maybe a warm site that has some data, but not thousands of GBs worth of data

Some questions appear when looking at some of the additional detail:

- Why are there thousands of GBs and thousands of dollars' worth of data being transferred out of this site when there is very little data stored in this location?
- The amount of data stored in this redundant/backup location does not appear to match up with what is expected of a $68,000 per month consumer of AWS cloud services.
- Compute costs are zero, or close to it. Has the data that is replicated there been validated? Has it been verified to work as planned? When was the last time it was checked and tested?

The solutions have both DynamoDB as well as RDS. In some cases, particularly in the cloud realm, different types of databases can be utilized for different purposes. For example, DynamoDB is only a NoSQL database where RDS can be one of six types. DynamoDB is a multi-tenant database solution with much lower costs. RDS is a single tenant solution at much higher costs. Both have completely different pricing models.

1. At the top of the same page in current view, there is a **Text Search** box. Please type dyn in the search box:

The filtered results immediately change to only show locations with DynamoDB deployed. Please confirm that views match the following screenshot:

The filtered detail shows that DynamoDB is deployed, or at least enabled, in all four locations in the billing file. There is very little, if any, activity in the last month, or maybe longer:

- Why are these services enabled and not used, or used very little?
- Do these services present any added risk, as they are likely partially configured, or set to basic defaults, and not locked down at this point?
- How do these relate to RDS, if at all? Is RDS also partially configured?
- Which service is primary for the business?
- Which site is primary and backup for the database service that is supposed to be utilized?

2. Please replace dyn in the **Text Search** box with RDS:

The filtered results immediately change to only show locations with RDS deployed. Please confirm that views match the following screenshot:

The filtered detail shows that RDS is only deployed in two locations based on the data in the billing file. US West 1 appears to be the primary location, with nearly $3000.00 in monthly spend associated. The only other site is in Europe with less than $250.00 in monthly spend. Again, with some answers found, more questions are added to the list:

- RDS can be set up in a multi-zone deployment. Based on the data, it does not appear to be true for this deployment. Should this be verified?
- How does a single-zone deployment of RDS affect suggestions for the future state?
- How would a multi-zone RDS deployment affect economics and risk?
- Which site appears to be primary, based on database activity?
- This may not be ideal when trying to find which location is production but has a very high probability based on the details seen so far.

As a cloud architect, many hats must be worn. We are investigators at times. The accountant, technician, risk manager, and strategist hats are never far away. Modern cloud architects must have as much or more skill in business finance and economics as they do technical prowess.

As the investigation into NeBu Systems' current state has progressed, the details examined continually must work to align NeBu Systems strategically, economically, and technically. NeBu appears to be overspending in areas and potentially not spending enough in others. The technical mix appears to be solid for the most part, with definite areas to improve. As described by NeBu Systems earlier, things do feel like they have grown quickly without the best governance and limited change management.

Up to this point, most of the examination has been across all locations included in the billing file. This has helped NeBu Systems gain a better understanding of where they are overall and what they are consuming, and has identified some ways to focus optimization efforts that may help control service sprawl and escalating costs.

In the next section, a deeper dive into individual locations within the billing file is needed. Comparing existing deployments to the current market will quickly provide insight that will help solidify direction and next steps for NeBu Systems as they continue their transformation to cloud.

Please click the first icon in the bottom-left corner to switch back to the design view. In the next section, current state data for the primary location will be considered and compared to current market real-time data to help expose additional insight:

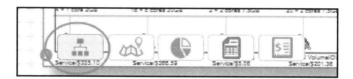

The view should switch to display all four NeBu Systems locations, with any infrastructure and services currently deployed at each location. Please confirm the view matches the following screenshot. From this view, each NeBu location and the services deployed there can be individually compared to the current market to identify options that NeBu can use to optimize designs item by item.

Each service has its own characteristics, deployment size, level of utilization, technical detail, and economic impact. Each compute service has its own performance characteristics and reliability/availability trends over time. Each of these data points will help the NeBu Systems cloud architects align strategy, economics, and technical requirements:

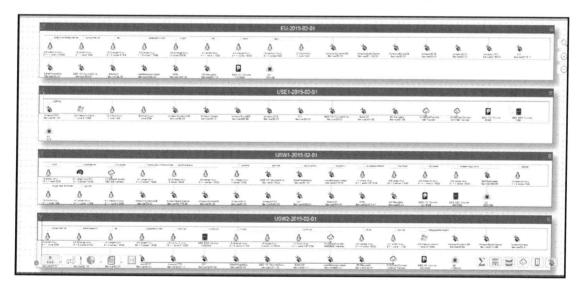

The primary locations appear to be USW1 and USW2. This next section will focus on the optimization of USW1. The current view shows compute, storage, services, and connectivity. Please click on the affectionately named hamburger menu at the top right of the USW1 current state design. Please confirm menu location in the following screenshot:

It will take a minute or two for the view to change. In real time, every line item is analyzed and compared to the current market. Once the view changes, a BOM view should show on the right, with the design visualization on the left. Please confirm the view has changed as shown in the following screenshot:

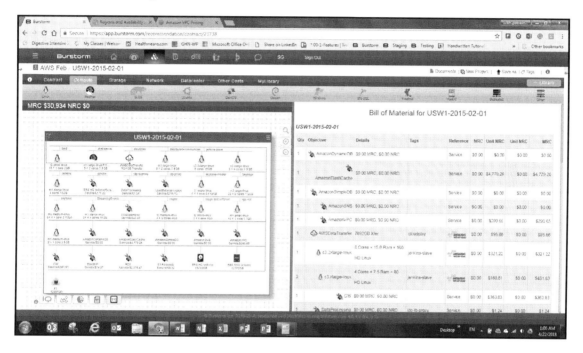

Please scroll through the line items on the right to the bottom of the page. Three ovals should now be visible. Please confirm the current view matches the following screenshot, with the three ovals now visible at the bottom of the page:

Again, what stories can be told with the data?

- The billing data shows nearly $31,000.00 total spent for this location during the billing period
- The **monthly recurring cost (MRC)** is $31,000.00
- The MRC equals the total, meaning that all services have a term of one month or less
- None of the spend is NRC, meaning NeBu Systems is not currently utilizing any reserve instances

The data mentioned provides a good high-level overview of the current state services and current state spending for NeBu Systems. More detail is needed as optimization efforts are explored:

- What is driving the cost of the solution?
- Are there any strategic, economic, or technical factors that highlight where the focus should be placed as future state considerations are made?
- How does performance factor in?
- Can the footprint be consolidated to help control cost?
- Are the correct or optimal instance types being used?
- Are consumption models matching up with strategy?

Please click on the middle icon at the bottom left of the screen. This will change the view to show how each service contributes to the overall cost of the solution. Larger blocks mean that items with larger block size account for larger portions of the overall spend. This provides a visual way for cloud architects to quickly identify places to focus and find alternatives to re-align strategy, economics, and technology:

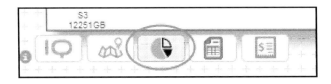

Please confirm that the view has changed to match the following screenshot. A couple of very large blocks quickly points out that a small number of services are contributing to a majority of the cost in the current state:

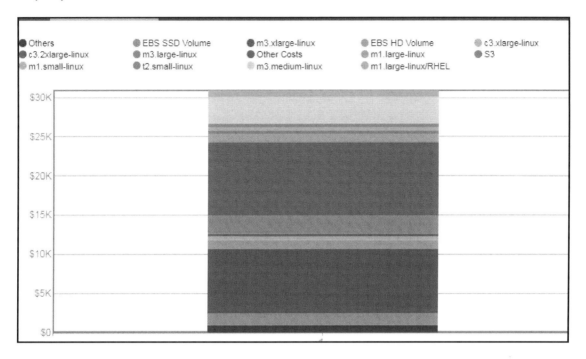

The purple block is **Other Costs**. These costs are AWS-specific services that may lead to vendor lock-in. These services are generally not the same from provider to provider. There may be alternatives that could be used by other providers. Additional time and effort are needed to investigate each of these further. The **Other Costs** block accounts for 31% of the total solution cost monthly.

The second large block (dark blue) is associated with the `m3-xlarge-linux` instance type. This single instance type is contributing 28% to the overall solution cost each month. There may be more than one instance deployed, but this type of instance is contributing significantly to the overall NeBu Systems solution in US West 1. Some interesting questions come to mind based on these two additional data points:

- What services are AWS-specific?
- Is lock-in to AWS an issue? Does it need to be resolved?
- The M3 instance types are older instances that have now been updated to newer versions. Should these be upgraded?
- Why have the M3 instances not been upgraded to a more current version?
- M3 instances are a general use compute type with SSD storage. Is it better to split the applications into more cost-effective compute types that match the applications?
- Would smaller instance types match NeBu System strategy better technically and/or economically?
- What are these instances doing? Are they still critical to the solution?
- As upgrades and changes for a future state are considered, what new services may align better strategically, economically, and technically to NeBu Systems' current direction?

A general idea is now understood regarding how NeBu Systems has deployed their infrastructure and services. Several questions have been raised with very good opportunities for optimization coming into focus quickly.

Please click on the first icon at the bottom left of the screen to change the view to the IQ view:

The view should change to show the **Summary** tab by default. This view provides high-level details such as location, cost, and price-to-performance for the entire solution. Please confirm the view has changed to match the following screenshot:

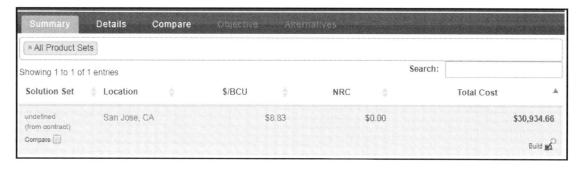

In this view, the location is confirmed as San Jose, CA, which is US West 1. Again, the total cost is shown. Two new pieces of data are shown in this view. First, it is shown as (from contract) in the first column under **Solution Set**. This distinguishes data that is from the current state billing file versus comparison market data that is compared in real time. The second new piece of data is the $/BCU red text in the middle of the screen. This red number is the **Burstorm Compute Unit** (BCU), an average cost per unit of performance based on the benchmark data discussed in depth at the end of the previous chapter. $/BCU will be used in later steps to compare solutions and individual solution components to current market options available. These comparisons will help quickly identify options that have lower price-to-performance ratios. Lower $/BCU numbers are more desirable if all other criteria are equal.

Please click on the **Details** tab in the gray bar at the top of the provider response window. The location of the tab is shown in the following screenshot:

The view should now have detailed solution data for each line item in the current state solution. Please confirm that the solution detail is shown. The following screenshot is included for reference:

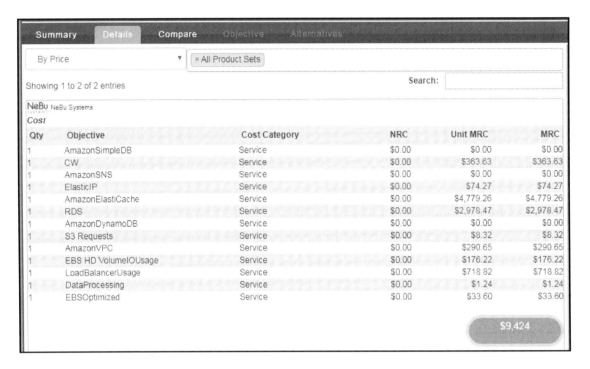

The preceding view shows the services portion of the current state bill related to Amazon-specific services. 30% of NeBu Systems' current monthly spend ($9,424.00) is associated with the AWS-specific services. Some of these services have already been discussed in detail earlier in this chapter.

Scrolling down through the same window shows the same level of detail for the infrastructure components and services. Please match views with the following screenshot. Scrolling to the bottom exposes two ovals. The green oval shows the total for the infrastructure components ($21,510.00). The second oval contains price-to-performance data. This view, by default, is set to prioritize based on price. The price-to-performance oval will show performance data as a cumulative total for the current state solution (2086.1):

| Summary | Details | Compare | Objective | Alternatives | | | |
|---|---|---|---|---|---|---|---|
| 14 | 135.5 | 1×1.7×160 | Other Linux Disto VM | m1.small-linux-co... | $0.00 | $31.58 | $442.12 |
| 1 | 29.5 | 8×15×160 | Other Linux Disto VM | c3.2xlarge-linux-... | $0.00 | $321.22 | $321.22 |
| 3 | 59.0 | 4×7.5×80 | Other Linux Disto VM | c3.xlarge-linux-c... | $0.00 | $160.61 | $481.83 |
| 5 | 69.1 | 2×7.5×840 | RHEL VM | m1.large-linux/RH... | $0.00 | $168.00 | $840.00 |
| 8 | 110.5 | 2×7.5×840 | Other Linux Disto VM | m1.large-linux-co... | $0.00 | $132.97 | $1,063.76 |
| 1 | 19.7 | 4×15×1680 | Other Linux Disto VM | m1.xlarge-linux-c... | $0.00 | $254.69 | $254.69 |
| 22 | 303.9 | 2×7.5×32 | Other Linux Disto VM | m3.large-linux-co... | $0.00 | $104.46 | $2,298.12 |
| 61 | 590.5 | 1×3.75×4 | Other Linux Disto VM | m3.medium-linux-c... | $0.00 | $55.74 | $3,400.14 |
| 21 | 413.1 | 4×15×80 | Other Linux Disto VM | m3.xlarge-linux-c... | $0.00 | $394.24 | $8,279.04 |
| 8 | 77.4 | 1×0.613×--- | Other Linux Disto VM | t1.micro-linux-co... | $0.00 | $30.20 | $241.60 |
| 4 | 55.3 | 2×4×--- | Other Linux Disto VM | t2.medium-linux-c... | $0.00 | $45.70 | $182.80 |
| 3 | 29.0 | 1×1×--- | Other Linux Disto VM | t2.micro-linux-co... | $0.00 | $12.56 | $37.68 |
| 18 | 174.2 | 1×2×--- | Other Linux Disto VM | t2.small-linux-co... | $0.00 | $25.33 | $455.94 |

*Storage*

| Qty | Amount (GB) | Protocols | Tech | Product | NRC | Unit MRC | MRC |
|---|---|---|---|---|---|---|---|
| 1 | 12,251 | | Striping | S3-storage(12251) | $0.00 | $397.55 | $397.55 |
| 1 | 12,372 | | Solid State | EBS SSD Volume-st... | $0.00 | $1,484.64 | $1,484.64 |
| 1 | 13,719 | | Striping | EBS HD Volume-sto... | $0.00 | $1,105.71 | $1,105.71 |

*Network*

| Qty | Type | Specs | Product | NRC | Unit MRC | MRC |
|---|---|---|---|---|---|---|
| 1 | | 3959.7/7691.8 GB | AWSDataTransfer-x... | $0.00 | $95.66 | $95.66 |

2086.1

$21,510

Compare ☐

Build

In the preceding compute details, some answers to previous questions can be answered. NeBu Systems noticed a very large portion of the bill was committed to `m3-xlarge-linux` instances. In this view, 21 instances are shown. The detail for each is also shown (4 cores, 15 GB RAM, 80 GB of storage). Quick math shows this to be the largest grouping of total cores and RAM (81 cores and 315 GB RAM). Depending on application requirements and the number of applications, this group may be able to be changed to more cost-effective and more specialized workloads that match the application and NeBu Systems' strategy better:

- Which instance type would be more beneficial based on performance and pricing data?
- Is there a way to re-stack applications to utilize a more advantageous instance type and/or size?
- What does this cost to deploy on updated infrastructure?
- Are there any applications that can now be purchased as a service?

Please change from prioritizing on price to prioritizing on price performance. Changing the prioritization of the data, compute can be compared looking for opportunities to optimize the instance type. Depending on actual utilization data, an `m3-large` may be more beneficial than an `m3-xlarge`. If RAM utilization is low, the `m3` may be the instance of choice:

| Summary | Details | Compare | Objective | Alternatives | | | |
|---|---|---|---|---|---|---|---|
| **Qty** | **$/BCU** | **Specs** | **OS** | **Product** | **NRC** | **Unit MRC** | **MRC** |
| 2 | $6.59 | 1×3.5×410 | Other Linux Disto VM | m1.medium-linux-c... | $0.00 | $63.84 | $127.68 |
| 14 | $3.26 | 1×1.7×160 | Other Linux Disto VM | m1.small-linux-co... | $0.00 | $31.58 | $442.12 |
| 1 | $10.90 | 8×15×160 | Other Linux Disto VM | c3.2xlarge-linux-... | $0.00 | $321.22 | $321.22 |
| 3 | $8.16 | 4×7.5×80 | Other Linux Disto VM | c3.xlarge-linux-c... | $0.00 | $160.61 | $481.83 |
| 5 | $12.16 | 2×7.5×840 | RHEL VM | m1.large-linux/RH... | $0.00 | $168.00 | $840.00 |
| 8 | $9.63 | 2×7.5×840 | Other Linux Disto VM | m1.large-linux-co... | $0.00 | $132.97 | $1,063.76 |
| 1 | $12.95 | 4×15×1680 | Other Linux Disto VM | m1.xlarge-linux-c... | $0.00 | $254.69 | $254.69 |
| 22 | $7.56 | 2×7.5×32 | Other Linux Disto VM | m3.large-linux-co... | $0.00 | $104.46 | $2,298.12 |
| 61 | $5.76 | 1×3.75×4 | Other Linux Disto VM | m3.medium-linux-c... | $0.00 | $55.74 | $3,400.14 |
| 21 | $20.04 | 4×15×80 | Other Linux Disto VM | m3.xlarge-linux-c... | $0.00 | $394.24 | $8,279.04 |
| 8 | $3.12 | 1×0.613×--- | Other Linux Disto VM | t1.micro-linux-co... | $0.00 | $30.20 | $241.60 |
| 4 | $3.31 | 2×4×--- | Other Linux Disto VM | t2.medium-linux-c... | $0.00 | $45.70 | $182.80 |
| 3 | $1.30 | 1×1×--- | Other Linux Disto VM | t2.micro-linux-co... | $0.00 | $12.56 | $37.68 |
| 18 | $2.62 | 1×2×--- | Other Linux Disto VM | t2.small-linux-co... | $0.00 | $25.33 | $455.94 |

Additional data that may also be helpful is how the individual types rank based on price performance data. The following real-time data is available by looking through the ongoing benchmark data. The arrows have been placed over the price-to-performance details for the `m3-xlarge` and the `m3-large` instance types:

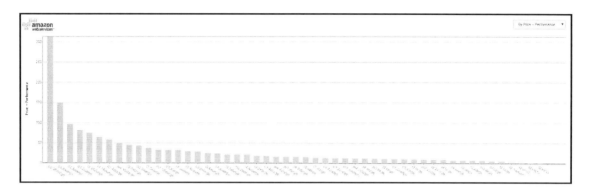

NeBu Systems applications tend to be more RAM-intensive. m3-large may not be the right instance type based on the workload type. What does the current market have available? Is there a high-performing, lower-cost instance type that matches up to the NeBu Systems workload?

Please click on the hamburger menu above the word **Summary** as follows:

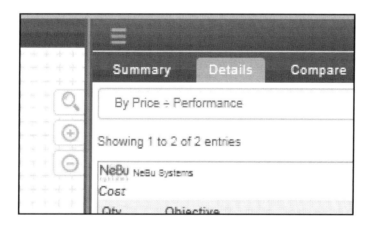

A menu will appear with a switch for **Exact-Match**. The switch should be on by default. Please click to flip the switch to **OFF**. Please use the following screenshot as a reference:

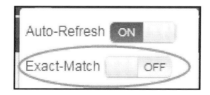

**Exact-Match | OFF** asks the platform to compare the solution to external solution providers. Showing a provider that is not an exact 100% match is allowed when the switch is off. Once the app has refreshed the new data view, the following screenshot should now match the current view:

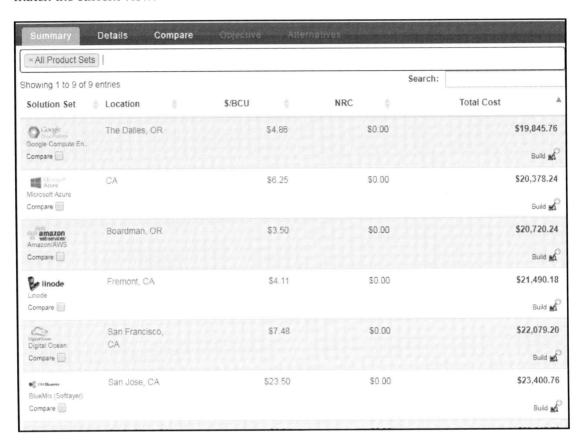

The new data allows for comparisons to be made using current market data. As in previous chapters, Google is lower cost than several others, including Azure and AWS. The following screenshot shows a few interesting insights:

- Google is the low-cost provider
- Azure and AWS are very similar in cost
- AWS, again, appears to be the higher-performing solution with a lower $/BCU
- The lowest-cost AWS solution is in US West 2 (Boardman, OR), not the NeBu current location of US West 1 (San Jose, CA)

Cloud architects must often weigh risk and economics. This book has discussed that economics must offset risk. The higher the risk, the lower the cost must be to make it worth absorbing the risk. Migrating to Boardman may feel a bit risky. However, it is still in the same region with the same provider. If the cost is significantly less and/or the performance is significantly high where applications can be consolidated or re-stacked, the move may be worth the effort. NeBu Systems has a strategy of getting the highest performance at the lowest cost. The move to Boardman may be a foundation piece for realigning strategy, economics, and technology:

| | | | | |
|---|---|---|---|---|
| Google — Google Compute En... — Compare | The Dalles, OR | $4.86 | $0.00 | $19,845.76 — Build |
| Microsoft Azure — Microsoft Azure — Compare | CA | $6.25 | $0.00 | $20,378.24 — Build |
| amazon webservices — Amazon/AWS — Compare | Boardman, OR | $3.50 | $0.00 | $20,720.24 — Build |

There should be a list of several solutions from several providers that match the following screenshot. In this section, a comparison between the current state billing file data for US West 1 and the current market. Please check the **Compare** box for AWS and the **Compare** box for (from contract) toward the bottom of the list. Please see the marked boxes in the following screenshot for reference:

Before comparing, there are a couple of interesting data points worth mentioning in this view. NeBu Systems is focused on finding the best performance at the lowest cost. Changing providers is an option if the price and/or performance is worth the risk:

- The current state bill is one of the most expensive options presented
- The current state option is $10,000+ higher than current market with the same provider
- The current state services are potentially much slower than current services from the same provider

The data in this view makes comparisons very easy for NeBu Systems. This data alone may lead NeBu to conclude that focusing on staying with AWS is the right option and migrating to Boardman may make a lot of sense as well. A direct comparison between the two AWS locations is the next logical step.

Please change to the **Compare** view at the top of the provider response table as follows:

The view will immediately change to align each unique line item side by side. The following screenshot is shown for reference if needed:

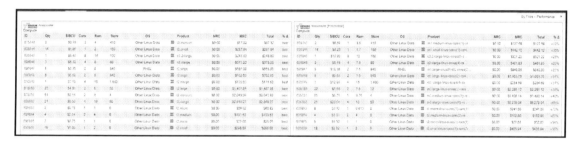

It becomes very clear quickly that staying with AWS and migrating to Boardman has many benefits. Please scroll to the bottom and look at the ovals with the summarized cost and price-to-performance data:

- Boardman has a much lower $/BCU ratio, $3.50 versus $8.83 for current state
- Boardman is lower infrastructure cost, $11,295 versus $21,510 for current state
- Changing the prioritized view from price performance to performance only shows that only Boardman is significantly faster, 2698.2 versus 2086.1 for current state

If these comparisons are difficult, refer to the first couple of sections of the hands-on labs, as each of these comparisons were detailed in those sections.

It is also very interesting to look at some of the side-by-side comparisons to see what is suggested based on the current state data available. Please look at the following example:

- The first line is the current state solution. A total of 21 `m3-xlarge` instances were deployed accounting for $8,279.04 with a performance score of 413.1.
- The second line is the potential future state solution utilizing 21 `t2-xlarge` instances for only $2848.27.
- The difference between the two options is 66% less cost and a 20% increase in performance.
- T2 instances may work very well for NeBu Systems' strategy as most of the applications are RAM-intensive, not CPU-intensive. The T2 series instances could stay at base CPU performance levels, controlling costs quite well. The T2 prices are very depending on how CPU performance and load increases. Staying at base performance would allow NeBu systems to utilize the RAM fully without increasing costs. Key note: understanding how economics and technology relate enables the simultaneous alignment of strategy, economics, and technology:

# Summary

NeBu Systems needed to revisit their transformation in progress and current deployment that has grown quickly. In this lab, price-to-performance became the key differentiator for nearly all the choices made.

These hands-on labs intentionally took a very infrastructure-centric view of the world. Infrastructure has long been ignored in favor of more sexy and endearing things such as applications. Applications are what users interact with. They are the things that are most often seen and commented on, not the infrastructure underneath.

Infrastructure is getting cheaper by the day. The race-to-zero is just beginning for compute. Network has been on its way for a while. Storage is also beginning the run. With infrastructure declining in price and the cost of management and operations rising exponentially, the cost of a mistake at the infrastructure level can be very costly, with changes in strategy and technical direction nearly cost-prohibitive. Get the foundation set right. Then build on the foundation.

This lab started with data at very high levels, abstracting most of the detail away. By doing this, the strategy could be quickly analyzed and confirmed. The first part of the lab was investigative work, matching up the stories the billing data was telling with the expectations of what NeBu Systems thought they were doing. The middle portion of the lab was used to look for deeper-level data to confirm stories and find opportunities to change the narrative. The last part of the lab showed how to confirm direction by answering questions raised during the beginning and middle of the lab.

Not all questions raised were answered. That was never the intent. The intent was to build a process and pattern for thinking, raising questions, searching for relevant data, and answering questions that help accomplish the simultaneous alignment of strategy, economics, technology, and risk. Cloud architecture is about quickly triaging data, identifying relevance, and remaining keenly aware of real-time insight.

# 20
# Cloud Architecture – Lessons Learned

If you are completely successful in navigating the complex and competing priorities levied on every cloud computing solution, your efforts will fail unless a successful implementation follows. Although implementation is outside the scope of this solution design text, we would like to share with you the lessons we have learned in these early years of cloud computing architecting:

- To be a successful cloud solution architect, you need to obtain and maintain *executive sponsorship*. Make sure governance control points are *built into* the transition process (an example control point: ensure financial controls on *pay-as-you-go* elastic compute model do not result in runaway costs!).

- Analysis of an organization's application portfolio as a whole is key to efficiency and the breadth of value delivered by transitioning to a cloud platform. Management oversight and review processes for legacy application transitions to IaaS platforms should be modified to reflect their *software-only* nature.

- Most customers are only aware of a few large cloud service providers (for example, AWS, Azure, Google, Salesforce, and IBM). They also may be limited to selecting a single CSP platform (that is, C2S). This does not reduce or eliminate the need to evaluate the economics and performance aspects of a transition strategy to the broader marketplace.

- Lack of IT standards or a failure to enforce those standards results in differences between your development, test, and production environments. This significantly reduces your ability to leverage automated testing tools and delays your cloud transition. Developers must be educated on **Application Performance Monitoring (APM)** capabilities, service management/monitoring capabilities, web and mobile analytics, and alerting and notification solutions.
- The most severe challenge when adopting cloud computing is around cultural change. A focused and dedicated informational and educational campaign should be in place to support this type of transition. A lack of cloud computing education and understanding is one of the most significant organizational risks.

# Epilogue

Where should NeBu Systems go next? They have successfully broken apart their monolithic application and now utilize cloud services. Is it a case of congratulations on finishing? Or is it congratulations on starting? Did NeBu successfully migrate or transform?

Migrations are a series of things that get done. Migrations seem tangible: from this to that, from here to there. Transformations, interestingly, are mental and emotional. Transformations require a change in mindset. Transformations require constant data that can be continuously compared to expose insights and establish perceived value.

Migrations are planned and executed. Transformations are adopted. Without adoption, transformation fails. Adoption requires a change in mindset, often created from a continuous digestion of highly valued relevant data and insight. This means continuously sensing the environment and continuously changing your actions to better align with goals, which are also changing continuously. We, the authors, call this being **senso-morphic**. Businesses and people tasked with adapting and driving change must become senso-morphic.

Today, many are flooded with data, yet remain uninformed. Many know they are in the wrong place, yet struggle to know where they are. The only sustainable path for positive transformation is to become senso-morphic. In the world of cloud computing, this means being senso-morphic across many domains, simultaneously. The senso-morphic domains are shown in the following table:

| Domain | Transition From | Transition To |
|---|---|---|
| Security Framework | Infrastructure-centric | Data-centric |
| Application Development | Tightly Coupled | Loosely Coupled |
| Data | Mostly Structured | Mostly unstructured |
| Business Processes | Mostly Serial | Mostly Parallel |
| Security Controls | Enterprise responsibility | Shared responsibility |
| Economic model | Mostly CAPEX | Mostly OPEX |
| Infrastructure | Mostly physical | Mostly virtual |
| IT Operations | Mostly manual | Mostly automated |
| Technology Operational scope | Local/Regional | International/Global |

This book is but the first step in a long journey. Our wish is that we've prepared you well. Good luck.

Kevin L. Jackson                                        Scott Goessling

# Other Books You May Enjoy

If you enjoyed this book, you may be interested in these other books by Packt:

**Google Cloud Platform Cookbook**
Legorie Rajan PS

ISBN: 978-1-78829-199-6

- Host a Python application on Google Compute Engine
- Host an application using Google Cloud Functions
- Migrate a MySQL DB to Cloud Spanner
- Configure a network for a highly available application on GCP
- Learn simple image processing using Storage and Cloud Functions
- Automate security checks using Policy Scanner
- Understand tools for monitoring a production environment in GCP
- Learn to manage multiple projects using service accounts

## Architecting Microsoft Azure Solutions – Exam Guide 70-535
Sjoukje Zaal

ISBN: 978-1-78899-173-5

- Use Azure Virtual Machines to design effective VM deployments
- Implement architecture styles, like serverless computing and microservices
- Secure your data using different security features and design effective security strategies
- Design Azure storage solutions using various storage features
- Create identity management solutions for your applications and resources
- Architect state-of-the-art solutions using Artificial Intelligence, IoT, and Azure Media Services
- Use different automation solutions that are incorporated in the Azure platform

# Leave a review - let other readers know what you think

Please share your thoughts on this book with others by leaving a review on the site that you bought it from. If you purchased the book from Amazon, please leave us an honest review on this book's Amazon page. This is vital so that other potential readers can see and use your unbiased opinion to make purchasing decisions, we can understand what our customers think about our products, and our authors can see your feedback on the title that they have worked with Packt to create. It will only take a few minutes of your time, but is valuable to other potential customers, our authors, and Packt. Thank you!

# Index

# M

machine learning  36
managed service provider (MSP)  45
marketing resource management (MRM)  157
mean time between failure (MTBF)  278
mean time to repair (MTTR)  278
metering  233
microservice architecture  258
mobile applications
  about  159
  cloud service components  162
  enterprise network components  164
  mobile device components  161
  public network components  161
mobile architecture components  159
Mobile device management (MDM)  162
monitoring  233
monthly recurring cost (MRC)  322
multi-cloud analysis platform (MCAP)  259
multi-data center architecture  133

# N

National Institute of Standards and Technology
  (NIST)  16
native applications  207
NeBu Systems
  decisions, based on non-negotiable concepts
  303
network address translations (NAT)  214
network attached storage (NAS)  211
network functions virtualization (NFV)  201
network virtualization (NV)  201
networking interface cards (NICs)  214
neural networks  36
node-based availability  196
Non-personally identifiable information (non-PII)
  268
non-redundant three-tier architecture  127

# O

once-in-a-lifetime workloads  112
open authorization (OAUTH)  168
open client  234
Operational Expenditure (OPEX)  56

operational level agreements (OLAs)  55
Operations Technology (OT)  187
Organization Normative Framework (ONF)
  management process  270
organizational assessment  121
organizations
  governance  235
  management  235
OSI model and layer description
  about  130
  autoscaling architecture  131
  logical and physical design  131

# P

performance  235
personally identifiable information (PII)  267
Platform-as-a-Service (PaaS)
  about  65, 166, 222
  background  26
  considerations  27, 28
portability
  about  232
  applications  232
  data  232
  infrastructure  233
  management  233
  platforms  232
  publication and acquisition  233
privacy addresses  234
privacy and data protection (P and DP) laws  266
private cloud  30
Product life cycle management (PLM)  156
provider exit strategy plan  236
public cloud
  about  29
  benefits  30
  considerations  30
public network
  about  151
  cloud provider network components  151
  enterprise network components  151
  security components  152
Puppet  257

# R

Radio Frequency Identification (RFID) 156
random access memory (RAM) 210
Really Simple Syndication (RSS) 118
Recovery Point Objective (RPO) 57
Recovery Time Objective (RTO) 57
Red Hat Enterprise Linux (RHEL) 49
Red Hat Enterprise Virtualization (RHEV) 200
redundant three-tier architecture
  about 128
  horizontal scaling 129
  redundancy, versus resiliency 129
  single points of failure 128
regulatory requisites 119
Representational State Transfer (REST) 117, 253
request for proposal (RFP) 110
request for quote (RFQ) 110
resiliency 234
REST
  about 118
  advantages 118
Return on Investment (ROI)
  about 79, 80
  driving factors 81, 82, 83
risk
  assessing 276, 277, 278
  framing 275
  monitoring 279
ROI metrics
  cost 86
  margin optimization 86
  quality 86
  time 86
role, data privacy
  controller 266
  data owner 266
  data subject 266
  processor 266

# S

Salt 258
Security Assertion Markup Language (SAML) 168
security components 152
security control

  about 236, 238
  administrative 237
  logical 237
  physical 237
security
  requisites 119
server side, cloud applications
  JAVA 256
  LAMP 256
  WISA stack 256
serverless architecture 258
service level agreements (SLAs) 23, 85, 176, 221, 222, 249, 260, 279
service orientation 253
service tier 152
service-oriented architecture (SOA) 253
shadow IT 17
Simple Mail Transfer Protocol (SMTP) 229
Simple Object Access Protocol (SOAP) 117
single point of failure (SPOF) 278
Single Sign-On (SSO) 168
single-site architecture
  about 127
  non-redundant three-tier architecture 127
  redundant three-tier architecture 128
SLAs 236
SOAP
  about 117
  advantages 118
software defined networking (SDN) 201
Software Development Kit (SDK) 181
software development kits (SDKs) 161
Software-as-a-Service (SaaS) 166
  about 65
  background 24
  considerations 25
  offering 225
static workloads 112
storage area networks (SAN) 211
storage services, IaaS
  archival storage 214
  key-value storage 213
  object/blob storage 212
  volume/block storage 212

2634S746R00215

Printed in Great Britain
by Amazon